Contents

Workbook/Laboratory Manual
Volume 1
to accompany

¿Qué tal?
AN INTRODUCTORY COURSE
Seventh Edition

Alice A. Arana
Formerly of Fullerton College

Oswaldo Arana
Formerly of CSU Fullerton

María Sabló-Yates
Delta College

Boston   Burr Ridge, IL   Dubuque, IA   Madison, WI   New York   San Francisco   St. Louis
Bangkok   Bogotá   Caracas   Kuala Lumpur   Lisbon   London   Madrid   Mexico City
Milan   Montreal   New Delhi   Santiago   Seoul   Singapore   Sydney   Taipei   Toronto

McGraw-Hill Higher Education

A Division of The McGraw-Hill Companies

Workbook/Laboratory Manual (Volume 1)
to accompany ¿Qué tal?
An Introductory Course

Published by McGraw-Hill, an imprint of The McGraw-Hill Companies, Inc.,
1221 Avenue of the Americas, New York, NY 10020. Copyright © 2007 by The
McGraw-Hill Companies, Inc. All rights reserved. No part of this publication
may be reproduced or distributed in any form or by any means, or stored
in a database or retrieval system, without the prior written consent of The
McGraw-Hill Companies, Inc., including, but not limited to, in any network
or other electronic storage or transmission, or broadcast for distance learning.

This book is printed on acid-free paper.

1 2 3 4 5 6 7 8 9 0 QPD QPD 0 9 8 7 6

ISBN-13: 978-0-07-320798-8
ISBN-10: 0-07-320798-5

Vice president and Editor-in-chief: *Emily Barrosse*
Publisher: *William R. Glass*
Senior sponsoring editor: *Christa Harris*
Director of development and media technology: *Scott Tinetti*
Development editor: *Pennie Nichols*
Executive marketing manager: *Nick Agnew*
Senior production supervisor: *Richard DeVitto*
Senior supplements producer: *Louis Swaim*
Production editor: *Mel Valentín*
Illustrators: *David Bohn, Wayne Clark, Anica Gibson, Rick Hackney,
    Sally Richardson, Dave Sullivan*
Compositor: *Techbooks*
Typeface: *10/12 Palatino*
Paper: *45# Scholarly Matte*
Printer and binder: *Quebecor World Printing, Dubuque*

http://www.mhhe.com

☷ To the Student

Welcome to Volume I of the combined Workbook/Laboratory Manual to accompany *¿Qué tal? An Introductory Course*, Seventh Edition. Each chapter of this Workbook/Laboratory Manual is based on the corresponding chapter of the text, so that you may practice and review on your own what you are learning in class. For ease of identification, the exercises appear under the same headings as in *¿Qué tal?* Once a section from the textbook has been introduced, you can do the same section in the Workbook/Laboratory Manual with the assurance that no new vocabulary or structures from later sections of that chapter will be encountered.

Special Feature

This Workbook/Laboratory Manual also contains a unique and convenient feature: within each chapter, each individual **paso** can be torn out and handed in without disturbing the remainder of the chapter. This means that you can have your instructor check your work on previous **pasos** while you continue to practice current class material. It also means that the study materials are clearly organized and easy for you to use.

Integrated Written and Oral Exercises

Because your different senses and skills (writing, reading, listening, and speaking) reinforce one another, written and oral exercises for each point in the text appear together in the Workbook/Laboratory Manual. Oral exercises are coordinated with the Audio Program, available in compact disc format, which you can use at home or at your school's language laboratory. They are marked with a headphones symbol:

To get the most out of the Audio Program, you should listen to the CDs after your instructor covers the corresponding material in class, and you should listen as often as possible. You will need the Workbook/Laboratory Manual much of the time when you listen to the CDs, since many of the exercises are based on visuals, realia (real things—such as advertisements, classified ads, and so on that you would encounter in a Spanish-speaking country), and written cues.

Organization

The structure of **Capítulo preliminar** of the Workbook/Laboratory Manual parallels that of **Capítulo preliminar** in the main text. **Capítulos 1–9** are organized as follows:

- **Paso 1: Vocabulario** allows you to practice the thematic vocabulary of each chapter through a variety of fun and interesting exercises. Here and in **Pasos 2** and **3,** written and oral exercises appear together for each point. The **Pronunciación y ortografía** pronunciation and spelling exercises provide focused practice of Spanish pronunciation, with explanations all in English. In **Los hispanos hablan** sections, students from Spain and Latin America answer questions about their life in their countries and their impressions of life in this country. These sections are followed by comprehension questions, such as true-false, short answer, or personal reaction.

- **Paso 2: Gramática** presents a variety of exercises on each grammar point in the corresponding section of the main text.
- **Paso 3: Gramática,** as in **Paso 2,** gives you the opportunity to practice chapter structures through written and oral exercises. In addition, **Un poco de todo** combines grammar points and vocabulary introduced in the current chapter as well as in previous chapters.
- **Paso 4: Un paso más** provides additional practice and focuses on integrating chapter vocabulary and grammar. Its main features are the following:
  - **Videoteca** reinforces the Video Program to accompany ¿Qué tal? Each section includes comprehension activities for the **Entrevista cultural** and **Entre amigos** videoclips.
  - **Enfoque cultural,** a cultural review section that focuses on Hispanic countries, is also practiced with comprehension exercises.
  - **¡Repasemos!** includes a focused review of grammar and vocabulary from preceding chapters, including reading selections, tense transformation, and paragraph completion. This section also contains a *Listening Passage,* with pre- and post-listening activities designed to guide and facilitate comprehension of the *Listening Passage.* These passages are cultural in nature and contain information on a variety of topics related to the Hispanic world. Their themes are related to the theme of each chapter. A section called **Antes de escuchar,** in which you will practice a variety of listening strategies, often precedes them. Comprehension or follow-up exercises are offered in **Después de escuchar.** Each **¡Repasemos!** section includes an oral interview, in which you write your responses to personalized questions. Answers for **¡Repasemos!** sections are *not* provided in the Appendix.
  - **Mi diario** is a chapter-culminating activity in which you are encouraged to write freely about your own experiences, applying the material you have been studying in that chapter.
  - **Paso 4** also includes a final section called **Póngase a prueba.** In this section, you will find first a short quiz called **A ver si sabe... ,** which focuses on some of the more mechanical aspects of the language-learning process, such as memorization of verb forms and syntax. By taking this quiz, you can evaluate your knowledge of the most basic aspects of the language before moving on to the **Prueba corta,** where you will complete a brief quiz that contains more contextualized written and oral practice.

Answers

Answers to most oral exercises are given on the Audio Program. In a few cases, as required, they appear in the Appendix at the back of this Workbook/Laboratory Manual. Answers to most written activities also appear in the Appendix. No answers are provided for exercises requiring personalized answers, indicated with this symbol: ❖

Acknowledgments

The authors wish to offer their sincere thanks to the following individuals:

- Ana María Pérez-Gironés (Wesleyan University), who wrote the listening passages in the **¡Repasemos!** sections
- Manuela González-Bueno (University of Kansas), who made many helpful suggestions for improving the **Pronunciación y ortografía** sections
- the Hispanic exchange students whose answers were the basis of the passages in the **Los hispanos hablan** sections
- William R. Glass, whose reading of previous editions of the separate Workbook/Laboratory Manual provided welcome suggestions and advice
- Christa Harris, for her valuable suggestions, helpful comments, and continued assistance and good humor in the editing of this edition
- Pennie Nichols, whose comments, suggestions, and superior editing made this combined Workbook/Laboratory Manual and Audio Program possible
- Thalia Dorwick, whose continuing work on *¿Qué tal?* reflects her abiding love of language learning and teaching

We sincerely hope that beginning Spanish will be a satisfying experience for you!

Alice A. Arana
Oswaldo Arana
María Sabló-Yates

About the Authors

Alice A. Arana is Associate Professor of Spanish, Emeritus, Fullerton College. She received her M.A.T. from Yale University and her Certificate of Spanish Studies from the University of Madrid. Professor Arana has taught Spanish at the elementary and high school levels, and has taught methodology at several NDEA summer institutes. She is coauthor of the first edition of *A-LM Spanish,* of *Reading for Meaning—Spanish,* and of several elementary school guides for the teaching of Spanish. In 1992, Professor Arana was named Staff Member of Distinction at Fullerton College and was subsequently chosen as the 1993 nominee from Fullerton College for Teacher of the Year. In 1994, she served as Academic Senate President.

Oswaldo Arana is Professor of Spanish, Emeritus, at California State University, Fullerton, where he has taught Spanish American culture and literature. He received his Ph.D. in Spanish from the University of Colorado. Professor Arana has taught at the University of Colorado, the University of Florida (Gainesville), and at several NDEA summer institutes. He served as a language consultant for the first edition of *A-LM Spanish* and is coauthor of *Reading for Meaning—Spanish* and of several articles on Spanish American narrative prose.

The Aranas are coauthors of the first through seventh editions, Workbook to accompany *Puntos de partida: An Invitation to Spanish,* the Workbook/Laboratory Manual to accompany *Puntos en breve,* Second Edition (McGraw-Hill, 2007), and of previous editions of the *¿Qué tal?* Workbook/Laboratory Manual.

María Sabló-Yates is a native of Panama. She holds a B.A. and an M.A. from the University of Washington (Seattle). She has taught at the University of Washington and Central Michigan University (Mt. Pleasant, Michigan), and currently teaches at Delta College (University Center, Michigan). She is the coauthor of previous editions of the *¿Qué tal?* Workbook/Laboratory Manual, of the first through seventh editions of the Laboratory Manual to accompany *Puntos de partida: An Invitation to Spanish,* and coauthor of the Workbook/Laboratory Manual to accompany *Puntos en breve,* Second Edition (McGraw-Hill, 2007).

Primer paso

Saludos y expresiones de cortesía

A. Saludos. Greet the following people in an appropriate manner.

1. a classmate, at any time of day _____

2. la señora Alarcón, at 9:30 P.M. _____

3. el señor Ramírez, at 2:00 P.M. _____

4. la señorita Cueva, at 11:00 A.M. _____

¡RECUERDE! (*REMEMBER!*)

¿Tú o (*or*) usted?

1. What form do you use when speaking to a professor?   **tú** ☐   **usted** ☐

2. What form do you use when speaking to another student?   **tú** ☐   **usted** ☐

3. To ask a classmate his or her name, say: ¿_____?

4. To ask your instructor his or her name, say: ¿_____?

B. ¡Hola, Carmen! On your way to class, you meet Carmen, a student from Spain, and exchange greetings with her. Complete the brief dialogue.

USTED: Hola, Carmen, ¿_____[1]?

CARMEN: Bien, gracias. ¿_____[2]?

USTED: Regular.

CARMEN: Adiós, _____[3] mañana.

USTED: Adiós, Carmen. _____[4]

C. Diálogo. Complete the following dialogue between you and your new Spanish instructor. Be sure to use your own name and that of your instructor in the appropriate blanks.

USTED: _____[1] noches, profesor(a) _____. ¿Cómo

_____[2]?

PROFESOR(A):   Bien, _____[3] ¿Cómo _____[4] usted?

USTED: _____[5] (*your name*).

PROFESOR(A):   Mucho _____[6]

USTED: _____[7]

D. Diálogos

Paso 1. In the following dialogues, you will practice greeting others appropriately in Spanish. The dialogues will be read with pauses for repetition. After each dialogue, you will hear two summarizing statements. Circle the letter of the statement that best describes each dialogue. First, listen.

1.   MANOLO: ¡Hola, Maricarmen!
    MARICARMEN: ¿Qué tal, Manolo? ¿Cómo estás?
    MANOLO: Muy bien. ¿Y tú?
    MARICARMEN: Regular. Nos vemos, ¿eh?
    MANOLO: Hasta mañana.

Comprensión: **a. b.**

2.   ELISA VELASCO: Buenas tardes, señor Gómez.
    MARTÍN GÓMEZ: Muy buenas, señora Velasco. ¿Cómo está?
    ELISA VELASCO: Bien, gracias. ¿Y usted?
    MARTÍN GÓMEZ: Muy bien, gracias. Hasta luego.
    ELISA VELASCO: Adiós.

Comprensión: **a. b.**

3.   LUPE: Buenos días, profesor.
    PROFESOR: Buenos días. ¿Cómo te llamas?
    LUPE: Me llamo Lupe Carrasco.
    PROFESOR: Mucho gusto, Lupe.
    LUPE: Igualmente.

Comprensión: **a. b.**

4.   MIGUEL: Hola, me llamo Miguel René. ¿Y tú? ¿Cómo te llamas?
    KARINA: Me llamo Karina. Mucho gusto.
    MIGUEL: Mucho gusto, Karina. Y, ¿de dónde eres?
    KARINA: Yo soy de Venezuela. ¿Y tú?
    MIGUEL: Yo soy de México.

Comprensión: **a. b.**

Paso 2. Now you will participate in a conversation, partially printed in your Workbook/Laboratory Manual, in which you play the role of Karina. Complete the conversation using the written cues. When you hear the corresponding number, say Karina's line. Then you will hear Miguel's response. Continue until you complete the conversation. (If you wish, pause and write the answers.) Here are the cues for your conversation.

buenas tardes	cómo te llamas	de dónde eres
me llamo	mucho gusto	yo soy

Now, begin the conversation.

KARINA: **1.** _____ .

MIGUEL: Muy buenas.

KARINA: **2.** _____ Karina. **3.** ¿_____?

MIGUEL: Me llamo Miguel.

KARINA: **4.** _____ , Miguel. **5.** ¿_____?

MIGUEL: Soy de Puerto Rico. ¿Y tú?

KARINA: **6.** _____ de Puerto Rico también.

E. ¿Formal o informal? You will hear a series of expressions. Indicate whether each expression would be used in a formal or in an informal situation.

1. **a.** formal   **b.** informal
2. **a.** formal   **b.** informal
3. **a.** formal   **b.** informal
4. **a.** formal   **b.** informal
5. **a.** formal   **b.** informal

F. Situaciones

Paso 1. You will hear a series of questions or statements. Each will be said twice. Circle the letter of the best response or reaction to each.

1. **a.** Me llamo Ricardo Barrios.   **b.** Bien, gracias.
2. **a.** Encantada, Eduardo.   **b.** Muchas gracias, Eduardo.
3. **a.** Regular. ¿Y tú?   **b.** Mucho gusto, señorita Paz.
4. **a.** Con permiso, señor.   **b.** No hay de qué.
5. **a.** De nada, señora Colón.   **b.** Buenas noches, señora Colón.
6. **a.** Soy de Guatemala.   **b.** ¿Y tú?

Paso 2. Now, listen to the questions and statements again and read the correct answers in the pauses provided. You will hear each item only once. Be sure to repeat the correct answer after you hear it.

1. ...   2. ...   3. ...   4. ...   5. ...   6. ...

El alfabeto español

A. El alfabeto español. Answer the following questions about the Spanish alphabet.

1. What is the one letter in the Spanish alphabet that does not exist in the English alphabet?

   _____

2. What letter in the Spanish alphabet is never pronounced? _____

B. ¿Cómo se escribe... ? (*How do you write . . . ?*) Write only the name of the underlined letter.

   MODELO: ¿Se escribe J̲osé con (*with*) ge o con jota? → Con *jota.*

1. ¿Se escribe g̲eneral con ge o con jota? Con _____.

2. ¿Se escribe Oli̲via con be o con ve (uve)? Con _____.

3. ¿Se escribe e̲xperto con equis o con ese? Con _____.

4. ¿Se escribe Pére̲z con ese o con zeta? Con _____.

5. ¿Se escribe C̲ecilia con ese o con ce? Con _____.

6. ¿Se escribe optim̲ista con i o con i griega? Con _____.

7. ¿Se escribe h̲asta con o sin (*without*) hache?_____ _____.

❖**C. ¿Cómo se llama usted?** Spell your complete name in Spanish.*

   MODELO: Me llamo Juan Martínez. → Jota -u -a -ene, eme- a -ere- te- i acentuada- ene- e -zeta

   Me llamo _____.

Nota comunicativa: Los cognados

❖ **A. Pronunciación.** Read aloud the following pairs of words. The stressed syllable is italicized. Note how the stress shifts in most of the Spanish words. These adjectives can be used to describe a man or a woman.

	ENGLISH	SPANISH		ENGLISH	SPANISH
1.	*nor*mal	nor-*mal*	8.	*ter*rible	te-*rri*-ble
2.	*e*motional	e-mo-cio-*nal*	9.	res*pon*sible	res-pon-*sa*-ble
3.	*el*egant	e-le-*gan*-te	10.	*val*iant	va-*lien*-te
4.	*cru*el	cru-*el*	11.	*hor*rible	ho-*rri*-ble
5.	pesi*mis*tic	pe-si-*mis*-ta	12.	im*por*tant	im-por-*tan*-te
6.	opti*mis*tic	op-ti-*mis*-ta	13.	in*tel*ligent	in-te-li-*gen*-te
7.	materia*lis*tic	ma-te-ria-*lis*-ta	14.	re*bel*lious	re-*bel*-de

---

*Exercises marked with this symbol (❖) do *not* have answers at the back of the Workbook/Laboratory Manual nor on the Audioscript.

B. Los cognados

❖ **Paso 1.** Scan the following selection, then underline all the cognates and other words that look familiar to you.

Paso 2. Based on your understanding of the article, circle **C** for **cierto** (*true*) or **F** for **falso** (*false*). ¡OJO! The sentences can help you understand the meaning of the paragraph.

> **Un producto natural, protector de la salud**
>
> El aceite de oliva, especialmente el aceite de oliva virgen, es un producto que cada día gana mayor aceptación en la preparación de las comidas. Contiene mucha vitamina E, un antioxidante por excelencia. Además, el aceite de oliva virgen no contiene colesterol. En efecto, su uso reduce la concentración de colesterol en la sangre. Por lo tanto, es preferible a las grasas de origen animal, que son malas para el sistema cardiovascular.

1. C F Virgin olive oil is gaining more acceptance in the preparation of meals.

2. C F One of the benefits of this oil is that it contains a lot of vitamin C.

3. C F Olive oil contains as much cholesterol as animal fats.

4. C F Animal fats are unhealthy because they are bad for the heart.

5. C F The use of olive oil reduces the amount of cholesterol in our blood.

6. C F Olive oil is beneficial for the cardiovascular system.

C. Descripción. In this exercise, you will practice "gisting," that is, getting the main idea—an important skill in language learning. Although some of the vocabulary you hear will not be familiar to you, concentrate on the words that you *do* know. After the exercise, pause and choose the statement that best describes the passage.

1. ☐ This person is describing her country and the sports that are played there.
2. ☐ This person is describing herself, her studies, and her outside interests.

Now resume listening.

D. Dictado:* ¿Cómo son? (*What are they like?*) You will hear five sentences. Each will be said twice. Listen carefully and write the missing words.

1. El hotel es _____.   4. El museo es muy _____.

2. El estudiante es muy _____.   5. Íñigo no es _____.

3. El _____ no es difícil (*difficult*).

■ ¿Cómo es usted?

❖**A. Adjetivos.** Read aloud the following adjectives, then choose those that best describe you and use them to complete the sentence.

arrogante	impaciente	optimista	realista
egoísta	independiente	paciente	rebelde
emocional	inteligente	pesimista	responsable
idealista	irresponsable		

Yo soy _____, _____, _____ y _____.

---

*Answers to all **Dictado** exercises are given in the Appendix.

B. ¿Qué opina usted? (*What do you think?*) Describe the following people by using appropriate adjectives from the preceding list and from the list in **Los cognados** in your textbook.

1. Gloria Estefan es _____, _____ y _____.

2. Enrique Iglesias es _____, _____ y _____.

3. Madonna es _____, _____ y _____.

4. Antonio Banderas es _____, _____ y _____.

❖**C. Mi mejor amigo/a** (*My best friend*). Tell your best friend what you think he/she is like. What verb form will you use with **tú: soy, eres, es**?

Tú (soy / eres / es) _____, _____, _____ y _____.

❖**D. Encuesta** (*Survey*). You will hear a series of questions. For each question, check the appropriate answer. No answers will be given. The answers you choose should be correct for you!

1. ☐ Sí, soy independiente.   3. ☐ Sí, soy eficiente.
   ☐ No, no soy independiente.   ☐ No, no soy eficiente.
2. ☐ Sí, soy sentimental.   4. ☐ Sí, soy flexible.
   ☐ No, no soy sentimental.   ☐ No, no soy flexible.

E. Preguntas (*Questions*). Ask the following persons about their personalities using **¿Eres... ?** or **¿Es usted... ?** as appropriate and the cues you will hear. Follow the model. (Remember to repeat the correct question. If you prefer, pause and write the questions.) You will hear answers to your questions.

MODELO: (*you see*) Marcos   (*you hear*) tímido →
(*you say*) Marcos, ¿eres tímido?   (*you hear*) Sí, soy tímido.

1. Ramón, ¿_____?

2. Señora Alba, ¿_____?

3. Señor Castán, ¿_____?

4. Anita, ¿_____?

Nota cultural: Spanish in the United States and in the World

A. Emparejar (*Matching*). Match the geographical area of the United States with the largest Spanish-speaking group(s) that has (have) settled in each area.

Northeast _____   a. Central Americans
                       b. Cubans
Southwest _____   c. Mexicans
                       d. Puerto Ricans
Southeast _____

❖ **B. Pregunta.** Do you know people who have come from Spanish-speaking countries? Which countries?

_____

Pronunciación y ortografía: El alfabeto español

A. El alfabeto español. You will hear the names of the letters of the Spanish alphabet, along with a list of place names. Listen and repeat, imitating the speaker. Notice that most Spanish consonants are pronounced differently than in English. In future chapters, you will have the opportunity to practice the pronunciation of most of these letters individually.

a	a	la Argentina		ñ	eñe	España
b	be	Bolivia		o	o	Oviedo
c	ce	Cáceres		p	pe	Panamá
d	de	Durango		q	cu	Quito
e	e	el Ecuador		r	ere	el Perú
f	efe	Florida		rr	erre	Monterrey
g	ge	Guatemala		s	ese	San Juan
h	hache	Honduras		t	te	Toledo
i	i	Ibiza		u	u	el Uruguay
j	jota	Jalisco		v	ve	Venezuela
k	ca	(*Kansas*)		w	doble ve	(*Washington*)
l	ele	Lima		x	equis	Extremadura
m	eme	México		y	i griega	el Paraguay
n	ene	Nicaragua		z	zeta	Zaragoza

B. Repeticiones. Repeat the following words, phrases, and sentences. Imitate the speaker and pay close attention to the difference in pronunciation between Spanish and English.

1.	c/ch	Colón	Cecilia	Muchas gracias.	Buenas noches.
2.	g/gu	Ortega	gusto	Miguel	guitarra
3.	h	La Habana	Héctor	hotel	historia
4.	j/g	Jamaica	Jiménez	Geraldo	Gilda
5.	l/ll	Lupe	Manolo	Sevilla	me llamo
6.	y	Yolanda	yate	Paraguay	y
7.	r/rr	Mario	arte	Roberto	carro
8.	ñ	Begoña	Toño	señorita	Hasta mañana.

C. Más repeticiones. Repeat the following Spanish syllables, imitating the speaker. Try to pronounce each vowel with a short, tense sound.

1.	ma	fa	la	ta	pa
2.	me	fe	le	te	pe
3.	mi	fi	li	ti	pi
4.	mo	fo	lo	to	po
5.	mu	fu	lu	tu	pu
6.	sa	se	si	so	su

D. Las vocales. Compare the pronunciation of the following words in both English and Spanish. Listen for the schwa, the *uh* sound in English, and notice its absence in Spanish.

English: *banana*   Spanish: **banana**
           capital   **capital**

Now, repeat the following words, imitating the speaker. Be careful to avoid the English schwa. Remember to pronounce each vowel with a short and tense sound.

1.	hasta	tal	nada	mañana	natural
2.	me	qué	Pérez	usted	rebelde
3.	sí	señorita	permiso	imposible	tímido
4.	yo	con	cómo	noches	profesor
5.	tú	uno	mucho	Perú	Lupe

E. ¿Español o inglés? You will hear a series of words. Each will be said twice. Circle the letter of the word you hear, either a Spanish word (**español**) or an English word (**inglés**). Note that Spanish vowels are short and tense; they are never drawn out with a *u* or *i* glide as in English.

ESPAÑOL   INGLÉS

1.	**a.** mi		**b.** me
2.	**a.** fe		**b.** Fay
3.	**a.** es		**b.** ace
4.	**a.** con		**b.** cone
5.	**a.** ti		**b.** tea
6.	**a.** lo		**b.** low

F. Dictado

Paso 1. You will hear a series of words that are probably unfamiliar to you. Each will be said twice. Listen carefully, concentrating on the vowel sounds, and write in the missing vowels.

1. r____d____ll____

2. M____r____b____l

3. ____n____l____t____r____l

4. s____lv____v____d____s

5. ____lv____d____d____z____

Paso 2. Imagine that you work as a hotel receptionist in Miami. Listen to how some Hispanic guests spell out their last names for you. Write down the names as you hear them.

1. _____

2. _____

3. _____

4. _____

Segundo paso

■ Los números 0–30; *hay*

A. Cantidades (*Quantities*). Write out the numbers indicated in parentheses. Remember that the number **uno** changes to **un** before a masculine noun and to **una** before a feminine noun.

1. (1) _____ clase (*f.*)

2. (4) _____ dólares

3. (7) _____ días

4. (13) _____ personas

5. (11) _____ señoras

6. (1) _____ estudiante (*m.*)

7. (20) _____ señoras

8. (23) _____ personas

9. (26) _____ clases

10. (21) _____ señores (*m.*)

11. (21) _____ pesetas (*f.*)

12. (30) _____ estudiantes

B. Problemas de matemáticas. Complete each equation, then write out the missing numbers in each statement.

1. $14 + $ _____ $ = 22$ Catorce y _____ son veintidós.

2. $15 - 4 = $ _____   Quince menos cuatro son _____.

3. $2 + 3 = $ _____   Dos y tres son _____.

4. $8 + $ _____ $ = 14$ Ocho y _____ son catorce.

5. $13 + $ _____ $ = 20$ Trece y _____ son veinte.

6. $15 + 7 = $ _____   Quince y siete son _____.

7. _____ $ - 3 = 27$ _____ menos tres son veintisiete.

❖**C. Preguntas.** Answer the following questions that a friend has asked about your university.

1. ¿Cuántas clases de Español I hay? _____

_____

2. ¿Cuántos estudiantes hay en tu (*your*) clase de español? _____

_____

3. ¿Y cuántos profesores hay en el Departamento de Español? _____

4. ¿Hay clase de español mañana? _____

5. ¿Hay un teatro en la universidad? _____

D. ¿Cuántos hay? (*How many are there?*) Read the following phrases when you hear the corresponding numbers. (Remember to repeat the correct answer.)

1. 21 personas (*f.*)
2. 18 profesores
3. 1 señora (*f.*)
4. 21 días (*m.*)
5. 30 cafés

E. ¿Qué hay en la sala de clase? (*What is there in the classroom?*) You will hear a series of questions. Each will be said twice. Answer based on the following drawing. (Remember to repeat the correct answer.)

1. ... 2. ... 3. ... 4. ...

Gustos (*Likes*) y preferencias

A. Gustos y preferencias. Imagine that you are asking your instructor and several classmates whether they like the following things. Form your questions by combining phrases from the first column with items and activities in the other two. Then write the answers you think they *might* give.

le gusta	la música jazz	esquiar
te gusta	el chocolate	beber café
(no) me gusta	el programa «American Idol»	estudiar
		jugar a la lotería / al tenis / al fútbol

1. —Profesor(a), ¿_____?

   —Sí (No), _____.

2. —Profesor(a), ¿_____?

   —Sí (No), _____.

3. —_____, ¿_____?
      (*classmate's name*)

   —Sí (No), _____.

4. —_____, ¿_____?

   —Sí (No), _____.

5. —_____, ¿_____?

   —Sí (No), _____.

6. —_____, ¿_____?

   —Sí (No), _____.

❖**B. Diálogo.** You meet another student who asks you the following questions. Write your answers in Spanish.

ESTUDIANTE: ¿Eres estudiante?

USTED: _____.

ESTUDIANTE: ¿Cómo te llamas?

USTED: _____.

ESTUDIANTE: ¿De dónde eres?

USTED: _____.

ESTUDIANTE: ¿Cómo se llama tu (*your*) profesor(a) de español?

USTED: _____.

ESTUDIANTE: ¿Cómo es él/ella? ¿impaciente? ¿inteligente? ¿interesante? ¿ ?

USTED: _____.

ESTUDIANTE: ¿Te gusta la clase?

USTED: _____.

C. Gustos y preferencias. You will hear a series of questions. Each will be said twice. You should be able to guess the meaning of the verbs based on context. Answer based on your own experience. You will hear a possible answer. (Remember to repeat the answer.)

MODELO: (*you see*) jugar
(*you hear*) ¿Te gusta jugar al tenis? →
(*you say*) Sí, me gusta jugar al tenis. OR No, no me gusta jugar al tenis.

1. jugar **2.** estudiar **3.** tocar **4.** comer

¿Qué hora es?

A. Son las... Match the following statements with the clock faces shown below.

1. _____ Son las cinco y diez de la tarde.

2. _____ Son las diez menos veinte de la noche.

3. _____ Es la una y cuarto de la mañana.

4. _____ Son las once y media de la mañana.

5. _____ Son las cuatro menos cuarto de la tarde.

6. _____ Son las nueve y veinte de la noche.

a. **b.** **c.** **d.** **e.** **f.**

Nota comunicativa: Para expresar la hora

¿**Qué hora es?** Write the sentences in Spanish, spelling out the times indicated. Use **de la mañana, de la tarde, de la noche,** and so on as required.

1. It's 12:20 A.M. ————————————————————————————————————

2. It's 1:05 P.M. —————————————————————————————————————

3. It's exactly 2:00 A.M. ———————————————————————————————

4. The reception (**La recepción**) is at 7:30 P.M. ——————————————

5. The class is at 10:50 A.M. —————————————————————————————

6. It's 9:45 P.M. —————————————————————————————————————

7. It's 1:30 A.M. —————————————————————————————————————

8. It's 8:15 A.M. —————————————————————————————————————

¡OJO!

In Spain, as in most of Europe, times in transportation schedules are given on a 24-hour clock. A comma is often used instead of a colon.

Convert the following hours from the 24-hour system to the A.M./P.M. system.

a. 16,05 = _____   b. 20,15 = _____   c. 22,50 = _____

B. ¿A qué hora es… ? You will hear a series of questions about Marisol's schedule. Answer based on her schedule. (Remember to repeat the correct answer.) First, pause and look at the schedule.

> MODELO: (*you hear*) ¿A qué hora es la clase de español? →
> (*you say*) Es a las ocho y media de la mañana.

Horario escolar*

Nombre: Marisol Abad
Dirección: Calle Alfaro, 16
Teléfono: 72-45-86

8:30	Español
9:40	Ciencias
11:00	Matemáticas
12:25	Inglés
2:15	Arte

*School schedule

---

1. … 2. … 3. … 4. …

C. ¿Qué hora es? You will hear a series of times. Each will be said twice. Circle the letter of the clock face that indicates the time you hear.

MODELO: (you hear) Son las diez de la mañana. → (you circle the letter a)

a.

b.

1. a.

   b.

2. a.

   b.

3. a.

   b.

4. a.

   b.

A leer: La geografía del mundo hispánico

Un poco de (*A little bit of*) **geografía.** Match these geographical names with the category to which they belong.

1. _____ los Andes   **a.** una cordillera

2. _____ Titicaca   **b.** un mar

3. _____ Cuba   **c.** un lago

4. _____ el Caribe   **d.** una península

5. _____ el Amazonas   **e.** un río

6. _____ Yucatán   **f.** una isla

Los hispanos hablan: ¿Qué tipo de música te gusta más?

In this section of the Workbook/Laboratory Manual, you will hear authentic passages from Hispanics about a variety of subjects, including their school experiences, food preferences, hobbies, and so on. As you listen, try not to be distracted by unfamiliar vocabulary. Concentrate instead on what you *do* know and understand.*

In addition to the types of music that most young people listen to here in the United States (soft rock, heavy metal, and so on), Hispanic students also listen to music that is typical of their own country or region. Have you heard of **la salsa, el merengue,** or **el tango**? These are all types of music from different regions of Spanish America. Note that the word **conjunto** means *musical group*.

You will hear a passage in which a student tells about her likes and dislikes in music. First, listen to get a general idea of the content. Then, go back and listen again for specific information. Then you will hear a series of statements. Circle **C** (**cierto**) if the statement is true or **F** (**falso**) if it is false.

Habla Teresa: Me gusta más el *rock* en inglés y en español. Mis cantantes favoritos son Sting y Whitney Houston. Mis conjuntos favoritos son Metálica y Hombres G, un conjunto que canta en español. Me gusta la música instrumental y me encanta la música latina por su ritmo y su sabor… y porque es nuestra. Me gustan la salsa y el merengue. Me gusta la música en inglés y español. ¡Amo toda la música!

1. C F   **2.** C F   **3.** C F

---

*The listening text for the **Los hispanos hablan** sections will appear in the Workbook/Laboratory Manual through **Capítulo 2.**

Un paso más

Videoteca*

Entre amigos. You will hear two conversations between students who are studying at the Universidad Iberoamericana. Listen carefully and supply the following information. Do not be distracted by unfamiliar vocabulary. Instead, focus on what you *do* know. Check your answers in the Appendix.

	EDAD (*age*)	PAÍS (*country*) DE ORIGEN
1. Miguel René	_____	_____
2. Tané	_____	_____
3. Rubén	_____	_____
4. Karina	_____	_____

¡Repasemos!

A. *Listening Passage: ¿Qué idiomas se hablan en Latinoamérica?*[†]

> The first listening passage, as well as the passages in other chapters of the Workbook/Laboratory Manual, will be preceded by prelistening exercises (**Antes de escuchar**). They will involve strategies such as predicting and guessing content before you listen, reading the true/false statements before listening, and so on. You should always do the prelistening section *before* you listen to the passage. Don't be distracted by unfamiliar vocabulary. Focus on what you *do* know. In most cases, you will be asked to listen for specific information.

Antes de escuchar (*Before listening*). Before you listen to the passage, pause and do the following prelistening exercises.

Paso 1. Read the true/false statements. As you read them, try to infer the information you will hear in the passage, as well as listen for specific information.

1. Julia es de México.
2. Tegucigalpa es la capital de Honduras.
3. Julia habla guaraní.
4. No se habla portugués en Latinoamérica.
5. Las palabras (*words*) **español** y **castellano** son sinónimas.
6. El español es la única (*only*) lengua que se habla en Latinoamérica.

Paso 2. What can you infer from the true/false statements? Check all that apply.

☐ Julia will probably tell us where she is from and what language she speaks.

☐ There may be more than one word to describe the Spanish language.

☐ It is possible that more than one language is spoken throughout Latin America.

Now resume listening.

---

*The **Videoteca** videoclips are available on the Video on CD to accompany *¿Qué tal?*, Seventh Edition.
[†]The text for the Listening Passages will appear in the Workbook/Laboratory Manual through **Capítulo 2.**

Listening Passage. Now, you will hear a passage about the Spanish language and where it is spoken. First, listen to get a general idea of the content. Then, go back and listen again for specific information.

¡Hola! Me llamo Julia y soy de Tegucigalpa. ¡Sí! Tegucigalpa. ¿Es un nombre difícil? Tegucigalpa es la capital de Honduras. Honduras está en Centroamérica. En mi país se habla el castellano o español. **Español** y **castellano** son palabras sinónimas para hablar del mismo idioma. El castellano también se habla en España y en toda Latinoamérica. Bueno, no en toda Latinoamérica, porque en el Brasil se habla portugués y en Belice se habla inglés. Además del castellano, en el mundo hispánico se hablan otros idiomas también. Por ejemplo, en el Paraguay hay dos lenguas oficiales, el español y el guaraní. El guaraní es una lengua indígena original de la región. Mi amiga Susana es paraguaya y habla español y guaraní.

El español es una lengua muy importante en el mundo, porque lo hablan muchas personas. ¿Se habla español en tu estado?

Now pause and do the exercises in **Después de escuchar.**

Después de escuchar (*After listening*)

Paso 1. Here are the true/false statements. Circle **C** (**cierto**) if the statement is true or **F** (**falso**) if it is false. Then, correct the statements that are false, according to the passage.

1. C F Julia es de México.

   _____

2. C F Tegucigalpa es la capital de Honduras.

   _____

3. C F Julia habla guaraní.

   _____

4. C F No se habla portugués en Latinoamérica.

   _____

5. C F Las palabras **español** y **castellano** son sinónimas.

   _____

6. C F El español es la única lengua que se habla en Latinoamérica.

   _____

Paso 2. Go back and listen to the passage again. Then, pause and complete the following sentences with words chosen from the list.

castellano   español   inglés   lengua   paraguaya

1. La palabra **idioma** es sinónimo de _____.
2. Julia es de Honduras: es **hondureña.** Susana es de Paraguay: es _____.
3. Susana habla guaraní y _____ (o _____).
4. En Belice se habla _____.

Now resume listening.

B. Entrevista. You will hear a series of questions. Each will be said twice. Answer, based on your own experience. Pause and write the answers.

1. _____
2. _____
3. _____
4. _____
5. _____
6. _____
7. _____

Mi diario

It is a good idea to have a separate notebook for your **diario** entries. Before you begin writing, reread the pages about **Mi diario** in To the Student (page vi). Include at least the following information in your first entry.

- First, write today's date in numerals. Note that in Spanish the day comes first, then the month, and finally the year. Thus, 29/8/06 is August 29, 2006.
- Now greet your diary as you would a friend and introduce yourself.
- Write down what time it is. (Write out the hour.)
- Describe your personality, using as many adjectives as you can from pages 4 and 5 of the Workbook/Laboratory Manual.
- List two things you like (or like to do) and two things you do *not* like (or do not like to do).

Póngase a prueba

A ver si sabe...

A. ¿Cómo es usted? (*What are you like?*) Fill in the blanks with the appropriate form of **ser.**

1. yo _____   3. usted, él, ella _____

2. tú _____

B. Saludos y expresiones de cortesía. Complete the following phrases.

1. To a friend:

   ¡_____! ¿Qué tal?

2. Fill in the blanks with the correct form of **bueno.**

   _____ días.

   _____ tardes.

   _____ noches.

3. To ask a classmate her name, you say:

   ¿Cómo _____?

4. The responses to **muchas gracias** are:

   _____.

   _____.

C. **Gustos y preferencias.** Fill in the blanks with the appropriate word(s).

—¿Te _____¹ el chocolate?

—No, no _____.²

D. **¿Qué hora es?**

1. To ask what time it is, you say:

   ¿_____?

2. To answer, use:

   _____ la una (y cuarto, y media).

   _____ las dos (tres, etcétera).

Prueba corta

A. **Preguntas.** Conteste en español.

1. Ask your instructor what his or her name is. _____

2. Ask the student next to you what his or her name is. _____

3. Now ask where he/she is from. _____

4. What do you say when someone gives you a gift? _____

5. How does that person respond? _____

6. Tell your best friend what he or she is like. Use at least three adjectives.

   _____

7. Ask your instructor if he or she likes **el jazz**. _____

8. Ask a classmate if he or she likes **el chocolate**. _____

   _____

9. Write out the numbers in the following series: tres, _____, nueve, _____,

   _____, dieciocho, _____, veinticuatro, veintisiete, _____.

10. Express 11:15 P.M. in Spanish: _____

B. **Hablando** (*Speaking*) **de las clases.** You will overhear a conversation between Geraldo and Delia. Listen carefully. Try not to be distracted by unfamiliar vocabulary; concentrate instead on what you do know. Then, you will hear a series of statements. Circle **C** if the statement is true (**cierto**) and **F** if it is false (**falso**).

1. C F   2. C F   3. C F   4. C F   5. C F

Paso 1 Vocabulario

En la clase

A. Identificaciones. Identify the person, place, or objects shown in each drawing.

1. _____ 2. _____ 3. _____ 6. _____

4. _____ 7. _____

5. _____ 8. _____

9. _____ 14. _____ 20. _____

10. _____ 15. _____ 21. _____

11. _____ 16. _____ 22. _____

12. _____ 17. _____ 23. _____

13. _____ 18. _____

19. _____

B. **¡Busque el intruso!** (*Look for the intruder!*) Write the item that does not belong in each series of words and explain why.

Categorías posibles

una cosa

un lugar

una persona

MODELO: el bolígrafo / el estudiante / el profesor / el hombre →
El bolígrafo, porque (*because*) es una cosa. No es una persona.

1. la consejera / la profesora / la calculadora / la compañera de clase

   _____

2. la residencia / la librería / la biblioteca / la mochila

   _____

3. el papel / el lápiz / el hombre / el bolígrafo

   _____

4. el diccionario / el libro / el cuaderno / el edificio

   _____

5. la bibliotecaria / la cafetería / la biblioteca / la oficina

   _____

C. **Dictado: ¿Qué necesita?** (*What does she need?*) Luisa is making a list of things that she will need for her classes this semester. Listen carefully to her list and check the items that she needs. If she mentions a number, write it in the space provided. Don't be distracted by unfamiliar vocabulary; concentrate instead on the words that you *do* know. ¡OJO! Not all items will be mentioned. First, listen to the list of possible items.

COSAS	SÍ	NO	¿CUÁNTOS O CUÁNTAS?
mochila(s)			
lápiz (lápices)			
bolígrafo(s)			
libro(s) de texto			
cuaderno(s)			
diccionario(s)			
calculadora(s)			
papel			
pizarra(s)			

D. Identificaciones. Identify the following items when you hear the corresponding number. Begin each sentence with **Es el...** or **Es la...** (Remember to repeat the correct answer.)

1. ...　2. ...　3. ...　4. ...　5. ...

6. ...　7. ...　8. ...　9. ...　10. ...

Las materias

A. Materias. What classes would you take if you were majoring in the following areas? Choose your classes from the list.

Antropología　Computación　Gramática alemana　Sociología urbana
Astronomía　Contabilidad (*Accounting*)　La novela moderna　Trigonometría
Biología 2　Física　Química orgánica
Cálculo 1　Francés 304　Sicología del adolescente

1. Lenguas y literatura

   a. _____

   b. _____

   c. _____

2. Matemáticas y administración de empresas

   a. _____

   b. _____

   c. _____

   d. _____

3. Ciencias sociales

   a. _____

   b. _____

   c. _____

4. Ciencias naturales

   a. _____

   b. _____

   c. _____

   d. _____

❖**B. ¿Qué estudias?** (*What are you studying?*) Write about the courses you need or like or do not like to study by combining phrases from the two columns.

Necesito estudiar (No) Me gusta estudiar	+	chino, español, inglés, italiano, japonés, ruso cálculo, computación, contabilidad ciencias políticas, historia biología, química sicología

MODELO: Necesito estudiar inglés.

1. _____

2. _____

3. _____

Nota comunicativa: Palabras interrogativas

A. Palabras interrogativas. Complete the sentences with the most appropriate interrogative word or phrase from the following list. In some cases more than one answer is possible. Write your answers in the spaces provided. To use this exercise for review, cover the answers with a piece of paper.

¿A qué hora?	¿Cuándo?	¿Dónde?
¿Cómo?	¿Cuánto?	¿Qué?
¿Cuál?	¿Cuántos?	¿Quién?

1. ¿_____ es por el libro (*for the book*)? ¿Tres o cuatro dólares?

2. ¿_____ es la clase de historia? ¿A la una o a las dos?

3. Buenos días, Sr. Vargas. ¿_____ está Ud. hoy?

4. ¿_____ es la capital de la Argentina? ¿Buenos Aires o Lima?

5. ¿_____ estudias (*do you study*), en casa (*at home*) o en la biblioteca (*library*)?

6. —¿_____ es Ud.? —Soy María Castro.

7. ¿_____ es el examen, hoy o mañana?

8. ¿_____ es esto? ¿una trompeta o un saxofón?

B. El Cine Bolívar. Your friend asks you some questions about a movie (**una película**) at the Cine Bolívar. Use an appropriate interrogative phrase to complete each of his questions.

AMIGO: ¿_____[1] se llama la película?

USTED: *Casablanca.*

AMIGO: ¿_____[2] es el actor principal?

USTED: Humphrey Bogart.

AMIGO: ¿_____[3] es la película?

USTED: Es romántica.

AMIGO: ¿_____[4] es por la entrada (*for the admission*)?

USTED: Siete pesos.

AMIGO: ¿_____[5] está el Cine Bolívar?

USTED: Está en la Avenida Bolívar.

AMIGO: ¿_____[6] es la película?

USTED: A las siete de la tarde.

AMIGO: ¿_____[7] hora es ahora?

USTED: Son las cinco y cuarto.

C. Preguntas y respuestas (*Questions and answers*). Imagine that your friend Marisa has just made some statements that you didn't quite understand. You will hear each statement twice. Circle the letter of the interrogative word or phrase you would use to obtain information about what she said.

1. a. ¿a qué hora?   b. ¿cómo es?
2. a. ¿quién?   b. ¿cómo es?
3. a. ¿cuál?   b. ¿dónde está?
4. a. ¿cuántas?   b. ¿cuándo?
5. a. ¿qué es?   b. ¿cómo es?
6. a. ¿cómo está?   b. ¿qué es?

Pronunciación y ortografía : Diphthongs and Linking

A. Vocales. Complete the sentences.

1. Spanish has _____ (*number*) vowels.

2. The strong vowels are _____.

3. The weak vowels are _____.

4. A diphthong consists of one _____ vowel and one _____ vowel, or two successive _____ vowels pronounced in the same syllable.

B. ¿Cuáles son diptongos? Underline the diphthongs in the following words.

1. es-tu-dian-te
2. dic-cio-na-rio
3. puer-ta
4. cua-der-no
5. bi-lin-güe
6. gra-cias
7. es-cri-to-rio
8. sie-te
9. seis

C. Repaso: Las vocales. Repeat the following words, imitating the speaker. Pay close attention to the pronunciation of the indicated vowels.

WEAK VOWELS

(i, y)	Pili	silla	soy	y
(u)	gusto	lugar	uno	mujer

STRONG VOWELS

(a)	calculadora	Ana	banana	lápiz
(e)	trece	papel	clase	general
(o)	profesor	hombre	Lola	bolígrafo

D. Diptongos. Diphthongs are formed by two successive weak vowels (**i** or **y, u**) or by a combination of a weak vowel and a strong vowel (**a, e, o**). The two vowels are pronounced as a single syllable. Repeat the following words, imitating the speaker. Pay close attention to the pronunciation of the indicated diphthongs.

1. (ia)	med**ia**	grac**ias**		7. (ui)	m**uy**	f**ui** (*I was/I went*)
2. (ie)	b**ie**n	s**ie**te		8. (uo)	c**uo**ta	ard**uo**
3. (io)	Jul**io**	edific**io**		9. (ai)	**ai**re	h**ay**
4. (iu)	c**iu**dad (*city*)	v**iu**da (*widow*)		10. (ei)	v**ei**nte	tr**ei**nta
5. (ua)	c**ua**derno	Manag**ua**		11. (oi)	s**oy**	est**oy**
6. (ue)	b**ue**nos	n**ue**ve		12. (au)	**au**to	p**au**sa
				13. (eu)	de**u**da (*debt*)	C**eu**ta

E. Más sobre (*about*) **los diptongos**

Paso 1. Diphthongs can occur within a word or between words, causing the words to be "linked" and pronounced as one long word. Repeat the following phrases and sentences, imitating the speaker. Pay close attention to how the words are linked.

1. (oi/ia)   Armando y Alicia
                 las letras o y hache
2. (ei/ie)   el tigre y el chimpancé
                 Vicente y Elena
3. (oi/ie/ai/io) Soy extrovertida y optimista.
4. (ai/iu)   Elena y Humberto necesitan una mochila y unos libros.

Paso 2. Linking also occurs naturally between many word boundaries in Spanish. Repeat the following sentences, imitating the speaker. Try to say each without pause, as if it were one long word.

1. ¿Es usted eficiente?
2. ¿Dónde hay un escritorio?
3. Tomás y Alicia están en la oficina.
4. Están en la Argentina y en el Uruguay.
5. No hay estudiantes en el edificio a estas horas (*at these hours*).

F. Dictado. You will hear a series of words containing diphthongs. Each will be said twice. Listen carefully and write the missing vowels.

1. c_____nc_____s   3. s_____s   5. _____to

2. Patric_____   4. b_____nos   6. s_____

Los hispanos hablan: ¿Qué materias te gusta estudiar?

You will hear three Hispanic students describe the courses they like or don't like. As you listen to each one, complete the following chart with **sí** or **no.** Use **sí** to indicate that the student likes a given subject, and **no** to indicate that he or she does not. You will hear the students in the order given in the chart. **¡OJO!** The students may mention subjects other than those listed in the chart. Check your answers in the Appendix.

1. *Habla José:* Me gustan mucho la química, la física, la biología, la sicología y la literatura. ¡No me gustan para nada las matemáticas!
2. *Habla Raúl:* No me gustan los idiomas. Pienso que todo el mundo debería hablar el mismo idioma, el español, claro. Me gustan mucho las ciencias porque las entiendo bien.
3. *Habla Julia:* Me gustan las matemáticas y la sicología. Me gustan mucho los números y también me gusta saber lo que está pensando la gente. No me gustan la historia y la química. Realmente no me interesa el pasado y detesto las fórmulas y los laboratorios.

MATERIAS	1. JOSÉ	2. RAÚL	3. JULIA
Historia			
Matemáticas			
Sicología			
Química			
Física			
Biología			
Idiomas			
Ciencias			

Paso 2 Gramática

 **1. Identifying People, Places, Things, and Ideas •
Singular Nouns: Gender and Articles**

A. **¿*El* o *la*?** Escriba el artículo definido apropiado, **el** o **la.**

1. _____ tarde   5. _____ día

2. _____ libertad   6. _____ mujer

3. _____ nación   7. _____ clase

4. _____ profesor   8. _____ hombre

B. **¿*Un* o *una*?** Escriba el artículo indefinido apropiado, **un** o **una.**

1. _____ diccionario   5. _____ día

2. _____ universidad   6. _____ mochila

3. _____ lápiz   7. _____ mesa

4. _____ dependienta   8. _____ programa

C. **Una cuestión de gustos.** Indicate how you feel about the following places or things. Remember to use the article **el** or **la.**

 MODELO: programa «Sixty Minutes» → (No) Me gusta el programa «Sixty Minutes».

1. clase de español   _____

2. universidad   _____

3. música de Bach   _____

4. Mundo de Disney   _____

5. limonada   _____

6. comida (*food*) mexicana _____

7. física   _____

8. programa «CSI»   _____

D. **¿Qué te gusta?** Tell a friend what you like, using the oral cues and the correct definite article. (Remember to repeat the correct answer.)

 MODELO: (*you hear*) profesora → (*you say*) Me gusta la profesora.

1. ... 2. ... 3. ... 4. ... 5. ...

E. Minidiálogo: En la clase del profesor Durán: El primer día

Paso 1. Dictado. The dialogue below will be read twice. Listen carefully the first time; the second time, write in the missing words.

PROFESOR DURÁN: Aquí está _____¹

_____² del curso.

Son necesarios _____³

_____⁴ de texto y

_____⁵ diccionario. También hay

_____⁶ _____⁷

de _____⁸ y libros

de poesía.

ESTUDIANTE 1: ¡Es una lista infinita!

ESTUDIANTE 2: Sí, y los libros cuestan demasiado.

ESTUDIANTE 1: No, _____⁹ _____¹⁰ no es el precio de los libros. ¡Es
_____¹¹ _____¹² para leer los libros!

Paso 2. ¿Cierto o falso? Now pause and read the following statements about the dialogue. Circle **C** (**cierto**) if the statement is true or **F** (**falso**) if it is false.

1. C F En la clase del profesor Durán es necesario leer muchos libros.

2. C F Para los estudiantes, el problema es el tiempo para leer los libros.

3. C F Los estudiantes necesitan una calculadora para la clase.

Now resume listening.

F. ¿Qué hay en estos (*these*) **lugares?** Identify the items in each drawing after you hear the corresponding number. Begin each sentence with **Hay un...** or **Hay una...** (Remember to repeat the correct answer.)

MODELO: (*you see*) diccionario → (*you say*) Hay un diccionario en la mesa.

1.

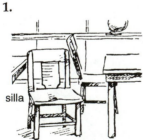

silla

2.

bolígrafo

3.

estudiante

4.

consejero

 ## 2. Identifying People, Places, Things, and Ideas • Nouns and Articles: Plural Forms

A. Singular → plural. Escriba la forma plural.

1. la amiga _____

2. el bolígrafo _____

3. la clase _____

4. un profesor _____

5. el lápiz _____

6. una extranjera _____

7. la universidad _____

8. un programa _____

B. Plural → singular. Escriba la forma singular.

1. los edificios _____

2. las fiestas _____

3. unas clientes _____

4. unos lápices _____

5. los papeles _____

6. las universidades _____

7. unos problemas _____

8. unas mujeres _____

C. Daniel, un estudiante típico. ¿Qué hay en el escritorio de Daniel? Use el artículo indefinido.

MODELO: Hay un radio en el escritorio.

1. _____

2. _____

3. _____

¿Qué necesita Daniel? (*What does Daniel need?*)

4. Necesita _____

5. _____

6. _____

7. _____

❖¿Y qué necesita Ud.?

8. Necesito _____.

D. Descripción: El cuarto de Ignacio. You will hear Ignacio describe his room. As you listen, circle the number of the drawing that best matches his description. First, pause and look at the drawings.

1.   2.   3.

E. Cambios (*Changes*). You will hear a series of nouns and articles. Give the plural forms of the first four nouns and articles and the singular forms of the next four. (Remember to repeat the correct answer.)

SINGULAR → PLURAL   PLURAL → SINGULAR

1. … **2.** … **3.** … **4.** … **5.** … **6.** … **7.** … **8.** …

F. Los errores de Inés. You will hear some statements that your friend Inés makes about the following drawing. She is wrong and you must correct her. (Remember to repeat the correct answer.)

MODELO: (*you hear*) Hay dos libros. → (*you say*) No. Hay tres libros.

1. … **2.** … **3.** … **4.** … **5.** … **6.** …

G. Dictado. You will hear a series of sentences. Each will be said twice. Listen carefully and write the missing words. You will be listening for words that are either singular or plural.

1. Hay _____ _____ en _____ _____.

2. _____ _____ están en _____ _____.

3. No hay _____ en _____ _____.

4. ¿Hay _____ _____ en _____ _____?

Paso 3 Gramática

3. Expressing Actions • Subject Pronouns; Present Tense of -ar Verbs; Negation

A. Los pronombres personales. What subject pronouns would you use to speak *about* the following persons?

1. your female friends _____
2. your brother _____
3. yourself _____
4. your friends Eva and Jesús _____
5. your male relatives _____
6. you and your sister _____

B. Más sobre (*about*) **los pronombres.** What subject pronouns would you use to speak *to* the following persons?

1. your cousin Roberto _____

2. your friends (*m.*) _____   _____
                   (*in Spain*)   (*in Latin America*)

3. your instructors _____

4. the store clerk _____

5. your friend _____   _____
            (*in Spain*)   (*in Latin America*)

C. ¡No, no! Correct the following statements by making them all negative. Use subject pronouns in your answers. Then write two sentences telling about things *you* do *not* do. Use only verbs that you have studied so far.

1. Shaquille O'Neal trabaja en una oficina.

   _____

2. Gloria Estefan canta en japonés.

   _____

3. Tomamos cerveza en la clase.

   _____

4. La profesora regresa a la universidad por la noche.

   _____

5. Los estudiantes bailan en la biblioteca.

   _____

6. Enseño español.

   _____

❖7. _____

❖8. _____

D. En la universidad. Describe what the following people are doing, using the verbs given. Not all verbs will be used.

bailar
cantar
hablar
pagar
tocar
tomar
trabajar

1. *En el bar:* Yo _____ por teléfono. Madonna _____ en la televisión y Jaime y Ana _____. Tomás y Carlos _____ cerveza y

   Carlos _____ las bebidas.ᵃ El meseroᵇ _____ mucho.

ᵃ*drinks* ᵇ*waiter*

buscar
escuchar
necesitar
pagar

2. *En el laboratorio de lenguas:* María y yo _____ la lección de español. Luis

   _____ el casete #2. Él _____ preparar la lección de francés.

desear
enseñar
estudiar
practicar
regresar

3. *En la clase:* La profesora Cantellini _____ italiano, y los estudiantes

   _____ y _____ mucho. A las nueve y media, ella

   _____ a suᵃ oficina.

ᵃ*her*

❖ 4. Now write three sentences that describe what you and your friends do on a typical weekend. Use only verbs that you have studied so far. (Use **nosotros** forms.)

   En un fin de semana típico, _____

   _____.

E. ¿Quién habla? You will hear a series of sentences. Each will be said twice. Listen carefully and circle the letter of the *subject* of each sentence. In this exercise, you will practice listening for specific information.

1. **a.** yo   **b.** ella   **4. a.** Alberto   **b.** Alberto y tú
2. **a.** él   **b.** tú   **5. a.** Uds.   **b.** nosotras
3. **a.** Ana y yo   **b.** los estudiantes

F. ¿Quién… ? Answer the following questions using the oral cues. (Remember to repeat the correct answer.)

1. ¿Quién canta bien?

   MODELO: (*you hear*) Juan → (*you say*) Juan canta bien.

   a. …   **b.** …   **c.** …   **d.** …

2. ¿Quién practica deportes (*sports*)?

   MODELO: (*you hear*) yo → (*you say*) Yo practico deportes.

   a. …   **b.** …   **c.** …   **d.** …

G. Mis compañeros y yo. Form complete sentences about yourself and others, using the oral and written cues. (Remember to repeat the correct answer.)

MODELO: (*you see and hear*) yo (*you hear*) pagar la matrícula →
(*you say*) Pago la matrícula.

1. Ana y yo   3. el estudiante de Chile   5. profesor, Ud.…
2. Chela y Roberto   4. Jaime, tú…

Nota comunicativa: The verb *estar*

A. ¿Dónde están todos ahora? Tell where you and your classmates are. Form complete sentences by using the words provided in the order given.

MODELO: Ud. **/** cafetería → Ud. está en la cafetería.

1. Raúl y Carmen **/** oficina _____

2. yo **/** biblioteca _____

3. tú **/** clase de biología _____

4. Uds. **/** laboratorio de lenguas _____

B. ¿Dónde están y qué hacen (*what are they doing*)? Complete las oraciones con el verbo apropiado de la lista.

bailar	escuchar	tocar
cantar	estar	tomar

1. Mis (*My*) amigos y yo _____ en una fiesta.

2. José, Elena, Roberto y Carmen _____.

3. Isabel y Julio _____ «La bamba».

4. Yo _____ la guitarra.

5. Pablo _____ cerveza y

   _____ la música.

Un poco de todo

A. Situaciones. You and your friend have just met Daniel, a new student at the university. It is about half an hour before class. He asks you the following questions. Answer them in complete sentences.

1. ¿Estudian Uds. español? _____

2. ¿Quién enseña la clase? _____

3. ¿De dónde es él/ella? _____

4. ¿Cuántos estudiantes hay en la clase? _____

5. ¿Te gusta la clase? _____

6. ¿El profesor/La profesora habla inglés en la clase? _____

7. ¿Uds. necesitan practicar en el laboratorio todos los días? _____

   _____

8. ¿A qué hora es la clase? _____

B. De compras (*Shopping*). Martín necesita comprar unos libros. Conteste las preguntas según el dibujo (*according to the drawing*).

1. ¿Dónde compra libros Martín? _____

2. ¿Hay libros en italiano en la librería? _____

3. ¿Qué otras cosas hay? _____

   _____

4. ¿Cuántos libros compra Martín? _____

5. ¿Hablan alemán la dependienta y Martín? _____

6. ¿Paga Martín doce dólares? _____

♫Paso 4 Un paso más

▉ Videoteca*

Entrevista cultural: Los hispanos en los Estados Unidos

You will hear an interview with Carlos Rivera. After listening, pause and choose the letter of the phrase that best completes each statement.

1. Carlos Rivera es...
   a. estudiante.
   b. profesor.
   c. jugador (*player*) de béisbol.

2. Él enseña (*teaches*)...
   a. dos clases de literatura.
   b. una clase de literatura.
   c. dos clases de composición.

3. A Carlos Rivera...
   a. le gusta ser profesor.
   b. no le gusta ser profesor.
   c. le gusta ser interesante.

4. Carlos Rivera trae (*brings*)...
   a. una clase de composición.
   b. un hispano.
   c. una gorra de béisbol.

Entre amigos: ¿Qué clases tomas?

Tané, Miguel René, Rubén, and Karina will be asked four questions about how they are feeling, what they study, and what they like to do on the weekends. Listen carefully and complete the chart. The names are listed in the order in which each of the questions is answered. Check your answers in the Appendix.

1. ¿Cómo estás hoy?

	BIEN	MUY BIEN	CANSADO/A	CONTENTO/A
Miguel René				
Tané				
Karina				
Rubén				

2. ¿Eres estudiante y qué estudias?

	CIENCIAS SOCIALES	COMUNICACIÓN SOCIAL	INGENIERÍA
Karina			
Rubén			
Miguel René			
Tané			

3. ¿Cuántos cursos tomas?

	NO.	COMPUTACIÓN	HISTORIA...	INFORMÁTICA	INGLÉS	LITERATURA	MATEMÁTICAS
Rubén							
Karina							
Tané							
Miguel René							

4. ¿Qué te gusta hacer los fines de semana?

	BAILAR	DESCANSAR	ESTUDIAR	IR AL CINE	LEER	TRABAJAR
Tané						
Miguel René						
Rubén						
Karina						

*The **Videoteca** videoclips are available on the Video on CD to accompany *¿Qué tal?*, Seventh Edition.

Enfoque cultural: Los hispanos en los Estados Unidos

¿Cierto o falso?

1. **C F** Hay más de 35 millones de hispanos en los Estados Unidos.

2. **C F** La palabra **hispánico** se refiere a la raza o grupo étnico.

3. **C F** César Chávez fue (*was*) líder de los trabajadores agrícolas.

4. **C F** César Chávez se graduó (*graduated*) en la Universidad de Stanford en 1962.

❖¡Repasemos!

A. ¿Cómo se dice en español? Siga (*Follow*) el modelo. Use un verbo conjugado + un infinitivo.

> MODELO: I need to study. → Necesito estudiar.

1. I want to work. _____

2. We need to work. _____

3. We need to buy a dictionary. _____

4. We need to pay for the dictionary. _____

5. He needs to look for some books. _____

B. En la cafetería. En español, por favor. Escriba el diálogo en otro papel.

ANA: Hi, Daniel! How are you?

DANIEL: Fine, thanks. (At) What time are you going (returning) home today?

ANA: At two o'clock. I work at four.

DANIEL: How many (**¿Cuántas**) hours do you work today?

ANA: Six. And tonight (**esta noche**) I need to study. Tomorrow there is an exam in (**un examen de**) history.

DANIEL: Poor thing! (**¡Pobre!**) You work a lot.

ANA: Well, I need to pay for my (**mis**) books and the registration fee. See you tomorrow.

DANIEL: Good-bye. See you later.

C. *Listening Passage:* **¿Cómo son las universidades hispánicas?**

Antes de escuchar. Before you listen to the passage, pause and do the following prelistening exercises.

Paso 1. The passage contains some general information about Hispanic universities and how they differ from universities in the United States. Check the specific information that you expect to find in the passage.

- ☐ how the academic year is divided (that is, into semesters, quarters, and so on)

- ☐ the number of courses or credits that students are required to take

- ☐ the length of the academic year

- ☐ how much professors are paid

- ☐ how soon students need to declare their major

- ☐ whether or not foreign students attend Hispanic universities

Paso 2. The passage also contains information about Julia's course of studies. What information do you think she will give you?

- ☐ her major
- ☐ which courses she has to take for her major
- ☐ which professors she likes best
- ☐ the name of the university she attends

Now resume listening.

Listening Passage. Now you will hear a passage about Hispanic universities. In this passage, Julia talks about her major, **su especialización,** and some of the differences between Hispanic and U.S. universities.

¡Hola! ¿Qué tal? Soy tu amiga Julia, la hondureña. Estudio en la Universidad de Salamanca, en España. Mi carrera es ciencias políticas. La carrera es la especialización académica, como *major* o concentración.

En el mundo hispánico las universidades son muy diferentes de las de los Estados Unidos. Por lo general, no hay semestres. El año académico dura nueve meses. Los estudiantes toman de cuatro a siete cursos en un año. Además, los estudiantes no esperan dos años para declarar su carrera o especialización.

Yo tomo muchos cursos en relación con las ciencias políticas. ¿Cuáles? Pues, cursos de historia, filosofía, economía, estadística, etcétera. También tomo inglés. Estudio mucho, porque, como en todas las universidades, es necesario estudiar mucho en las universidades de España para pasar los cursos.

A pesar de eso, me gusta la vida universitaria. En Salamanca hay muchos estudiantes extranjeros, y muchos son de los Estados Unidos, como mi amiga Heather, que es de Carolina del Norte. Nosotras practicamos el español y el inglés muchas tardes después de las clases. ¿Con quién practicas tú el español?

Después de escuchar. Go back and listen to the passage again. Then, pause and complete the following sentences with words chosen from the list.

el alemán	ciencias naturales	especialización	el inglés
carrera	ciencias políticas	extranjeros	semestres

1. Para expresar el concepto de *major,* se usa la palabra _____

   (o _____) en español.

2. Por lo general, no hay _____ en el año académico hispánico.

3. Julia toma cursos en relación con las _____.

4. También toma una lengua extranjera: _____.

5. En Salamanca, hay muchos estudiantes _____.

Now resume listening.

D. Entrevista. You will hear a series of questions about your classes and your life at the university. Each will be said twice. Answer, based on your own experience. Pause and write the answers.

Note: The word **tu** means *your,* and **mi** means *my.*

1. _____

2. _____

3. _____

4. _____

5. _____

6. _____

❖■ Mi diario

Write the date first. (*Remember:* In Spanish the day comes first, then the month: 15/9/06.) Write about yourself. Be sure to write in complete sentences. Include the following information:

- your name and where you are from
- how you would describe yourself as a student (**Como estudiante, soy...**); review the cognates in **Primeros pasos** if you need to
- the courses you are taking this term (**este semestre/trimestre**) and at what time they are given
- the school materials and equipment that you have (**tengo...**) and those you need
- what you like to do (**me gusta...**) at different times of the day (**por la mañana, por la tarde, por la noche**).

Limit yourself to vocabulary you have learned so far. Do *not* use a dictionary!

Póngase a prueba

 A ver si sabe...

A. Gender and Articles. Escriba el artículo apropiado.

DEFINITE ARTICLES (*the*) INDEFINITE ARTICLES (*a, an, some*)

SINGULAR PLURAL SINGULAR PLURAL

1. *m.* _____ _____ 3. *m.* _____ _____

2. *f.* _____ _____ 4. *f.* _____ _____

B. Present Tense of -ar Verbs. Escriba la forma correcta del verbo **buscar.**

1. yo _____   4. nosotros/as _____

2. tú _____   5. vosotros/as _____

3. Ud., él, ella _____ 6. Uds., ellos, ellas _____

C. Negation. Place the word **no** in the appropriate place.

1. Yo _____ deseo tomar _____ café.

2. _____ hablamos _____ alemán en la clase.

D. Palabras interrogativas. Write the appropriate interrogative word. Be sure to write accent marks and question marks.

1. Where? _____ 4. Who? (*singular*) _____

2. How? _____ 5. What? _____

3. When? _____ 6. Why? _____

E. El verbo *estar*. Escriba la forma plural.

yo estoy → _____ _____¹

tú estás → vosotros _____²

Uds. _____³

él está → _____ _____⁴

Prueba corta

A. Los artículos definidos. Dé el artículo definido.

1. _____ papel
2. _____ mochila
3. _____ universidad
4. _____ libro de texto
5. _____ nación
6. _____ días
7. _____ lápices
8. _____ programas

B. Los artículos indefinidos. Dé el artículo indefinido.

1. _____ librería
2. _____ señores
3. _____ hombres
4. _____ problema
5. _____ clase
6. _____ tardes
7. _____ mujer
8. _____ horas

C. Los verbos. Complete las oraciones con la forma apropiada de un verbo de la lista.

enseñar   estudiar   hablar   necesitar   practicar   regresar   tocar

1. Los estudiantes _____ en la biblioteca.

2. Yo _____ español en el laboratorio de lenguas.

3. En la clase de español (nosotros) no _____ inglés.

4. ¡Alberto es fantástico! _____ el piano como (*like*) un profesional.

5. La profesora García _____ ciencias naturales.

6. Perdón, señor. (Yo) _____ comprar un diccionario.

7. ¿A qué hora _____ el consejero a su (*his*) oficina?

D. Cosas de todos los días

Paso 1. Practice talking about your university, using the written cues. When you hear the corresponding number, form sentences using the words provided in the order given, making any necessary changes or additions. (Remember to repeat the correct answer.)

MODELO: (*you see*) **1.** profesores / llegar / temprano / a / universidad   (*you hear*) uno →
(*you say*) *Los* profesores *llegan* temprano a *la* universidad.

2. consejeros / trabajar / en / oficina
3. mi amiga y yo / estudiar / en / biblioteca
4. en clase / nosotros / escuchar / a / profesores
5. fin de semana / mis amigos y yo / bailar / en / discoteca
6. por la mañana / (yo) / practicar / vocabulario
7. por la noche / (yo) / mirar / televisión

Paso 2. ¿Qué recuerda Ud.? Now you will hear a series of questions. Each will be said twice. Answer based on the preceding sentences. If you prefer, pause and write the answers. (Remember to repeat the correct answer.)

1. _____

2. _____

3. _____

4. _____

Paso 1 Vocabulario

 La familia y los parientes

A. Identificaciones. Identifique a los parientes y mascotas de Julián.

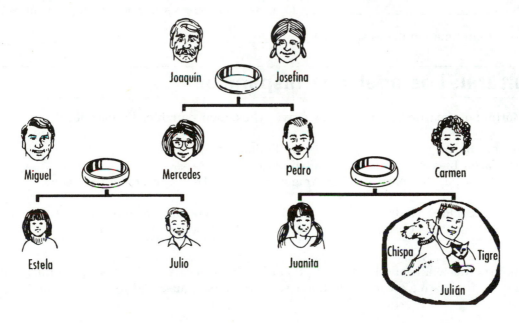

MODELO: Pedro *es el padre de Julián.*

1. Joaquín _____.

2. Julio _____.

3. Miguel y Mercedes _____.

4. Estela y Julio _____.

5. Josefina _____.

6. Pedro y Carmen _____.

7. Chispa _____.

8. Tigre _____.

B. ¿Qué son? Complete the sentences logically. Use each item only once. Some items will not be used.

abuela   hermana   mascota   padres   sobrino

abuelos   hermano   nieta   parientes tía

1. El hijo de mi hermano es mi _____.

2. La madre de mi primo es mi _____.

3. Los padres de mi madre son mis _____.

4. La madre de mi madre es mi _____.

5. Yo soy la _____ de mis abuelos.

6. Hay muchos _____ en mi familia. Tengo seis tíos y veintiún primos.

7. El perro o gato de una familia es su (*their*) _____.

Nota cultural: Los apellidos hispánicos

1. Miguel Martín Soto married Carmen Arias Bravo. Thus, their daughter Emilia's legal name is _____.
   - **a.** Emilia Soto Bravo
   - **b.** Emilia Martín Bravo
   - **c.** Emilia Martín Arias
   - **d.** Emilia Soto Arias
2. Ángela Rebolleda Castillo married César Aragón Saavedra. Their son Francisco's name, therefore, is _____.
   - **a.** Francisco Castillo Saavedra
   - **b.** Francisco Aragón Rebolleda
   - **c.** Francisco Saavedra Castillo
   - **d.** Francisco Rebolleda Saavedra

C. La familia Muñoz. You will hear a brief description of Sarita Muñoz's family. Listen carefully and complete the following family tree according to the description. First, pause and look at the family tree.

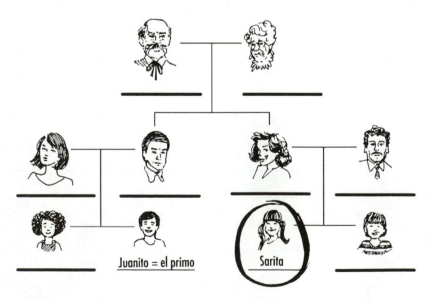

Juanito = el primo

Sarita

D. Definiciones. You will hear a series of definitions of family relationships. Each will be said twice. Listen carefully and write the number of the definition next to the word defined. First, listen to the list of words.

_____ mi (*my*) abuelo   _____ mi hermano   _____ mi tío

_____ mi tía   _____ mi prima   _____ mi abuela

Los números 31–100

A. Situaciones. You've been asked to make a list of some equipment and supplies in the university library. Write out the numbers. ¡RECUERDE! (*Remember!*) **Uno** becomes **un** before a masculine noun and **una** before a feminine noun.

1. 100 _____ discos compactos

2. 31 _____ computadoras

3. 57 _____ enciclopedias

4. 91 _____ diccionarios

5. 76 _____ escritorios

Nota comunicativa: Expressing Age

❖ **¿Cuántos años tienen?** (*How old are they?*) Complete las oraciones con información acerca de (*about*) su (*your*) familia o amigos: **padre, madre, abuelo/a, amigo/a, ¿ ?**

1. Mi _____ tiene _____ años.

2. Mi _____ tiene _____ años.

3. Mi _____ tiene _____ años.

4. Y yo tengo _____ años.

B. Dictado: El inventario. Imagine that you and a friend, Isabel, are taking inventory at the university bookstore where you work. Write out the numerals as she dictates the list to you. She will say each number twice. ¡OJO! Items are given in random order. First, listen to the list of words.

_____ mochilas

_____ lápices

_____ cuadernos

_____ novelas

_____ calculadoras

_____ libros de español

Adjetivos

❖A. ¿Qué opina Ud.? Do you agree with the following statements? Check the appropriate box.

		ESTOY DE ACUERDO.	NO ESTOY DE ACUERDO.
1.	David Letterman es cómico.	☐	☐
2.	Danny DeVito es alto y delgado.	☐	☐
3.	Eminem es moreno y gordo.	☐	☐
4.	Brad Pitt es guapo.	☐	☐
5.	El Parque Yosemite es impresionante.	☐	☐

B. ¿Cómo son Ricardo y Felipe? Ricardo is the opposite of Tomás, and Felipe is the opposite of Alberto. What are Ricardo and Felipe like?

1. Tomás es alto, guapo, tonto y perezoso, pero Ricardo es _____,

    _____, _____ y _____.

2. Alberto es casado, joven, antipático y rubio, pero Felipe es _____,

    _____, _____ y _____.

C. Descripciones

Paso 1. ¿Cómo son estas personas famosas? Escriba todos los adjetivos apropiados.

1. Billy Crystal es _____.

2. Arnold Schwarzenegger es _____.

3. James Gandolfini es _____.

4. El presidente _____.

❖Paso 2. Now write sentences that describe a male friend, a male member of your family, or your favorite male actor. Include that person's age, if you know it.

1. ¿Quién es? _____

2. ¿Cómo es? _____

D. Anuncios personales. Lea (Read) los anuncios y corrija (correct) los comentarios falsos.

Profesor, 48 años, rubio, guapo. Me gusta el ciclismo, la música clásica. Tel: 2-95-33-51, Luis	Ejecutivo, Banco Internacional, 32 años, graduado en MIT, soltero, delgado. Aficiones: basquetbol, viajar, bailar, ciencia ficción. Tel: 9-13-66-42, Carlos	Secretario ejecutivo bilingüe, alto, moreno, 28 años. Me gusta la playa, el camping, la comida francesa. Tel: 7-14-21-77, David

1. David es joven y rubio. _____

2. Luis tiene cincuenta y ocho años. _____

3. Carlos es casado y gordo. _____

4. A Luis le gusta escuchar la música rock. _____

5. El teléfono de David es el siete, cuarenta, veintiuno, setenta y siete. _____

    _____

E. ¿Cuál es? You will hear a series of descriptions. Each will be said twice. Circle the letter of the item or person described.

1. a.   b.

2. a.   b.

3. a.   b.

4. a.   b.

5. a.   b.

Pronunciación y ortografía:
Stress and Written Accent Marks (Part 1)

¡RECUERDE!

Circle the letter of the correct answer.

1. A word that ends in **-n, -s,** or a vowel is normally stressed on _____.
      a. the next-to-last syllable   **b.** the last syllable
2. A word that ends in any other consonant is normally stressed on _____.
      a. the next-to-last syllable   **b.** the last syllable

A. El acento. Underline the stressed syllable in each of the following words.

1. doctor	5. permiso	9. universidad	13. usted
2. mujer	6. posible	10. Carmen	14. libertad
3. mochila	7. general	11. Isabel	15. origen
4. actor	8. profesores	12. biblioteca	16. animal

B. Repeticiones. Repeat the following words, imitating the speaker. The highlighted syllable receives the stress in pronunciation.

1. If a word ends in a vowel, **n,** or **s,** stress normally falls on the next-to-the-last syllable.

   sin**ce**ra   intere**san**te   cua**der**nos   e**xa**men

2. If a word ends in any other consonant, stress normally falls on the last syllable.

   es**tar**   libe**ral**   profe**sor**   pa**pel**

C. Más repeticiones. Repeat the following words, imitating the speaker. The words have been divided into syllables for you. Pay close attention to which syllable receives the spoken stress.

1. Stress on the next-to-the-last syllable

   li-bro   si-lla   cla-se   me-sa   Car-men

   con-se-je-ra   li-te-ra-tu-ra   o-ri-gen   com-pu-ta-do-ra   cien-cias

2. Stress on the last syllable

   se-ñor   mu-jer   fa-vor   ac-tor   co-lor

   po-pu-lar   li-ber-tad   ge-ne-ral   sen-ti-men-tal   u-ni-ver-si-dad

D. Dictado. You will hear the following words. Each will be said twice. Listen carefully and circle the syllable that receives the spoken stress.

1. con-trol
2. e-le-fan-te
3. mo-nu-men-tal
4. com-pa-ñe-ra
5. bue-nos
6. us-ted

Los hispanos hablan: Dinos algo acerca de (*Tell us something about*) tu familia*

You will hear the following passage in which a student tells you about his family. Then you will hear a series of statements. Circle **C** (**cierto**) if the statement is true or **F** (**falso**) if it is false. If the information is not contained in the passage, circle **ND** (**No lo dice** [*It doesn't say*]).

Habla Antonio: Me llamo Antonio y soy de España. Ahora estudio en los Estados Unidos. Tengo tres hermanos que estudian aquí también, dos hermanos y una hermana. Tengo diecisiete años. En cuanto a los gustos, los cuatro somos un poco diferentes. A mí me gusta practicar deportes; a mi hermana le gusta cantar; a uno de mis hermanos le encanta escuchar música y al otro hermano le gusta mucho mirar deportes en la televisión. Físicamente somos muy similares, aunque creo que algunos vamos a ser más altos que otros. En cuanto a la personalidad, somos muy diferentes. Por ejemplo, yo soy una persona muy introvertida y pacífica. Sin embargo, mi hermana es muy extrovertida y gregaria.

1. C   F   ND   2. C   F   ND   3. C   F   ND   4. C   F   ND

---

*This is the last **Los hispanos hablan** section to include a transcript of the spoken text in the Workbook/Laboratory Manual.

Paso 2 Gramática

 4. Describing • Adjectives: Gender, Number, and Position

A. María Gabriela. The following sentences describe some aspects of the life of María Gabriela, a student from Argentina. In each item, scan through the adjectives to see which ones, by *form* and *meaning*, can complete the sentence. Write the appropriate ones in the space provided.

1. La ciudad de Buenos Aires es _____.

   bonita, corta, grande, interesante, largo, pequeños

2. Los compañeros de María Gabriela son _____.

   amable, casado, delgados, jóvenes, simpáticos, solteras

3. Su amiga Julia es _____.

   delgada, gordo, importantes, nervioso, pequeña, trabajadora

4. Sus profesoras son _____.

   altas, impacientes, inteligentes, morena, perezosos, simpáticos

B. Personas, cosas y lugares internacionales. Complete the following sentences with the appropriate adjective of nationality.

1. Berlín es una ciudad _____.

2. El Ferrari es un coche _____.

3. Ted Kennedy es un político _____.

4. Londres (*London*) es la capital _____.

5. Guadalajara es una ciudad _____.

6. Shakespeare y Charles Dickens son dos escritores (*writers*) _____.

7. París y Marsella son dos ciudades _____.

C. En busca de... (*In search of . . .*) Describe what you or your friends are looking for by inserting the adjectives given in parentheses *in their proper position* in these sentences. Be sure that the adjectives agree with the nouns they modify.

1. Ana busca coche. (italiano, otro) _____

2. Buscamos motocicleta. (alemán, uno) _____

3. Paco busca las novelas. (francés, otro) _____

4. Busco el drama *Romeo y Julieta*. (grande, inglés) _____

5. Jorge busca esposa. (ideal, uno) _____

D. Hablando (*Speaking*) **de la familia.** Imagine that your friend Graciela is describing her family. Listen to her description and check the adjectives that apply to each member of her family. ¡OJO! Not all the adjectives will be used, and not all adjectives in the description appear in the chart. In this exercise, you will practice listening for specific information.

	ACTIVOS	BAJO	ALTAS	JÓVENES	SOLTERO	CASADA
su tío						
los abuelos						
sus primos						
su hermana						
su padre						

E. ¿Cómo son? Practice describing various people, using the oral and written cues. Remember to change the endings of the adjectives if necessary. (Remember to repeat the correct answer.)

MODELO: (*you see and hear*) mi profesora (*you hear*) listo →
(*you say*) Mi profesora es lista.

1. mi compañero de cuarto
2. la profesora de español
3. Bernardo
4. Amanda
5. yo (*f.*)

F. ¿De dónde son (*are*) **y qué idioma hablan?** Imagine that your friend Carmen is asking you about some of the exchange students on campus. You will hear each of her questions twice. Answer according to the model, giving the nationality of the persons she mentions and the language they might speak. First, listen to the list of nationalities. You will need to change the endings in some cases. (Remember to repeat the correct answer.)

alemán   español   francés   inglés   italiano   portugués

MODELO: (*you hear*) ¿Evaristo es de Portugal? → (*you say*) Sí, es portugués y habla portugués.

1. …   2. …   3. …   4. …   5. …

■ 5. Expressing *to be* • Present Tense of *ser;* Summary of Uses

A. Estudiantes españoles. Muchos estudiantes en la universidad son de España. Imagine que Ud. es uno de ellos. Jorge es de Madrid. ¿De dónde son los otros estudiantes? Use la forma apropiada de **ser.**

Yo _____.¹
(Barcelona)

Miguel y David _____.²
(Valencia)

Tú _____.³
(Granada)

Nosotros _____.⁴
(Sevilla)

Uds. _____.⁵
(Toledo)

Vosotras _____.⁶
(Burgos)

❖ **B. ¿De dónde son?** Indicate what state (or country, if appropriate) the following people are from. Use the correct form of **ser.**

    1. Yo _____.

    2. Mi mejor (*best*) amigo/a _____.

    3. Mi profesor(a) de español _____.

    4. Muchos estudiantes en mi clase _____.

C. ¿De quién son estas cosas? Ask Jorge to whom the following things belong. Then write Jorge's response.

Sr. Ortega

MODELO: UD.:   ¿De quién es el cuaderno?
                JORGE: Es del Sr. Ortega.

1.

            la profesora

    UD.: _____

    JORGE: _____

2.

            Cecilia

    UD.: _____

    JORGE: _____

3.

            Sr. Alonso

    UD.: _____

    JORGE: _____

4.

            Sres. Olivera

    UD.: _____

    JORGE: _____

D. Regalos. Imagine that you are giving presents to the following people. Justify each choice by using one of these phrases. Add other details if you wish.

es gordo/a   su (*their*) televisor es viejo

desea comprar un *iPod*   tienen (*they have*) cuatro niños

      MODELO: diccionario bilingüe **/** Alberto →
              El diccionario bilingüe es para Alberto. Es estudiante de lenguas.

1. programa de «Weight Watchers» **/** mi hermana _____

_____

2. casa grande **/** los Sres. Walker _____

_____

3. dinero **/** mi hermano _____

_____

4. el televisor nuevo **/** mis abuelos _____

_____

E. Minidiálogos: Presentaciones. Manolo y su esposa hablan de quiénes son.

Paso 1. You will hear a brief passage about Manolo Durán and his wife Lola Benítez. As you listen, try not to be distracted by unfamiliar vocabulary. Concentrate instead on what you *do* know and understand. You may want to take notes on the information in the passage.

_____

_____

_____

Paso 2. ¿Qué recuerda Ud.? Now pause and complete the following sentences based on the passage and your notes. ¡OJO! Use a form of the verb **ser** in the first blank of each sentence.

1. Marta _____ la _____ de Lola y Manolo.

2. Lola _____ profesora de _____.

3. Lola y Manolo _____ de _____.

4. Lola _____ morena y _____; Manolo es _____ y moreno.

Now resume listening.

F. ¿De dónde son? Practice telling where you and your imaginary family and friends are from, using the written cues. (Remember to repeat the correct answer.)

      MODELO: (*you see and hear*) mi amigo Aristides **/** Colombia →
              (*you say*) Mi amigo Aristides es de Colombia.

1. mi amigo Lorenzo **/** la Argentina   3. mis abuelos **/** Cuba

2. tú **/** Costa Rica   4. mi hermano y yo **/** Chile

Paso 3 Gramática

 ## 6. Expressing Possession • Possessive Adjectives (Unstressed)

¡RECUERDE!

Uso de la preposición **de** para expresar posesión.

¿Cómo se dice en español?

    MODELO: It's Raúl's family. → Es la familia de Raúl.

1. She's Isabel's sister. _____

2. They're Mario's relatives. _____

3. They're Marta's grandparents. _____

A. ¿Cómo es su vida (*life*)**?** Escoja (*Choose*) la forma correcta del adjetivo posesivo y luego (*then*) complete la oración con todos los adjetivos posibles según (*according to*) la forma.

  1. Mi/Mis familia es _____.

     grande, mediana (*average*), pequeña, pobre, rica

  2. Nuestra/Nuestro universidad es _____.

     grande, moderna, nueva, pequeña, vieja

  3. Muchos de mi/mis amigos son _____.

     casados, estudiosos, listos, perezosos, trabajadores

  4. El coche de mi/mis padres es _____.

     grande, nuevo, pequeño, viejo

  5. Mi/Mis clases son _____.

     aburridas (*boring*), grandes, interesantes, pequeñas

  6. La madre de mi/mis mejor (*best*) amigo/a es _____.

     alta, baja, delgada, generosa, gorda, morena, rubia, simpática

B. Hablando (*Speaking*) **de la familia.** Answer affirmatively, using a possessive adjective.

    MODELO: ¿Son ellos los hijos de tu hermana? → Sí, son sus hijos.

  1. ¿Es ella la suegra de Tomás? _____

  2. ¿Es Carlos el hermano de Uds.? _____

  3. ¿Son ellos los padres de tu novia? _____

  4. ¿Son Uds. los primos de Marta? _____

  5. ¿Es Carmen la sobrina de tu mamá? _____

  6. ¿Eres el nieto / la nieta de los señores? _____

C. ¿Cómo es la familia de Vicente? Tell what Vicente's family is like, using the written cues and the correct form of the possessive adjective **su.** Say the sentence when you hear the corresponding number. ¡OJO! Watch for singular or plural forms of the verb **ser.** (Remember to repeat the correct answer.)

MODELO: (*you see*) **1.** tíos / bajos   (*you hear*) uno →
(*you say*) Sus tíos son bajos.

2. tías / simpáticas
3. primos / altos
4. abuela / delgada

5. hermanos / mayores
6. madre / bonita

D. ¿Cómo es su universidad? Describe your university to an exchange student who has recently arrived on campus, using the written cues and the appropriate form of **nuestro** and the verb **ser.** Say the sentence when you hear the corresponding number. (Remember to repeat the correct answer.)

MODELO: (*you see*) **1.** universidad / vieja   (*you hear*) uno →
(*you say*) Nuestra universidad es vieja.

2. profesores / buenos
3. clases / pequeñas
4. biblioteca / grande

5. consejeros / amables
6. estudiantes / buenos

7. Expressing Actions • Present Tense of *-er* and *-ir* Verbs; More About Subject Pronouns

A. En el centro estudiantil (*student union*). Use los verbos indicados para describir las acciones de los estudiantes.

beber Coca-Cola
comer mucho
escribir una carta
estudiar francés
leer un periódico
mirar un vídeo

1. _____
2. _____
3. _____
4. _____
5. _____
6. _____

❖**B. ¿Y Ud.?** Now imagine that you are at the student union. Write two more sentences telling what you and your friends usually do (or do not do) there. Remember to use the **nosotros** form.

1. _____
2. _____

C. Una carta de Ramón. Ramón y Pepe son dos hermanos mexicanos. Ahora viven en California. Complete el comienzo (*beginning*) de una carta que escribe Ramón a su familia en Morelia, México.

Queridos[a] padres:

Pepe y yo _____[1] (**vivir**) bien aquí en California, en la casa de una señora muy simpática. Yo _____[2] (**asistir**) a clases cinco días a la[b] semana. Mis clases son difíciles, pero los profesores son buenos. En la clase de inglés _____,[3] _____[4] y _____[5] (*nosotros:* **hablar, leer, escribir**). Todos los días _____[6] (*nosotros:* **aprender**) algo nuevo. Sin embargo,[c] hay estudiantes que[d] nunca _____[7] (**abrir**) los libros para estudiar.[e]

Pepe y yo _____[8] (**comer**) en la cafetería estudiantil por la mañana. Por la noche _____[9] (*nosotros:* **deber**) regresar a casa porque la señora nos[f] _____[10] (**preparar**) la comida. ¡Es muy amable!

[a]*Dear* [b]*a... per* [c]*Sin... However* [d]*who* [e]*para... to study* [f]*for us*

D. Un sábado típico de la familia Robles. Describe what happens on a typical Saturday at the Robles household, using the written and oral cues. Remember that subject pronouns are not always used in Spanish. (Remember to repeat the correct answer.)

MODELO: (*you hear*) nosotros (*you see*) estar en casa → (*you say*) Estamos en casa.

1. leer el periódico
2. escribir cartas
3. asistir a un partido (*game*) de fútbol
4. abrir una carta de mi prima
5. comer a las seis

E. ¿Quién... ? Answer the following questions using the oral cues. Use subject pronouns only if necessary. (Remember to repeat the correct answer.)

1. ¿Quién come en la cafetería?

MODELO: (*you hear*) Evita → (*you say*) Evita come en la cafetería.

a. ... b. ... c. ... d. ...

2. ¿Quién vive en una residencia?

MODELO: (*you hear*) yo → (*you say*) Vivo en una residencia.

a. ... b. ... c. ... d. ...

Nota comunicativa: Telling How Frequently You Do Things

❖ **Ud. y sus amigos.** Tell about what you and your friends do or do not do. Form complete sentences by using one word or phrase from group A and one from group B. Be sure to limit yourself to writing only those things you have learned how to say in Spanish. Use the **nosotros** verb form.

> MODELO: comer → A veces comemos en la cafetería. Casi nunca comemos en casa.

A. nunca, casi nunca, a veces, con frecuencia, todos los días

B. asistir, beber, deber, estudiar, leer y escribir, practicar, trabajar

1. _____

2. _____

3. _____

4. _____

5. _____

 # Un poco de todo

❖**La escena** (*scene*) **universitaria.** Imagine that you have just returned home after your first few weeks at the university. Describe the people, places, and things you have seen. Form complete sentences by using one word or phrase from each column. Make five sentences with nouns from the second column and two with nouns that you supply. Watch out for agreement of adjectives! Do not use the same adjective more than once.

| mi mis el la los las | + | laboratorio de lenguas edificios estudiantes biblioteca coche de mi amigo clases profesores ¿ ? | + | (no) es (no) son | + | nuevo / viejo simpático / amable / antipático pequeño / grande / enorme tonto / inteligente alto / bajo feo / bonito joven / viejo interesante ¿ ? |

1. _____

2. _____

3. _____

4. _____

5. _____

6. _____

7. _____

Paso 4 Un paso más

Videoteca*

Entrevista cultural: México

Listen carefully to the interview of Dolores Suárez, then circle the letter of the phrase that best completes each statement. Do not be distracted by unfamiliar vocabulary. Instead, focus on what you do know.

1. Dolores Suárez es de...

    a. Panamá.   b. Colombia.   c. México.

2. Dolores Suárez tiene...

    a. seis hijos y ocho nietos.   b. seis nietos y ocho hijos.   c. siete hijos y dos nietos.

3. Según la Sra. Suárez, sus nietos son...

    a. inteligentes.   b. unidos.   c. bonitos.

Now resume listening.

Entre amigos: ¿Cuántos hermanos tienes?

Paso 1. Listen carefully as the four friends answer a question about their surnames. Then write each of the following surnames next to the corresponding first name. First, listen to the list of surnames.

Zamora Egert   Moreno Gómez   Ramírez Sánchez   Martínez Placencia

1. Miguel René _____   3. Karina _____

2. Tané _____   4. Rubén _____

Paso 2. Now pause and write the name of each of the students next to the appropriate parents. Remember to check your answers to **Paso 1** before beginning **Paso 2.**

	APELLIDOS DEL PADRE	APELLIDOS DE LA MADRE	EL AMIGO / LA AMIGA
1.	Ramírez Huérfano	Sánchez Díaz	
2.	Gómez Parra	Moreno Galás	
3.	Egert Martínez	Zamora Lorea	
4.	Martínez Blanco	Placencia Morales	

Enfoque cultural: México

¿Cierto o falso?

1. C F La UNAM es la famosa Universidad de Guanajuato.

2. C F La UNAM es del año (*dates from the year*) 1551 (mil quinientos cincuenta y uno).

3. C F Tenochtitlán era (*was*) la capital antigua del imperio mixteca.

4. C F La mayoría (*majority*) de a población mexicana es mestiza.

5. C F Los tres grandes muralistas del siglo (*century*) veinte son Orozco, Rivera y Siqueiros.

6. C F Hay un mural de José Clemente Orozco en los Estados Unidos.

*The **Videoteca** videoclips are available on the Video on CD to accompany *¿Qué tal?*, Seventh Edition.

❖ ■ ¡Repasemos!

A. La familia Rivera

Paso 1. Answer these questions about the Rivera family in complete sentences. You will need to invent information about several of the characters.

Palabras útiles: el ama de casa (*housewife*)

1. ¿Cuántas personas hay en la familia Rivera? _____

2. ¿De dónde son los padres? _____

3. ¿Dónde trabaja el padre ahora? ¿y la madre?

    _____

4. ¿Qué estudia el hijo mayor (*oldest*)? ¿Cuántos años tiene él? ¿Cómo es él?

    _____

5. ¿Quién es la otra señora? ¿Cuántos años tiene? ¿Cómo es?

    _____

6. ¿Cómo son el coche y la casa, y de quién(es) son?

    _____

Paso 2. On a separate sheet of paper, write a descriptive paragraph about the Rivera family by combining your answers and using connecting words such as **y, pero, por eso, también,** and **aunque** (*although*). Try to be as creative as possible.

B. *Listening Passage:* Las familias hispanas*

Antes de escuchar. Before you listen to the passage, pause and do the following prelistening exercises.

Paso 1. Read the following true/false statements. As you read them, try to infer the information the passage will give you, as well as the specific information for which you need to listen.

1. En las familias hispanas, más de (*more than*) dos generaciones viven en una sola casa.
2. Los abuelos no participan activamente en el cuidado (*care*) de los nietos.
3. Por lo general, las personas viejas viven en asilos (*nursing homes*).
4. Los abuelos cuidan (*care for*) a los nietos mientras (*while*) los padres trabajan.
5. Los hijos y los nietos cuidan a sus padres o a sus abuelos cuando estos (*the latter*) están viejos o enfermos.

---

*This is the last Listening Passage section to include a transcript of the spoken text in the Workbook/Laboratory Manual.

Paso 2. The passage contains information about Julia's family and about Hispanic families in general. Which statements do you think apply to the Hispanic family in general?

☐ The Hispanic family is typically smaller than a U.S. family.

☐ Many Hispanic families are extended families; that is, more than one generation live in the same household.

☐ The elderly and the sick are often sent to nursing homes.

☐ Grandparents are important in the daily lives of families.

☐ Many young couples live with their in-laws until they can become independent.

Now resume listening.

Listening Passage. Now you will hear a passage about Hispanic families. In this passage, Julia talks about Hispanic families in general and about her own family in particular. The following words and phrases appear in the passage.

estadounidenses	de los Estados Unidos
No sólo… sino que además	*Not only . . . but also*
las ventajas	*advantages*
se ayudan	*they help each other*
el cuidado	*care*
enfermas	*sick*
murió	*he died*
la cuidamos	*we take care of her*

Here is the passage. First, listen to it to get a general idea of the content. Then go back and listen again for specific information.

Las familias hispanas son más grandes que las familias estadounidenses, por lo general. No sólo es normal tener más hijos, sino que además, con frecuencia los abuelos viven con la familia.

En español existe un nombre específico para los padres del esposo o esposa. Son los suegros, el suegro y la suegra. A veces si un matrimonio joven no tiene mucho dinero, los nuevos esposos viven con los padres de uno de ellos (o sea, los suegros).

Para muchos norteamericanos esta es una situación extraña, ¿no? Pero es una situación que tiene sus ventajas también. Las familias hispanas conservan un contacto muy fuerte entre varias generaciones. Los miembros de la familia se visitan mucho y se ayudan constantemente con el cuidado de los niños y el de las personas viejas o enfermas.

Como ejemplo, yo puedo hablar de mi familia. Mi abuela materna vive con mi familia, porque su esposo, mi abuelo Rafael, murió joven. Sólo tenía 60 años. Mi abuela siempre ayudó a mi mamá con nosotros, sus nietos. Y ahora que mi abuela está vieja, mi mamá y nosotros la cuidamos. Es ley de la vida, ¿no? Mi abuela está contenta porque ahora también puede pasar tiempo con sus bisnietos, los hijos de mi hermano.

Now pause and do the **Después de escuchar** exercises.

Después de escuchar

Paso 1. Here are the true/false statements. Circle **C** (**cierto**) if the statement is true or **F** (**falso**) if it is false. Then correct the statements that are false, according to the passage.

1. C F   En las familias hispanas, más de dos generaciones viven en una sola casa.

   _____

2. C F   Los abuelos no participan activamente en el cuidado de los nietos.

   _____

3. C F Por lo general, las personas viejas viven en asilos.

_____

4. C F Los abuelos cuidan a los nietos mientras los padres trabajan.

_____

5. C F Los hijos y los nietos cuidan a sus padres o a sus abuelos cuando estos están viejos o enfermos.

_____

Paso 2. Go back and listen to the passage again. Then, pause and complete the following sentences with words chosen from the list.

bisnietos   grandes   materna   suegros

1. La madre de mi madre es mi abuela _____.

2. Mis _____ son los padres de mi esposo/a.

3. Los _____ son los hijos de los nietos.

4. Por lo general, las familias hispanas son más _____ que las familias estadounidenses.

Now resume listening.

C. Entrevista. You will hear a series of questions. Each will be said twice. Answer, based on your experience. Pause and write the answers.

1. _____
2. _____
3. _____
4. _____
5. _____
6. _____
7. _____

❖ ■ Mi diario

Write a description of your favorite relative. Include the following information. Use all the adjectives you can! Refer to the vocabulary list in your textbook for additional adjectives.

- name
- relationship to you
- age (**Tiene _____ años.**)
- where he/she is from
- what he/she does for a living
- appearance
- personality

Póngase a prueba

▉ A ver si sabe...

A. Adjectives: Gender, Number, and Position. Complete las siguientes tablas (*following charts*).

1. Escriba la forma correcta del adjetivo **casado.**

   a. hermana _____   **b.** primos _____   **c.** tías _____

2. Escriba la forma **plural** de los adjetivos.

   a. grande _____   **b.** sentimental _____   **c.** francés _____

B. Present Tense of *ser*. Match the following statements with the uses of **ser** given in the right-hand column.

1. Lola es de Puerto Rico.

2. La carta es para mi madre.

3. Los papeles son del profesor.

4. Alicia es mi prima.

a. _____ With **para**, to tell for whom or what something is intended.

b. _____ With **de**, to express possession.

c. _____ With **de**, to express origin.

d. _____ To identify people and things.

C. Possessive Adjectives (Unstressed). Express the following possessive adjectives and nouns in Spanish.

1. my brother _____   3. our grandparents _____

2. her uncle _____   4. their house _____

D. Present Tense of *-er* and *-ir* Verbs. Complete la tabla con la forma correcta de los verbos.

leer		escribir	
yo	_____	tú	_____
nosotros	_____	ella	_____
vosotros	_____	Uds.	_____

▉ Prueba corta

A. La nacionalidad. Complete the following sentences with the adjective of nationality that corresponds to the country in parentheses.

MODELO: Marta es *mexicana*. (México)

1. Paolo es un estudiante _____. (Italia)

2. París es una ciudad _____. (Francia)

3. El Volkswagen es un coche _____. (Alemania)

4. Diane y Margaret son dos mujeres _____. (Inglaterra)

B. Ser. Escriba la forma apropiada del verbo **ser.**

1. La mochila no _____ nueva.

2. Yo _____ de los Estados Unidos.

3. Burgos y Toledo _____ ciudades viejas y fascinantes.

4. ¿Tú _____ de México?

5. El profesor y yo _____ de California.

C. Los adjetivos posesivos. Complete las oraciones con el adjetivo posesivo apropiado.

La madre de _____¹ (*my*) sobrino Mauricio se llama Cecilia. Ella es

_____² (*my*) cuñada. _____³ (*My*) hermanos Enrique y Luis son

solteros. El padre de Cecilia se llama Marco; _____⁴ (*her*) madre se llama Elena.

Elena y Marco son italianos, pero viven en México. Ellos piensan (*They think*) que

_____⁵ (*our*) cultura es muy interesante. Todos _____⁶ (*their*)

nietos son mexicanos. ¿De dónde es _____⁷ (*your*) familia?

D. Los verbos. Complete las oraciones con la forma correcta del verbo apropiado de la lista.

asistir   beber   comprender   escuchar   estudiar   hablar   leer   recibir   vender

1. Nosotros no _____ mucho cuando la profesora _____ rápidamente (*quickly*).

2. ¿(Tú) _____ música mientras (*while*) (tú) _____?

3. Mi padre nunca _____ la sección de deportes del periódico.

4. ¿Siempre _____ Uds. los libros al final del semestre?

5. Mi hermana siempre _____ muchos regalos y tarjetas (*cards*) el día de su santo.

6. Yo no _____ café por la noche.

7. Nosotros _____ a esta clase todos los días.

E. La familia de doña Isabel. You will hear a passage about doña Isabel's family. Read the passage along with the speaker and circle the numbers you hear.

¡La familia de doña Isabel es muy grande y extendida! Ella tiene **30 / 20** nietos en total, y **16 / 26** bisnietos (*great-grandchildren*). Doña Isabel tiene **89 / 99** años. Su hijo mayor, Diego, tiene **67 / 77** años. Su hija menor, Alida, tiene **64 / 54**. Doña Isabel tiene **10 / 6** hijos en total. El próximo año, todos sus hijos, nietos y bisnietos celebran los **100 / 50** años de edad de doña Isabel.

F. Cosas de todos los días. Practice talking about your imaginary family, using the written cues. When you hear the corresponding number, form sentences using the words provided in the order given, making any necessary changes or additions. (Remember to repeat the correct answer.)

MODELO: (*you see*) **1.** mi **/** familia **/** ser **/** muy **/** simpático   (*you hear*) uno →
                (*you say*) *Mi* familia *es* muy *simpática.*

2. (nosotros) vivir **/** en **/** un **/** ciudad **/** pequeño
3. nuestro **/** casa **/** ser **/** bonito
4. mi **/** padres **/** siempre **/** leer **/** periódico **/** en **/** patio
5. (nosotros) siempre **/** comer **/** juntos (*together*)
6. este **/** noche **/** mi **/** hermanos **/** asistir **/** a **/** un **/** concierto
7. pero **/** yo **/** deber **/** estudiar **/** para **/** mi **/** clases

Paso 1 Vocabulario

 De compras: La ropa

A. La ropa. Identifique la ropa que llevan estas personas. Use el artículo indefinido.

1. a. _____
    b. _____
    c. _____
    d. _____
    e. _____
    f. _____

2. a. _____
    b. _____
    c. _____
    d. _____
    e. _____

B. De compras en México. Imagine that you are studying in Puebla, México. You ask your friend Rosa about where and how to shop. Complete her answer with the appropriate items from the following list.

almacén	gangas	regatear
centro	mercado	tiendas
fijos	rebajas	venden de todo

En el _____[1] comercial de la calle Bolívar, hay un _____[2]

grande donde _____.[3] Allí[a] los precios son _____[4] y muy

caros. Ahora, en las _____[5] del centro, hay muchas _____.[6]

O puedes ir[b] al _____.[7] Allí los precios no son fijos y es posible

_____.[8] También puedes encontrar[c] muchas _____.[9]

[a]*There* [b]*puedes... you can go* [c]*find*

C. **¿Qué opina Ud.?** Complete la narración en español. Use estas palabras: **algodón, lana, seda.**

1. La ropa interior de _____ es más fresca que (*cooler than*) la de nilón.

2. Las _____ de _____ son elegantes y bonitas.
   (*ties*)

3. Los _____ y las _____ de _____ son caros y abrigados (*warm*).
   (*sweaters*)   (*skirts*)

D. **Identificaciones.** Identify the items in the drawing after you hear the corresponding number. Begin each sentence with **Es un...**, **Es una...**, or **Son...**

1. ...   **2.** ...   **3.** ...   **4.** ...   **5.** ...   **6.** ...   **7.** ...   **8.** ...   **9.** ...

¿De qué color es?

A. **¿De qué color es?** Complete the sentences with the correct form of the words from the following list. Adjectives are given in the masculine singular form. Be sure to make the adjectives agree with the nouns they are describing. Some words can be used more than once.

amarillo	azul	color café	morado	rosado
anaranjado	blanco	gris	rojo	verde

1. Las plantas son _____.

2. La bandera (*flag*) mexicana es _____, _____ y _____.
   (*green*)   (*white*)   (*red*)

3. La bandera de los Estados Unidos es _____, _____ y

   _____.

4. La naranja (*orange*) es _____ y el limón es _____.

5. El color _____ es una combinación de blanco y negro.

6. El color _____ es una combinación de rojo y azul.

7. El color tradicional para las bebés (*baby girls*) es _____.

8. Muchos hombres hispanos llevan colores oscuros (*dark*): azul, negro y _____.

❖**B. Mi estilo personal.** ¿Qué ropa usa Ud. en estos lugares? Mencione los colores, cuando sea (*whenever it is*) posible.

> **Palabra útil:** la sudadera (*sweatshirt*)

1. En la universidad: _____

2. En una cena (*dinner*) elegante: _____

3. En la playa (*beach*): _____

Más allá del número 100

A. Los números. Write the following numbers in Arabic numerals.

1. ciento once _____

2. cuatrocientos setenta y seis _____

3. quince mil setecientos catorce _____

4. setecientos mil quinientos _____

5. mil novecientos sesenta y cinco _____

6. un millón trece _____

B. ¿Cuánto cuesta? You have been asked to write six checks for ads of different sizes to be published in a Mexican newspaper. Write out in words the prices in **nuevos pesos** (N$) for each ad (N$2.100,00 = dos mil cien nuevos pesos).

1. N$28.510,00 _____

2. N$14.625,00 _____

3. N$7.354,00 _____

4. N$3.782,00 _____

5. N$1.841,00 _____

6. N$920,00 _____

C. Dictado: El inventario del Almacén Robles. Imagine that you and a coworker are doing a partial inventory for a department store. Listen to what your coworker says, and write the numbers in numerals next to the correct items. You will hear each number twice. ¡OJO! The items are not listed in sequence. First, listen to the list of items.

ARTÍCULOS	NÚMERO (CANTIDAD)
pares de medias de nilón	
camisas blancas	
suéteres rojos	
pares de zapatos de tenis	
blusas azules	
faldas negras	

Pronunciación y ortografía: Stress and Written Accent Marks (Part 2)

¡RECUERDE!

Circle the letter of the correct answer.

1. A word that ends in **-n, -s,** or a vowel is normally stressed on
   a. the next-to-last syllable   **b.** the last syllable
2. A word that ends in any other consonant is normally stressed on
   a. the next-to-last syllable   **b.** the last syllable
3. Any exception to these rules will require a written accent on the stressed
   a. consonant   **b.** vowel

A. ¿Acento escrito (*written*) **o no?** The following words are stressed on the underlined syllables. If a written accent is required, add it above the stressed vowel.

1. ex-<u>a</u>-men
2. lu-<u>gar</u>
3. ma-<u>tri</u>-cu-la
4. bo-<u>li</u>-gra-fo
5. <u>jo</u>-ven
6. sen-ti-men-<u>tal</u>
7. <u>Pe</u>-rez
8. e-di-<u>fi</u>-cios
9. a-le-<u>man</u>

B. Palabras divididas. The following words have been divided into syllables for you. Read them when you hear the corresponding number. (Remember to repeat the correct answer.) ¡OJO! Some of the words will be unfamiliar to you. This should not be a problem because you have pronunciation rules to guide you.

1. nor-mal
2. prác-ti-co
3. á-ni-mo
4. a-na-to-mí-a
5. cu-le-bra
6. con-ver-ti-bles
7. ter-mó-me-tro
8. co-li-brí
9. con-di-cio-nal

C. Dictado. You will hear the following words. Each will be said twice. Listen carefully and write in a written accent where required. ¡OJO! Some of the words will be unfamiliar to you. This should not be a problem because you have the rules and the speaker's pronunciation to guide you.

1. metrica
2. distribuidor
3. anoche
4. Rosalia
5. actitud
6. sabiduria
7. jovenes
8. magico
9. esquema

Los hispanos hablan: ¿Qué importancia tiene la ropa para ti y tus amigos?

You will hear a student, Teresa, give an answer to the preceding question. After listening, pause and check all the statements that are true according to the passage. The following expressions appear in the passage.

una persona vale por lo que es	*a person's worth is determined by who he/she is*
aunque	*even though*
los harapos	*rags*

1. ☐ Teresa piensa que (*thinks that*) las modas son muy importantes.

2. ☐ Para ella, la persona es más importante que la ropa que usa.

3. ☐ La mayoría (*majority*) de sus amigos están de acuerdo con Teresa.

Paso 2 Gramática

8. Pointing Out People and Things • Demonstrative Adjectives and Pronouns

¡RECUERDE!
Formas de **este**
Escriba la forma apropiada: **este, esta, estos, estas.**
1. _____ (*this*) color
2. _____ (*these*) colores
3. _____ (*this*) camisa
4. _____ (*these*) camisas

A. ¿Este, ese o aquel? Complete las oraciones con la forma correcta de **este, ese** o **aquel**. Complete la última oración con su preferencia.

Ud. necesita comprar un coche. ¿Cuál le gusta más?

_____[1] coche es muy viejo; _____[2] coche es muy grande; _____[3]

coche es fantástico, pero también es muy caro. Pienso comprar _____[4] coche porque

_____.

B. ¿De quién son? You and a friend are trying to sort out to whom the following items belong. Answer your friend's questions with the appropriate demonstrative adjective.

Note: **Aquí** (*Here*) and **allí** (*there*), like **este** and **ese,** suggest closeness to, or distance from, the speaker.

> MODELO: Aquí hay unos zapatos. ¿Son de Pablo? → Sí, estos zapatos son de Pablo.
> Allí veo (*I see*) una bolsa. ¿Es de Chela? → Sí, esa bolsa es de Chela.

1. Aquí hay una chaqueta. ¿Es de Miguel? _____

2. Allí veo unos calcetines. ¿Son de Daniel? _____

3. Allí veo un impermeable. ¿Es de Margarita? _____

4. Aquí hay unos guantes. ¿Son de Ceci? _____

5. Aquí hay un reloj. ¿Es de Pablo? _____

6. Allí veo unos papeles. ¿Son de David? _____

C. Minidiálogo: Suéteres a buenos precios. You will hear a dialogue in which Susana goes shopping for a sweater. After listening, pause and read each statement about the dialogue. Circle **C** (**cierto**) if the statement is true or **F** (**falso**) if it is false. If the information is not contained in or cannot be inferred from the dialogue, circle **ND** (**No lo dice**).

1. C F ND Susana busca un suéter para su amiga.

2. C F ND Los suéteres de pura lana son más caros.

3. C F ND Los suéteres de pura lana cuestan 150 pesos.

4. C F ND Los suéteres de rayas (*striped*) son acrílicos y cuestan cien pesos.

Now resume listening.

D. ¿Cómo son estas cosas? Answer, using the oral cues and an appropriate form of the indicated demonstrative adjective. Remember to change the endings of the adjectives, and use **es** or **son,** as appropriate.

> MODELO: (*you see*) ese **/** corbatas (*you hear*) verde → (*you say*) Esas corbatas son verdes.

1. ese **/** botas
2. este **/** pantalones
3. aquel **/** trajes
4. aquel **/** faldas
5. ese **/** vestidos

E. Recuerdos de su viaje a México. Your friends want to know all about your trip to Mexico. Answer their questions, using an appropriate form of the demonstrative adjective **aquel** and the oral cues.

> MODELO: (*you hear and see*) ¿Qué tal el restaurante El Charro? (*you hear*) excelente →
> (*you say*) ¡Aquel restaurante es excelente!

1. ¿Qué tal el Hotel Libertad?
2. ¿Y los dependientes del hotel?
3. ¿Qué tal la ropa del Mercado de la Merced?
4. ¿Y los parques de la capital?

9. Expressing Actions and States • *Tener, venir, preferir, querer,* and *poder;* Some Idioms with *tener*

A. Diálogo

Paso 1. Complete the following dialogue between you and a friend to make plans to go to a movie.

—¿_____¹ (*Tú:* **Querer**) ir al cineª esta noche?

—Hoy no _____² (*yo:* **poder**) porque _____³ (**tener**) que estudiar

para un examen de sicología. _____⁴ (**Preferir**) ir mañana.

—Bien. Entoncesᵇ _____⁵ (*yo:* **venir**) por tiᶜ mañana a las siete y media. No

_____⁶ (*yo:* **querer**) llegar tarde.

ªir... *to go to the movies*   ᵇ*Then*   ᶜpor... *for you*

Paso 2. Now rewrite the same dialogue, replacing **yo** with the **nosotros** form and **tú** with the **Uds.** form. (Replace **por ti** with **por Uds.**)

_____

_____

_____

_____

_____

B. Conclusiones personales. Conteste con un modismo con **tener.**

1. Cuando Ud. trabaja toda la noche, ¿qué tiene en la mañana?

   _____

2. Si Ud. quiere aprender, ¿qué tiene que hacer (*do*)?

   _____

3. Si Ud. se encuentra con (*run into*) un hombre con revólver, instintivamente, ¿qué tiene Ud.?

   _____

4. Ud. necesita llegar a la oficina a las dos. Si son las dos menos uno, ¿qué tiene Ud.?

   _____

5. Si Ud. dice (*say*) que Buenos Aires es la capital de la Argentina, ¿qué tiene Ud.?

   _____

Buenos Aires

la Argentina

C. Luis habla con su compañero Mario. Complete el diálogo entre (*between*) Luis y Mario. *Note:* / / indica una oración nueva.

    LUIS: ¿a qué hora / (tú) venir / universidad / mañana?

    _____

    MARIO: (yo) venir / ocho y media / / ¿Por qué?

    _____

    LUIS: ¿(yo) poder / venir / contigo? / / no / (yo) tener / coche

    _____

    MARIO: ¡cómo no!ª / / (yo) pasar / por tiᵇ / siete y media / / ¿(tú) tener / ganas / practicar / vocabulario ahora?

    _____

    _____

    LUIS: no / / ahora / (yo) preferir / comer / algoᶜ / / ¿(tú) querer / venir? / / (nosotros) poder / estudiar / para / examen / despuésᵈ

    _____

    _____

    MARIO: bueno / idea / / (yo) creer / que / Raúl y Alicia / querer / estudiar / con nosotros

    _____

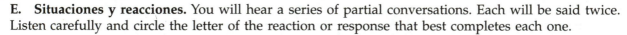

D. Es la semana de exámenes. Practice telling about what you and your friends do during exam week, using the written and oral cues. ¡OJO! Remember that subject pronouns are not always used in Spanish.

    MODELO: (*you hear*) nosotros (*you see*) tener muchos exámenes →
        (*you say*) Tenemos muchos exámenes.

    1. estar en la biblioteca
    2. siempre venir conmigo (*with me*)
    3. leer cien páginas
    4. ¡ya no poder leer más!
    5. querer regresar a la residencia
    6. ...pero no poder

E. Situaciones y reacciones. You will hear a series of partial conversations. Each will be said twice. Listen carefully and circle the letter of the reaction or response that best completes each one.

    1. **a.** Ay, ¡tú siempre tienes prisa!   **b.** Tienes razón, ¿verdad?
    2. **a.** ¿Por qué tienes sueño?   **b.** Sí, tienes razón, pero tienes que estudiar más.
    3. **a.** ¿Tienes que comer en un restaurante?   **b.** ¿Tienes ganas de ir (*go*) a un restaurante?
    4. **a.** ¿Cuántos años tienes?   **b.** La verdad es que tienes miedo, ¿no?
    5. **a.** No, no tengo ganas de comprar ropa.   **b.** ¿Cuántos años tiene la niña ahora?

ª¡cómo... *of course!* ᵇpor... *for you* ᶜ*something* ᵈ*later*

Paso 3 Gramática

 10. Expressing Destination and Future Actions •
Ir; ir + a + Infinitive; The Contraction al

A. Una fiesta familiar. Complete las oraciones con la forma apropiada del verbo **ir.**

Muchas personas van a ir a una fiesta. Toda la familia de Ana _____.[1] Los tíos y

los abuelos de Julio _____[2] con los padres de Ana. Tú _____[3]

también, ¿verdad? Miguel y yo _____,[4] pero yo _____[5] a

llegar tarde.

B. El cumpleaños (_birthday_) **de Raúl.** Using **ir + a +** an infinitive, indicate what the following people are going to do for Raúl's birthday.

    MODELO: La fiesta es este sábado. → La fiesta va a ser este sábado.

1. Eduardo y Graciela buscan un regalo. _____

_____

2. David y yo compramos las bebidas (_drinks_). _____

_____

3. Todos van a la fiesta. _____

4. Ignacio y Pepe vienen con nosotros. _____

_____

5. Por eso necesitamos tu coche. _____

_____

6. Desgraciadamente (_Unfortunately_) Julio no prepara la comida. _____

_____

C. Situaciones. Imagine that a friend of yours has made the statements listed below. Form a response using **vamos a +** one of the phrases from the following list. In each case you will be suggesting that you and your friend do something together: "Let's _____."

    MODELO: Este diccionario es malo. → Vamos a comprar otro.

        buscar algo más barato   estudiar esta tarde
        comprar otro   mirar en el Almacén Juárez
        descansar ahora

1. Mañana vamos a tener examen. _____

2. En esta tienda no venden buena ropa. _____

3. Estos precios aquí son muy caros. _____

4. No tengo ganas de trabajar más hoy. _____

D. Minidiálogo: ¿Adónde vas? You will hear a dialogue in which Casandra asks her roommate Rosa where she is going. Then you will hear the following statements. Write the letter of the person who made each statement next to the statement.

    a. Rosa   **b.** Casandra   **c.** Javier

1. _____ Voy a dar una fiesta este fin de semana.

2. _____ Voy al centro.

3. _____ Voy a comprar un vestido.

4. _____ Casandra y Rosa van a venir a mi fiesta.

E. ¿Adónde vas? You will hear a series of statements a friend might say about what you like to do or want to do. Using the words and phrases listed below, tell where you would go to do these activities. First, listen to the list.

    Almacén Robles

    biblioteca

    discoteca El Ciclón

    mercado

    Restaurante Gallego

    universidad

    MODELO: (*you hear*) Te gusta estudiar y aprender cosas nuevas. →
                (*you say*) Por eso voy a la universidad.

1. ...   **2.** ...   **3.** ...   **4.** ...   **5.** ...

F. Preguntas. You will hear a series of questions. Each will be said twice. Answer, using **ir** + **a** + infinitive and the written cues.

    MODELO: (*you hear*) ¿Qué vas a comprar en la librería?   (*you see*) unos cuadernos →
                (*you say*) Voy a comprar unos cuadernos.

1. tres horas
2. a casa de un amigo
3. en McDonald's
4. pantalones grises / un suéter rojo

Un poco de todo

A. De compras en San Sebastián. Complete the following paragraph with the correct form of the words in parentheses, as suggested by context. When two possibilities are given in parentheses, select the correct word.

En _____[1] (**el/la**) ciudad vasca[a] de San Sebastián, en el

norte de España, cuando la gente[b] necesita o _____[2]

(**querer**) ir de compras, tiene que _____[3] (**ir**) a

_____[4] (**pequeño**) tiendas que _____[5] (**vender**)

productos _____[6] (**especial**), porque en San Sebastián no permiten la construcción de

_____[7] (**grande**) almacenes. La gente _____[8] (**preferir**) proteger[c] a los comer-

ciantes vascos locales en vez de apoyar[d] a las grandes galerías _____[9] (**español**) como El

Corte Inglés o las Galerías Preciado. Por eso, hay en _____[10] (**este**) ciudad muchas tiendas

de ropa para niños, para mujeres y para hombres; también hay tiendas _____[11]

(**especializado**) como zapaterías, librerías o papelerías. Son muy _____[12] (**popular**) las

tiendas que venden artículos de piel[e] como bolsas, cinturones, gorras, guantes[f] y carteras. Claro,

también _____[13] (**existir**) pequeñas boutiques muy _____[14] (**elegante**) con pro-

ductos de moda de los más _____[15] (**famoso**) nombres de la moda mundial.[g]

[a]*Basque* [b]*people* [c]*to protect* [d]*en... instead of supporting* [e]*leather* [f]*gloves* [g]*moda... world fashion*

B. María Montaño. Imagine that you are a new student in Dr. Prado's class. Talk about yourself and the way you feel. Complete the sentences using idioms with **tener.**

Me llamo María Montaño. _____[1] 18 años y tengo _____[2] de

aprender español porque quiero hablar con mis abuelos y otros parientes que viven en México.

Desgraciadamente,[a] en clase tengo _____[3] de hablar. El profesor cree que debo

practicar más en el laboratorio. Él tiene _____,[4] pero no tengo mucho tiempo libre.[b]

Trabajo muchas horas y cuando quiero estudiar, tengo mucho _____[5] y a veces me

quedo dormida.[c]

[a]*Unfortunately* [b]*free* [c]*me... I fall asleep*

C. Entre amigas. Fill in the blanks with the correct form of the infinitive or with the correct word in parentheses to complete the dialogue between Susana and Paquita.

SUSANA: Hola, Paquita. ¿Qué tal?

PAQUITA: Bien. Y tú, ¿cómo _____[1](**estás / eres**)?

SUSANA: Muy bien. Aquí tengo algo para ti. Creo que _____[2] (**esos / estos**)

textos son _____[3] (**tu / tus**) libros de historia, ¿verdad?

PAQUITA: ¡Ay, qué bueno! Necesito _____[4] (**esos / aquellos**) libros para estudiar

para _____[5] (**nuestra / nuestro**) examen. Gracias.

SUSANA: ¿Adónde _____[6] (**ir**) ahora?

PAQUITA: Primero _____[7] (**ir**) a la biblioteca a buscar un libro y luego María y yo

_____[8] (**ir**) a estudiar. ¿Por qué no estudias con _____[9]

(**nosotros / nosotras**)?

SUSANA: Gracias por _____[10] (**tú / tu**) invitación, pero _____[11]

(**esta / este**) tarde dan[a] una película francesa y Enrique y yo _____[12]

(**querer**) ir. Tengo _____[13] (**razón / prisa**) porque él está esperándome[b]

ahora mismo.[c]

PAQUITA: Muy bien. _____[14](**Adiós / Vamos**).

[a]*they're showing*   [b]*waiting for me*   [c]*ahora... right now*

D. Buscando regalos para papá. Listen to a conversation between a brother and sister, José and Ana, who are looking for gifts for their father. Do not be distracted by unfamiliar vocabulary. As you listen, circle only the items that they decide to buy.

Paso 4 Un paso más

🎧 Videoteca*

Entrevista cultural: Nicaragua

Dictado. You will hear an interview with Delvia Arguello. As you listen, complete the following paragraph with information from the interview. Check your answers in the Appendix. First, pause and read the incomplete paragraph.

Delvia Arguello es de Managua, _____.¹ Ella tiene _____² años. Su familia tiene una _____³ de ropa para _____.⁴ En la tienda venden _____,⁵ camisas, _____⁶ y accesorios. Delvia trabaja en la tienda con su _____.⁷

Entre amigos: Está superfuera de moda (*out of style*).

The four friends answer questions about shopping and fashion. Listen to the questions and answers. Then pause and read the following statements. Circle **C** (**cierto**) if the statement is true or **F** (**falso**) if the answer is false.

1. C   F   A todos los amigos les gusta ir de compras.

2. C   F   A muchos de los amigos les gusta estar cómodos.

3. C   F   A uno de los amigos le gusta el color azul.

4. C   F   A todos los amigos les interesa ir de moda o estar de moda.

■ Enfoque cultural: Nicaragua

Complete las oraciones con la información apropiada.

1. _____ llegó (*arrived*) a Nicaragua en 1502.

2. El lago (*lake*) más grande de Centroamérica es _____. Hay más de (*more than*) _____ islas en el lago. (escriba el número en palabras)

3. Los nicaragüenses refieren al lago como su «mar dulce» porque es grande y tiene _____ dulce (*fresh, sweet*). Tiene los únicos (*only*) _____ de agua dulce del mundo (*world*).

4. En 1856 _____ se declaró (*he declared himself*) presidente de Nicaragua, pero dos años después, fue (*he was*) _____ por los nicaragüenses.

5. Nicaragua tiene una _____ turbulenta por las luchas (*struggles*) entre las fuerzas _____ y _____.

---

*The **Videoteca** videoclips are available on the Video on CD to accompany *¿Qué tal?*, Seventh Edition.

❖ ■ ¡Repasemos!

A. De compras

Paso 1. El Sr. Rivera necesita comprar dos artículos de ropa para sus vacaciones en México. Conteste las preguntas según los dibujos.

1.

2.

3.

4.

5.

6.

7.

1. ¿Qué quiere comprar el Sr. Rivera? ¿Qué tipo (*type*) de camisa busca?

   _____

2. ¿A qué hora llega a la tienda? _____

3. ¿Cómo son todas las camisas, caras o baratas? _____

   _____

4. ¿Qué camisa compra por fin (*finally*)? ¿una de veinte dólares? _____

   _____

5. Y, ¿cómo son las sandalias que venden? _____

6. ¿Adónde tiene que ir para comprar las sandalias? _____

   _____

7. ¿Regresa a casa contento o triste con sus compras? _____

   _____

Paso 2. Now, on a separate sheet of paper, convert your answers into a paragraph about Mr. Rivera's shopping trip. Use the following words to make your paragraph more coherent and connected: **pero, y, por eso, por fin, ya** (*already*).

B. Listening Passage: El Rastro

Antes de escuchar. Before you listen to the passage, pause and do the following prelistening exercise.

It is sometimes helpful to answer questions about yourself that are related to a passage that you will listen to or read. Answering the following questions will give you an idea of the information the passage might contain.

1. ¿Hay un mercado al aire libre en la ciudad donde tú vives?
2. Por lo general, ¿qué venden en los mercados al aire libre?
3. ¿Cómo crees que son los precios en un mercado al aire libre?
4. ¿Te gusta ir de compras?
5. ¿Te gusta regatear?
6. ¿Coleccionas algo? ¿Sellos (*Stamps*), monedas (*coins*), libros viejos, trenes (*trains*), muñecas (*dolls*)?

Now resume listening.

Listening Passage. Now, you will hear a passage about El Rastro, an open-air market in Madrid. The narrator is from Spain. The following words and phrases appear in the passage.

los sellos	*stamps*
las monedas	*coins*
los domingos	*on Sundays*
los puestos	*stalls*

Después de escuchar. Circle the letter of the phrase that best completes each sentence.

1. El Rastro es...
   a. una gran tienda.
   b. un centro comercial.
   c. un mercado con muchos puestos.

2. El Rastro está abierto (*open*)...
   a. todo el fin de semana.
   b. el domingo por la mañana.
   c. el domingo por la tarde.

3. En el Rastro venden...
   a. sólo ropa y zapatos.
   b. sólo cosas para coleccionistas (*collectors*).
   c. muchas cosas de todo tipo.

4. El Rastro está...
   a. en Madrid y es muy famoso.
   b. en España y es nuevo.
   c. en todas las ciudades de España.

Now resume listening.

C. Entrevista. You will hear a series of questions. Each will be said twice. Answer, based on your own experience. Pause and write the answers.

1. _____
2. _____
3. _____
4. _____
5. _____
6. _____
7. _____

Mi diario

Paso 1. Look in your closet and bureau drawers and take an inventory of the articles of clothing you own and the approximate number of each item. What colors are they? Now write the information in your diary.

> MODELO: Tengo diez camisetas: blancas, negras, rojas y una verde.

Paso 2. Now choose three of the following situations and write a description of the clothing you typically wear in each. Include the color and fabric, if possible.

Palabras útiles

los *jeans* rotos (*torn*)

de cuero (*leather*)

de manga larga (*long-sleeved*)

la manga (*sleeve*)

la sudadera (*sweatshirt*)

los zapatos de tacón alto (*high heels*)

> MODELO: Cuando estoy en la playa (*beach*), llevo...

1. en la universidad
2. en una entrevista (*job interview*)
3. en casa
4. en la playa
5. en una fiesta
6. en un *picnic* en el parque

Póngase a prueba

A ver si sabe...

A. **Demonstrative Adjectives and Pronouns.** Escriba el adjetivo demostrativo apropiado.

1. _____ (*this*) zapato

2. _____ (*these*) pantalones

3. _____ (*that*) bolsa

4. _____ (*those*) abrigos

5. _____ (*that, over there*) camiseta

6. _____ (*those, over there*) cinturones

B. *Ir; Ir + a + Infinitive.* Rewrite the following sentences, using **ir** + **a** + infinitive.

1. Ellos compran ropa. _____

2. ¿No comes? _____

3. Tienen una fiesta. _____

4. Voy de compras. _____

C. *Tener, venir, preferir, querer,* and *poder;* **Some Idioms with** *tener.*

1. Complete la tabla con la forma apropiada del presente.

INFINITIVO	YO	UD.	VOSOTROS	NOSOTROS
poder			podéis	
querer		quiere		
venir				

2. Exprese en español los siguientes modismos con **tener.**

a. to be afraid (of) _____

b. to be right (wrong) _____

c. to feel like _____

d. to have to _____

Prueba corta

A. Los demostrativos. Rewrite the sentences, substituting the noun provided and making all the necessary changes.

MODELO: ¿Necesitas aquel sombrero rojo? (corbata) →

¿Necesitas aquella corbata roja?

1. Quiero comprar esa camisa negra.

(impermeable) _____

2. ¿Buscas estos calcetines grises?

(traje) _____

3. Juan va a comprar esos zapatos blancos.

(chaqueta) _____

4. Mis padres trabajan en aquel almacén nuevo.

(tienda) _____

B. Los verbos. Complete las oraciones con la forma apropiada de uno de los verbos de la lista. (*Note:* Use each verb at least once.)

poder   preferir   querer   tener   venir

1. Mis amigos y yo _____ a esta biblioteca todos los días para estudiar. Nuestras

clases son difíciles y _____ que estudiar mucho.

2. —¿Qué (tú) _____ tomar, una Coca-Cola o un café? —Yo _____
un café.

3. Si Ud. _____ prisa, debe salir (*leave*) ahora.

4. En una librería, los estudiantes _____ comprar libros, cuadernos y mochilas.

C. Ir + a + infinitivo. Rewrite each sentence, changing the simple present tense to a construction with **ir + a + infinitive**, to tell what the following people are going to do.

MODELO: Estudio mucho. → Voy a estudiar mucho.

1. Roberto lleva traje y corbata. _____

2. Busco sandalias baratas. _____

3. Tenemos una fiesta. _____

4. ¿Vienes a casa esta noche? _____

D. Cosas de todos los días. Practice talking about the price of different items of clothing, using the written cues. When you hear the corresponding number, form sentences using the words provided in the order given, making any necessary changes or additions. Note: **Cuesta** means *it costs*, **cuestan** means *they cost*.

MODELO: (*you see*) **1.** este / pantalones / negro / cuestan / $80 (*you hear*) uno →
(*you say*) Estos pantalones *negros* cuestan *ochenta dólares.*

2. ese / chaqueta / azul / cuesta / $127
3. aquel / botas / de color café / cuestan / $215
4. este / vestido / amarillo / cuesta / $149
5. aquel / traje / gris / cuesta / $578
6. ese / ropa / cuesta / $1.069

E. ¿Qué van a llevar? You will hear a series of situations. Tell what each person might wear based on the information in each. First, listen to the possible items of clothing. ¡OJO! There is an extra item.

un abrigo de lana   un traje de baño

una camiseta de algodón   un traje y una corbata de seda

un cinturón   zapatos de tenis

MODELO: (*you hear*) Los pantalones que llevo son muy grandes. →
(*you say*) Voy a llevar un cinturón.

1. …   2. …   3. …   4. …   5. …

F. Apuntes (*Notes*):* **De compras con Luis.** Luis has just received a bonus from his boss. He plans to spend all of it on clothes. Listen carefully to his narration and, as you listen, write the information requested. Write out all numbers. First, pause and read the requested information.

1. El dinero que tiene Luis: _____

2. El precio de la chaqueta: _____

3. El precio del reloj de oro (*gold*): _____

4. El material de los pantalones: _____

5. El material de las dos corbatas: _____

6. Lo que (*what*) no puede comprar: _____

7. El dinero que le queda (*remains*): _____

_____

*Answers to all **Apuntes** exercises are given in the Appendix.

Paso 1 Vocabulario

 ## ¿Qué día es hoy?

A. El horario (*schedule*) **de David.** Escriba lo que (*what*) va a hacer David esta semana.

L	M	M	J	V	S	D
banco hablar con consejero	dentista	estudiar física	laboratorio de física	examen cenar[a] con Diana	de compras concierto	playa[b]

[a]*to have dinner* [b]*beach*

MODELO: El lunes tiene que ir al banco. (El lunes va a ir al banco.)

1. El lunes también... _____

2. _____

3. _____

4. _____

5. _____

6. _____

7. _____

B. ¿Qué día es hoy? Complete las oraciones con las palabras apropiadas.

1. Hay dos días en el _____ de semana: _____ y _____.

2. _____ es el primer (*first*) día de la semana en el calendario hispánico.

3. Si hoy es martes, mañana es _____.

4. El Día de Acción de Gracias es siempre el cuarto (*fourth*) _____ de noviembre.

5. Si hoy es miércoles, _____ es viernes.

6. No puedo venir _____ sábado porque _____ sábados trabajo.

7. Tengo que estudiar mucho porque la _____ semana tengo tres exámenes.

C. El horario de la profesora Velásquez

Paso 1. Dictado. Imagine that you are Professor Velásquez's secretary and that you are filling in her weekly calendar. Listen carefully as she tells you her schedule for this week, and fill in the blanks in the calendar. Some of the entries have already been made. First, pause and look at the calendar.

lunes	martes	miércoles	jueves	viernes
mañana 10:45 AM : Clase de conversación	mañana ___ : dentista ___ :	mañana ___ :	mañana ___ :	mañana ___ :
tarde ___ :	tarde ___ :	tarde ___ :	tarde 3:00 PM : clase de español	tarde ___ :

Paso 2. Preguntas. Now you will hear a series of questions. Each will be said twice. Answer based on the information in **Paso 1**. Be sure to check your answers to **Paso 1** in the Appendix before beginning **Paso 2**. Follow the model.

MODELO: (*you hear*) ¿Qué días enseña la profesora una clase de conversación? →
(*you say*) El lunes y el viernes.

1. … 2. … 3. … 4. …

Los muebles, los cuartos y otras partes de la casa

A. ¿Qué hay en esta casa? Identifique las siguientes partes de la casa.

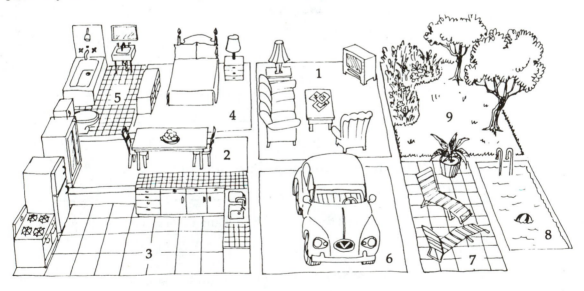

1. _____   4. _____   7. _____

2. _____   5. _____   8. _____

3. _____   6. _____   9. _____

❖**B. Describa su alcoba.** Mencione los muebles que hay y el color de las paredes y de la alfombra (si la hay). Luego use tres adjetivos para describir la alcoba en general.

_____

_____

_____

C. Identificación: ¿Qué hay en estos cuartos? Identify the following items when you hear the corresponding number. Begin each sentence with **Es un...** or **Es una...**

En la sala

1. ... **2.** ... **3.** ... **4.** ... **5.** ... **6.** ... **7.** ...

En la alcoba

8. ... **9.** ... **10.** ...

¿Cuándo? • Las preposiciones

A. ¿Antes o después? ¿Cuándo hace Ud. estas cosas? Siga el modelo.

MODELO: estudiar las lecciones / tomar el examen →
Estudio las lecciones antes de tomar el examen.

1. tener sueño / descansar

_____

2. regresar a casa / asistir a clase

_____

3. tener ganas de comer / estudiar

_____

4. preparar la comida / ir al supermercado

_____

5. lavar (*to wash*) los platos / comer

_____

B. ¿Cuándo? Tell when your imaginary friends do the following things using the oral cues. Follow the model.

MODELO: (*you see*) Anita estudia / la clase   (*you hear*) antes de →
(*you say*) Anita estudia antes de la clase.

1. Alicia escribe una carta / escuchar la radio
2. Rosa trabaja / asistir a clases
3. Mis amigos bailan / las once de la noche
4. José lee / ir a la universidad

Pronunciación y ortografía: *b* and *v*

Spanish **b** and **v** are pronounced exactly the same way. At the beginning of a phrase, or after **m** or **n,** **b** and **v** are pronounced like the English *b*, as a stop; that is, no air is allowed to escape through the lips. In all other positions, **b** and **v** are fricatives; that is, they are produced by allowing some air to escape through the lips. There is no equivalent for this sound in English.

A. Repeticiones. Repeat the following words and phrases, imitating the speaker. Note that the type of *b* sound you will hear is indicated at the beginning of the series.

1. [b]   bueno viejo barato baño hombre
2. [ƀ]   llevar libro pobre abrigo universidad
3. [b/ƀ] bueno / es bueno busca / Ud. busca bien / muy bien en Venezuela / de Venezuela visita / él visita
4. [b/ƀ] beber bebida vivir biblioteca vívido

B. Dictado. You will hear five sentences. Each will be said twice. Listen carefully and write what you hear.

1. _____
2. _____
3. _____
4. _____
5. _____

Los hispanos hablan: Apuntes (*Notes*): ¿Qué cosas tienes en tu alcoba?

This question is answered by Xiomara. As you listen to the passage, jot down some of the things that she has in her room. The following words appear in the passage.

el abanico	*fan*
el tocador	*dressing table*
los cuadros	pinturas
la gata de peluche	*stuffed toy cat*
me regaló	*he gave me (as a gift)*

Lo que Xiomara tiene en su alcoba

_____
_____
_____
_____
_____

Paso 2 Gramática

11. Expressing Actions • *Hacer, oír, poner, salir, traer, and ver*

A. Las actividades de Roberto. Complete las oraciones con la forma apropiada del verbo.

1. Los domingos _____ (*yo:* **ver**) una película con mi hermano Enrique.

2. Ricardo y yo _____ (**salir**) con amigos los fines de semana.

3. _____ (*yo:* **poner**) el televisor antes de ir a clases.

4. Los sábados, _____ (*yo:* **traer**) a mi perro a este parque (*park*).

5. Jimena y Alberto _____ (**oír**) las noticias (*news*) por la radio.

6. Antes del examen de español, _____ (*yo:* **hacer**) los ejercicios del libro.

7. _____ (*yo:* **salir**) de la clase de matemáticas a las once de la mañana.

B. Un sábado típico. Complete the following paragraph with the correct form of **hacer, oír, poner, salir, traer,** or **ver** to tell about a typical Saturday. ¡OJO! Not all of the verbs will be used.

Por la mañana (yo) _____ [1] la radio y _____ [2] la tarea[a] para el lunes.

Por la tarde, un amigo normalmente _____ [3] sándwiches y cerveza y comemos

juntos.[b] Por la noche, (nosotros) _____ [4] con un grupo de amigos.

_____ [5] una película o _____ [6] a bailar.

[a]*homework* [b]*together*

❖**C. Preguntas personales.** Conteste con oraciones completas.

1. ¿A qué hora sale Ud. de casa los lunes para ir a la universidad?

   _____

2. ¿Ve películas en casa o prefiere salir a ver películas en el cine?

   _____

3. En clase, ¿hace Ud. muchas preguntas o prefiere estar callado/a (*quiet*)?

   _____

4. Si Ud. quiere escuchar música, ¿qué pone Ud., la radio o un CD? ¿Tiene Ud. una estación de

   radio favorita? ¿Cuál es? _____

   _____

5. ¿Qué cosas trae Ud. a clase en su mochila? _____

6. ¿A qué hora oye Ud. las noticias (*news*)? _____

D. Minidiálogo: Los jóvenes de hoy

Paso 1. Dictado. You will hear the following passage in which an adult complains about today's youth. It will be read twice. Listen carefully and fill in the missing words.

«¡Estos muchachos sólo quieren _____!¹ No _____² sus

cosas en orden en sus cuartos… Los jóvenes de hoy día no

_____³ nada bien; no son responsables… ¡Hasta quieren

_____⁴ muchachas a sus cuartos!»

Paso 2. Preguntas. Now you will hear a series of questions that an adult might ask a young person. Each will be said twice. Answer, based on your own experience. You will hear a possible answer. Pause and write your answers.

1. _____

2. _____

3. _____

4. _____

Now resume listening.

E. ¡Qué dedicada! You will hear a conversation between two students on campus, followed by a series of statements. Circle **C** (**cierto**) if the statement is true or **F** (**falso**) if it is false.

1. C F   2. C F   3. C F

❖F. Encuesta. You will hear a series of statements. For each statement, check **siempre, a veces** (*sometimes*), or **nunca**. No answers will be given. The answers you choose should be true for you.

	SIEMPRE	A VECES	NUNCA		SIEMPRE	A VECES	NUNCA
1.	☐	☐	☐	**4.**	☐	☐	☐
2.	☐	☐	☐	**5.**	☐	☐	☐
3.	☐	☐	☐	**6.**	☐	☐	☐

G. Mis compañeros y yo. Form complete sentences about yourself and others, using the oral and written cues. The last two sentences will be negative.

MODELO: (*you see*) Adela (*you hear*) hacer ejercicio →
(*you say*) Adela hace ejercicio.

1. yo   2. Tito y yo   3. tú   4. ellos   5. Marta

H. Soy buen compañero. Imagine that you want to impress your friend Sam, who is looking for a roommate. When you hear the corresponding number, form sentences that tell Sam what a good roommate you are. Make any necessary changes or additions. Repeat the correct sentence.

MODELO: (*you see*) **1.** (*you hear*) uno (*you see*) escuchar / noticias / por la mañana →
(*you say*) Escucho las noticias por la mañana.

2. no hacer / mucho / fiestas
3. siempre / hacer / cama
4. no salir / tarde / sábados

5. no poner / televisor / doce / noche
6. siempre / poner / ropa / armario

12. Expressing Actions • Present Tense of Stem-Changing Verbs

 ¡RECUERDE!

Stem-Changing Verbs You Already Know. Complete the verb chart.

	yo	tú	Ud., él, ella	nosotros	Uds., ellos, ellas
querer	_____	_____	_____	queremos	_____
preferir	_____	prefieres	_____	_____	_____
poder	_____	_____	puede	_____	_____

❖**A. ¿Cierto o falso?** Indique si cada oración es cierta o falsa para Ud.

1. C F Pienso ir de compras esta noche.
2. C F Todos los días vuelvo a casa antes de las cinco.
3. C F Cuando salgo a comer, siempre pido una cerveza.
4. C F Mis amigos y yo nunca pedimos vino.
5. C F Almuerzo en casa todos los días.
6. C F En mi casa servimos la cena (*dinner*) a las siete.
7. C F Mi primera clase empieza a las ocho.
8. C F No entendemos cuando el profesor / la profesora de español habla rápidamente.
9. C F Con frecuencia pierdo mis libros.

B. Preferencias. ¿Qué prefieren hacer Ud. y sus amigos? Complete las oraciones con la forma apropiada de los verbos entre paréntesis.

1. (**pensar**) Isabel y Fernando _____ almorzar en casa, pero Pilar y yo

   _____ salir. ¿Qué _____ hacer tú?

2. (**volver**) Nosotras _____ en tren con Sergio, pero Felipe _____

   en coche con Lola. ¿Cómo _____ Uds.?

3. (**pedir**) Por lo general Tomás _____ cerveza. Rita y Carmen

   _____ Coca-Cola. Pepe y yo _____ café.

C. Un día típico de Bernardo. Describe a typical school day for Bernardo. Form complete sentences, using the words provided in the order given. Make any necessary changes, and add other words when necessary.

MODELO: comer / casa / 6:00 → Come en casa a las seis.

1. salir / casa / 7:15

   _____

2. su / primera clase / empezar / 8:00

   _____

3. si no / entender / lección, / hacer / mucho / preguntas

   _____

4. con frecuencia / almorzar / en / cafetería

   _____

5. a veces / pedir / hamburguesa / y / refresco

   _____

6. lunes y miércoles / jugar / tenis / con / un / amigo

   _____

7. su madre / servir / cena (*dinner*) / 6:00

   _____

8. hacer / la tarea (*homework*) / por / noche / y / dormir / siete horas

   _____

D. Minidiálogo: Una fiesta para Marisa. You will hear a conversation in which Gracia and Catalina plan a surprise birthday party for their roommate, Marisa. After listening, pause and read each statement about the dialogue. Circle **C** (**cierto**) or **F** (**falso**). If the information is not contained in the dialogue, circle **ND** (**No lo dice**).

1. C F ND Marisa y Gracia preparan una fiesta de sorpresa para Catalina.
2. C F ND Marisa va a cumplir veinte años.
3. C F ND La cocina ya está arreglada.
4. C F ND Van a servir champán en la fiesta.
5. C F ND La fiesta de sorpresa va a ser muy grande.

Now resume listening.

E. Un sábado típico en mi casa. Tell about the activities of your fictitious family on a typical Saturday. Use the written and oral cues.

1. yo   2. mis padres   3. mi hermana y yo   4. tú

F. Entrevista con los Sres. Ruiz. Interview Mr. and Mrs. Ruiz about some of the things they like to do. Use the written cues. You will hear an answer to each of your questions.

MODELO: (*you hear*) jugar al tenis →
(*you say*) ¿Juegan al tenis?   (*you hear*) No, no jugamos al tenis.

1. … 2. … 3. … 4. …

Paso 3 Gramática

13. Expressing *-self/-selves* • Reflexive Pronouns

❖**A.** **¿Cierto o falso?** Indique si cada oración es cierta o falsa para Ud.

1. C F Me levanto tarde los fines de semana.

2. C F Me divierto con los amigos todas las noches.

3. C F A veces mi padre se duerme cuando mira la televisión.

4. C F Siempre me ducho por la noche.

5. C F Me pongo zapatos de tenis para ir a clase.

6. C F En la clase de español nos sentamos en un círculo.

7. C F Me cepillo los dientes antes de vestirme.

B. **Oraciones incompletas.** Complete las oraciones con la forma apropiada del pronombre reflexivo.

1. Yo _____ llamo Juan y mi hermana _____ llama Inés.

2. Nuestros padres _____ llaman Carlos y Luisa.

3. ¿Por qué _____ pones esa blusa? Está sucia (*dirty*).

4. ¿_____ despiertan Uds. tarde los sábados?

5. Después de levantarnos, _____ bañamos y _____ vestimos.

6. ¿Dónde _____ diviertes más, en el teatro o en el cine?

C. **Ud. y otra persona.** Cambie (*Change*) el sujeto **yo** por (*to*) **nosotros.** Haga todos los cambios necesarios.

1. Me despierto temprano. _____

2. Me visto después de ducharme. _____

3. Nunca me siento para tomar el desayuno. _____

    _____

4. En la universidad asisto a clases y me divierto. _____

    _____

5. Después de volver a casa hago la tarea. _____

    _____

6. A las doce tengo sueño, me cepillo los dientes y me acuesto. _____

    _____

7. Me duermo a las doce y media. _____

    _____

❖D. **Preguntas personales.** Conteste con oraciones completas.

1. ¿A qué hora se despierta Ud. los sábados? ¿Por qué? _____

    _____

2. Los lunes, ¿se levanta Ud. inmediatamente después de despertarse? _____

    _____

3. ¿Se afeita Ud.? ¿Cuántas veces por semana? _____

    _____

4. ¿Prefiere Ud. bañarse o ducharse? ¿Se baña (Se ducha) por la mañana o por la noche?

    _____

5. ¿Dónde prefiere sentarse para mirar la tele? ¿en un sillón? ¿en un sofá? ¿en la alfombra? ¿Y

    para estudiar? _____

6. ¿Dónde se divierte Ud. más? (en el cine, en una discoteca, en la playa [*beach*], practicando

    [*playing*] un deporte) _____

E. **¿Qué van a hacer estas personas?** When you hear the corresponding number, tell what the people in each drawing are going to do. **¡OJO!** You will be using the **ir** + **a** + infinitive construction, and you will attach the reflexive pronouns to the infinitives. First, listen to the list of verbs.

acostarse	afeitarse	ducharse	quitarse	sentarse

1.

2.

3.

4.

5.

❖**F.   Encuesta.** You will hear a series of statements about your habits. For each statement, check the appropriate response. No answers will be given. The answers you choose should be correct for you!

	SIEMPRE	CON FRECUENCIA	A VECES	¡NUNCA!
1.	☐	☐	☐	☐
2.	☐	☐	☐	☐
3.	☐	☐	☐	☐
4.	☐	☐	☐	☐
5.	☐	☐	☐	☐
6.	☐	☐	☐	☐

G.   Hábitos y costumbres. Practice telling about some of the habits of the members of your fictitious family. Use the oral and written cues.

1. yo
2. mi primo y yo

3. mi hermanito
4. mis abuelos

Un poco de todo

A.   El próximo sábado... Complete las oraciones con la forma correcta del verbo para describir las actividades de Juan Carlos el próximo sábado.

Los sábados _____¹ (*yo:* **levantarse**) a las nueve de la mañana, pero el sábado de la

próxima semana _____² (**tener**) que _____³ (**despertarse**) más

temprano porque _____⁴ (**querer**) ir a _____⁵ (**jugar**) al tenis con

mi amigo Daniel. Casi siempre, _____⁶ (*nosotros:* **empezar**) a las nueve y media; si

_____⁷ (*yo:* **poner**) la alarma a las ocho y media y _____⁸ (**salir**) de

la casa a las nueve, _____⁹ (**poder**) llegar a tiempo. Daniel y yo

_____¹⁰ (**almorzar**) después de jugar al tenis. Si Daniel _____¹¹

(**perder**) el juego, _____¹² (*él:* **tener**) que pagar el restaurante; si yo

_____¹³ (**perder**) el juego, yo _____¹⁴ (**tener**) que pagar. A las

dos, _____¹⁵ (*yo:* **volver**) a casa.

❖B. Un día típico. On a separate sheet of paper, write about your typical day this semester, what you do when.

Paso 1. Before you begin to write, read the verbs given below and cross out those that do not apply to you. Organize the verbs you plan to use by writing **m (mañana)**, **t (tarde)**, **n (noche)** next to the appropriate infinitives. Then put each group into a logical chronological sequence.

acostarse	hacer	quitarse
afeitarse	ir	salir
almorzar	leer	sentarse a (comer)
asistir	levantarse	tomar el desayuno
bañarse/ducharse	llamar por teléfono (a)	trabajar
despertarse	mirar	vestirse
dormirse	ponerse	volver
empezar		

Paso 2. Now begin to write. Use any of the phrases listed here, or any others, to tell *when* you do these activities and to help you organize your sentences. Connect them into three coherent paragraphs: **por la mañana, por la tarde, por la noche.**

primero, luego	siempre, todos los días	hasta	antes de
nunca	con frecuencia, a veces	durante	después de

C. ¿Cuál es su casa? You will hear a description of Raquel and Arturo's house, read by Raquel. Listen to the description and circle the number of the drawing that matches the description.

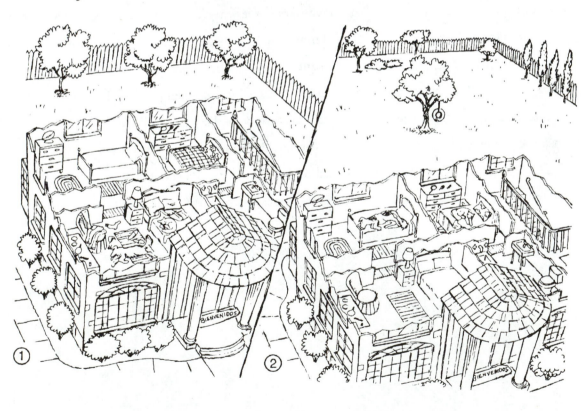

Paso 4 Un paso más

🎧 ◼ Videoteca*

Entrevista cultural: Costa Rica

You will hear an interview with Alexander Borbón. After listening, pause and choose the letter of the phrase that best completes each statement.

1. El Sr. Borbón trabaja en ____.
   a. Puerto Rico
   b. Costa Rica
   c. una universidad

2. Su compañía de bienes raíces (*real estate*) está en ____.
   a. San Juan
   b. San Francisco
   c. San José

3. Según el Sr. Borbón, en el centro hay más ____.
   a. casas con patios grandes
   b. mascotas, como perros
   c. condominios y apartamentos

4. Un condominio amueblado tiene ____.
   a. todos los muebles necesarios
   b. sólo (*only*) una cama
   c. una cocina

Entre amigos: Quiero cambiar de muebles.

Paso 1. The four friends will answer questions about where they live. Listen carefully and complete the following chart. The names are listed in the order in which they answer. Check your answers in the Appendix.

	¿CASA O APARTAMENTO†?	¿SOLO O CON OTRA(S) PERSONA(S)?	TAMAÑO (*SIZE*)	NÚMERO DE ALCOBAS††	NÚMERO DE BAÑOS	¿CON COCINA O NO?
Miguel René						
Karina						
Tané						
Rubén						

Now resume listening.

Paso 2. Now listen to how Rubén answers a question about his daily routine. Then pause and read the following statements. Circle **C** (**cierto**) if the statement is true or **F** (**falso**) if it is false.

1. C F Rubén se levanta a las ocho de la mañana.
2. C F Rubén trabaja por la mañana y por la tarde.
3. C F Rubén estudia entre las clases.
4. C F Rubén llega a casa a las dos de la tarde.
5. C F Cuando Rubén llega a casa, come y se acuesta.

---

*The **Videoteca** videoclips are available on the Video on CD to accompany *¿Qué tal?*, Seventh Edition.
†Words for **apartamento** include **departamento** and **piso**.
††Other words for *bedroom:* **el cuarto, la habitación, la recámara.**

Enfoque cultural: Costa Rica

A. Complete las oraciones con la información necesaria.

1. Costa Rica es una de las primeras _____ de las Américas.

2. Tuvo sus primeras elecciones en _____.

3. Costa Rica es la «Suiza» de las Américas porque se mantiene _____ en los conflictos entre naciones.

4. En 1987 el presidente de Costa Rica recibió (*received*) _____ de la Paz.

5. La Fundación Arias es una organización dedicada a _____.

B. ¿Cierto o falso?

1. C F La protección de las regiones naturales es muy importante en Costa Rica.

2. C F Aproximadamente un 50 por ciento (%) de Costa Rica está cubierto de bosques y selvas.

3. C F Más de la mitad (*half*) del territorio costarricense está dedicada para la preservación.

4. C F Costa Rica tiene un esfuerzo militar permanente muy grande.

❖■ ¡Repasemos!

A. **Una carta.** Complete this letter from Mariana to her pen pal in Bogotá, Colombia, with the correct form of the words in parentheses. When two possibilities are given in parentheses, select the correct word.

Querida Amalia:

Me preguntas[a] cómo pasamos[b] _____[1] (**nuestro / nuestros**) fines de semana. Pues,

_____[2] (**el / los**) viernes, _____[3] (**antes de / después de**)

clases, _____[4] (*yo:* **volver**) a casa o _____[5] (**ir**) a la

_____[6] (**biblioteca / librería**) porque es un lugar tranquilo para estudiar. Por

_____[7] (**el / la**) noche, yo voy _____[8] (**a la / al**) cine con

_____[9] (**mi / mis**) amigos o _____[10] (*nosotros:* **ir**) todos a una dis-

coteca. Los sábados trabajo en un almacén grande. No es un trabajo difícil,[c] pero

_____[11] (**a / son**) las seis _____[12] (**de / en**) la tarde, estoy

_____[13] (**cansada / cansado**). Los domingos, _____[14] (**mi / mis**)

padres, _____[15] (**mi / mis**) hermana y yo _____[16] (**ir**) a la iglesia,

_____[17] (**leer**) el periódico y _____[18] (**mirar**) la televisión.

_____[19] (**Por / De**) la tarde, muchas veces vamos a la casa de

_____[20] (**mi / mis**) tíos. Como _____[21] (*tú:* **ver**),

_____[22] (**el / los**) fines de semana todos nosotros _____[23] (**divertirse**).

Recuerdos cariñosos,[d]
Mariana

[a]Me... *You ask me*   [b]*we spend*   [c]*difficult*   [d]Recuerdos... *Affectionate regards*

B. *Listening Passage:* **Una casa hispana**

Antes de escuchar. Before you listen to the passage, pause and do the following prelistening exercises.

Paso 1. This passage will contain information about a house found in a Hispanic country. Check the specific information that you might expect to find in the passage.

☐ The speaker might talk about the different rooms in the house.

☐ The speaker might mention how many people are in his or her family.

☐ He or she might discuss the different architectural styles found in the Hispanic world.

Paso 2. Now complete the sentences with information that is true for your house or apartment. When a choice is given, circle the choice that is true for you.

1. Mi (casa/apartamento) tiene _____ alcoba(s) y _____ baño(s).

2. (Tiene / No tiene) sala.

3. (Tiene / No tiene) comedor.

4. Vivo allí con (mi familia / mis amigos/as). (Vivo solo/a [*alone*].)

5. Mi (casa/apartamento) (es / no es) típico/a de esta región o ciudad.

6. En la región donde vivo, (es necesario / no es necesario) tener calefacción (*heating*) en el invierno (*winter*).

7. Algo que (*Something that*) me gusta mucho de mi (casa/apartamento) es

   _____.

8. Algo que no me gusta es _____.

Now resume listening.

Listening Passage. Now you will hear a passage about Alma's house. The following words appear in the passage.

afueras	*outskirts*	árboles	*trees*
el vecindario	*neighborhood*	el clima	*climate*
recámaras	*bedrooms*	calefacción	*heating*
juntos	*together*		

Después de escuchar. Read the following true/false statements. Circle **C** (**cierto**) if the statement is true or **F** (**falso**) if it is false. If the information is not given in the passage, circle **ND** (**No lo dice**). Correct the statements that are false.

1. C F ND Todos los edificios en Panamá son de estilo colonial.

   _____

2. C F ND Alma vive en el centro de la Ciudad de Panamá.

   _____

3. C F ND Su casa es pequeña.

   _____

4. C F ND   Alma y su familia almuerzan en el comedor.

    _____

5. C F ND   La casa de Alma no tiene patio.

    _____

Now resume listening.

 C. Entrevista. You will hear a series of questions. Each will be said twice. Answer, based on your own experience. Pause and write the answers.

1. _____
2. _____
3. _____
4. _____
5. _____
6. _____
7. _____
8. _____

❖■ Mi diario

In your diary, write a description of your house (apartment, dorm, room, and so on). Be sure to include the following information.

- size
- name(s) and size of room(s)
- furniture in each room
- color of the walls, rug (if any), and furniture

- if there's a garage and/or yard, and what it or they are like
- your favorite place in your residence (or where you live) and why

Póngase a prueba

■ A ver si sabe...

A. *Hacer, oír, poner, salir, traer,* **and** *ver.* Complete la siguiente tabla.

INFINITIVO	YO	TÚ	NOSOTROS	ELLOS
hacer			hacemos	
traer				traen
oír		oyes		
poner				
ver				
salir				

B. Present Tense of Stem-Changing Verbs. Complete las oraciones con los siguientes verbos y preposiciones.

1. **(pensar servir)** ¿Qué _____ (tú) _____?

2. **(empezar a)** Ahora (yo) _____ _____ entender.

3. **(volver a)** ¿Uds. van a _____ _____ entrar?

4. **(pedir)** Voy a _____ otra Coca-Cola.

C. Reflexive Pronouns

1. Escriba el pronombre reflexivo apropiado.

   a. yo _____ levanto   c. él _____ despierta   e. vosotros _____ acostáis

   b. tú _____ acuestas   d. nosotros _____ divertimos   f. Uds. _____ bañan

2. Cambie el plural por el singular.

   a. Nosotros nos acostamos tarde.   _____

   b. ¿Cuándo se sientan a comer?   (tú) _____

   c. Nos vestimos en cinco minutos.   _____

▌Prueba corta

A. Oraciones. Complete las oraciones con la forma apropiada de los verbos de la lista. (*Note:* Use each verb once.)

divertirse   dormirse   hacer   levantarse   ponerse   salir   sentarse

1. Algunos (*Some*) estudiantes _____ en clase cuando están muy cansados.

2. Prefiero _____ cerca del escritorio del profesor.

3. Yo _____ mucho cuando salgo con mis amigos.

4. Si quieres llegar a tiempo, debes _____ temprano.

5. Para ir a un concierto al aire libre ella _____ un suéter y *jeans*.

6. (Tú) Siempre _____ muchas preguntas en clase, ¿verdad?

7. Los viernes por la noche mis amigos y yo _____ a comer y después vamos al cine.

B. Una lista. Complete las siguientes listas.

1. Escriba tres actividades que Ud. realiza (*that you do*) en la alcoba por la mañana:

   _____, _____ y _____.

2. Escriba tres actividades que Ud. realiza en el baño, después de despertarse:

   _____, _____ y _____.

3. Escriba el nombre de tres muebles de su sala: _____,

_____ y _____.

4. Escriba el nombre de tres cosas o muebles que Ud. piensa comprar para su casa:

_____, _____ y _____.

5. Escriba en qué cuartos de su casa realiza Ud. las siguientes actividades. Use oraciones completas.

almorzar _____

dormir _____

estudiar _____

C. Asociaciones. You will hear a series of statements. Circle the location with which you associate each statement.

1.	**a.**	la lámpara	**b.**	el comedor	**c.**	la cocina
2.	**a.**	la sala	**b.**	el baño	**c.**	la alcoba
3.	**a.**	el sofá	**b.**	el armario	**c.**	el lavabo
4.	**a.**	la piscina	**b.**	el almacén	**c.**	el garaje
5.	**a.**	la cocina	**b.**	el comedor	**c.**	la sala
6.	**a.**	la mesita	**b.**	el plato	**c.**	el sillón
7.	**a.**	la cómoda	**b.**	el estante	**c.**	el jardín

D. La rutina diaria. Practice talking about your daily routine, using the written cues. When you hear the corresponding number, form sentences using the words provided in the order given, making any necessary changes or additions.

MODELO: (*you see*) **1.** (yo) despertarse y levantarse / 7:00 A.M.   (*you hear*) uno →
(*you say*) Me despierto y me levanto a las siete de la mañana.

2. (yo) ducharse / vestirse / y / peinarse
3. hacer / el desayuno / y / sentarse a comer
4. hacer / la cama / y / salir / de casa / 8:00
5. después de las clases / ir / al gimnasio
6. hacer ejercicio / hasta / 3:30
7. volver a casa / y / poner el televisor
8. empezar / a preparar / comida
9. por fin / acostarse / 11:00 P.M. / y / dormirse

E. Apuntes. You will hear a brief paragraph that tells about a house for sale. Listen carefully and, while listening, write in the information requested. Write all numbers as numerals. First, listen to the new vocabulary and the requested information.

mide	*measures*	por	*by (as in 3 meters by 2 meters)*
el metro	*meter*	el vecindario	*neighborhood*

El número de alcobas: _____

El número de baños: _____

¿Cuántos metros mide la sala? _____

Esta casa está cerca de _____ y enfrente de _____.

La dirección (*address*) de la casa: _____

CAPÍTULO **5**

Paso 1 Vocabulario

¿Qué tiempo hace hoy?

A. **¿Qué tiempo hace?** Describe the weather conditions in each drawing.

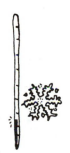 

1. _____
2. _____
3. _____
4. _____
5. _____

B. **¿Qué tiempo hace?**

1. Marta lleva impermeable y botas. _____

2. Joselito tiene frío y lleva abrigo, dos suéteres y botas. _____

3. Carmen tiene calor y lleva traje de baño. _____

4. Samuel lleva una chaqueta de lana, pero no lleva abrigo. _____

5. Todos llevan camisetas y pantalones y están en el parque. _____

6. Nadie (*No one*) hace ejercicio hoy. _____

C. ¿Qué tiempo hace? You will hear a series of weather conditions. Each will be said twice. Give the number of the drawing to which each corresponds, then repeat the description. First, pause and look at the drawings.

1.

2.

3.

4.

5.

6.

Los meses y las estaciones del año

A. Meses y estaciones. Complete las oraciones con las palabras apropiadas de esta sección.

1. El Día de los Inocentes (*April Fools' Day*) es _____ en los Estados Unidos.

2. Los tres meses del verano son _____, _____ y _____.

3. Diciembre es el primer mes del _____.

4. En la primavera hace buen tiempo, pero también _____ mucho.

5. Septiembre, octubre y noviembre son los tres meses del _____.

6. El _____ se celebra el Día de la Independencia de los Estados Unidos.

7. Por lo general, _____ mucho en las montañas durante el invierno.

8. Después de diciembre viene el mes de _____, y después de abril viene

   _____.

❖9. Mi cumpleaños es en (la estación de) _____.

B. ¿Cuándo es... ? Your Peruvian friend Evangelina wants to know when certain events take place, including a birth date (**una fecha de nacimiento**), an anniversary (**un aniversario**), and a national holiday (**una fiesta nacional**). Answer, using the written cues.

> MODELO: (*you hear*) ¿Cuándo es el cumpleaños de Nicolás? (*you see*) Sunday, May 4 →
> (*you say*) Es el domingo, cuatro de mayo.

1. Saturday, November 22
2. Wednesday, April 14

3. February 11, 1899
4. July 4, 1776

¿Dónde está? Las preposiciones

❖A. ¿Cierto o falso? ¿Qué hace Ud. en su clase de español?

1. C F Me siento delante del profesor.
2. C F Prefiero sentarme detrás de un estudiante alto.
3. C F Con frecuencia hablo con mis compañeros durante la clase.
4. C F Siempre pongo la mochila al lado de mi silla.
5. C F Me siento cerca de la puerta.
6. C F Pongo los pies (*feet*) encima de la silla delante de mí.
7. C F A veces olvido (*I forget*) libros debajo de mi silla.

B. ¿Dónde está España? Mire el mapa y luego complete la descripción con la(s) palabra(s) apropiada(s). Es necesario usar algunas (*some*) palabras más de una vez (*more than once*).

> al norte   al sur   al este   al oeste   cerca   lejos   en   entre

España y Portugal forman la Península Ibérica. Los Pirineos están _____[1] España

y Francia. Francia está _____[2] de España y África está _____[3] de

España. El Mar Mediterráneo está _____[4] de la península y el Océano Atlántico

está _____.[5]

Madrid, la capital, está en el centro del país.

La hermosa ciudad de Granada está

_____[6] de Madrid; Toledo está

_____.[7] La isla de Mallorca, una

de las Islas Baleares, está _____[8]

el Mar Mediterráneo. Las Islas Canarias están

_____[9] de África del Norte.

❖C. ¿Quién es?

Paso 1. Draw a seating plan of the people who sit directly around you in class, and write in their names. If no one sits in one of those seats, write **nadie.**

_____

_____ yo _____

_____

Paso 2. Ahora, en otro papel, escriba un párrafo para indicar (*indicate*) dónde se sientan sus compañeros de clase con respecto a Ud. Escriba también los nombres de las personas que se sientan más lejos (*farthest*) y más cerca de la puerta.

a mi derecha   a mi izquierda   delante de   detrás de   más lejos (cerca) de

MODELO: George se sienta delante de mí. María se sienta a mi derecha...

D. ¿Dónde está? You will hear a series of descriptions. Listen carefully and name the country, location, or item described. You will be listening for specific information about the location of the place or item. (Remember to repeat the correct answer.)

4. ...   5. ...   6. ...

1. ...   2. ...   3. ...

7. ... **8.** ... **9.** ...

 ## Pronunciación y ortografía: *r* and *rr*

The letter **r** has two pronunciations in Spanish: the trilled **r** (written as **rr** between vowels or as **r** at the beginning of a word), and the flap **r,** which appears in all other positions. Because mispronunciations can alter the meaning of a word, it is important to distinguish between these two pronunciations of the Spanish **r.** For example: **coro** (*chorus*) and **corro** (*I run*).

The flap **r** is similar to the sound produced by the rapid pronunciation of *tt* and *dd* in the English words *Betty* and *ladder*.

¡RECUERDE!

The trilled **r** is spelled _____ at the beginning of a word. It is spelled _____ in the middle of a word (between vowels).

A. El sonido *rr*. Underline the examples of the trilled **rr** sound in the following words and phrases.

1. Rosa	**4.** Roberto	**7.** una persona rara
2. caro	**5.** rebelde	**8.** Raquel es rubia.
3. perro	**6.** un horrible error	

B. Repeticiones. Listen to these word pairs. Then repeat them.

> *Petty* / pero
> *sadder* / Sara
> *motor* / moro

C. Más repeticiones. Repeat the following words, phrases, and sentences, imitating the speaker.

1. arte   gracias   para   vender   triste
2. ruso   Roberto   real   reportero   rebelde
3. burro   corral   carro   barra   corro
4. el extranjero
   el precio del cuaderno
   el nombre correcto
   Enrique, Carlos y Rosita
   las residencias
   una mujer refinada
   Puerto Rico
   El perro está en el corral.
   Soy el primo de Roberto Ramírez.
   Estos errores son raros.

D. ¿R o rr? You will hear a series of words. Each will be said twice. Circle the letter of the word you hear.

1. **a.** ahora   **b.** ahorra
2. **a.** caro   **b.** carro
3. **a.** coro   **b.** corro
4. **a.** coral   **b.** corral
5. **a.** pero   **b.** perro

Los hispanos hablan: ¿De dónde eres?

You will hear three brief answers to this question. As you listen, write the information in the spaces provided. First, pause and look at the information for which you need to listen. (Check your answers in the Appendix.)

Habla José.

Ciudad: _____ País: _____

El clima: _____

La gente (*people*): _____

¿Hay una universidad en la ciudad?   Sí   No

Habla Clara.

Ciudad: _____ País: _____

El clima: _____

La gente: _____

¿Hay una universidad en la ciudad?   Sí   No

Habla Diana.

Ciudad: _____ País: _____

El clima: _____

La gente: _____

¿Hay una universidad en la ciudad?   Sí   No

Paso 2 Gramática

14. *¿Qué están haciendo?* • **Present Progressive: estar + -ndo**

A. En este momento... ¿Qué están haciendo estas personas en este momento?

1. _____ Enrique Iglesias…
2. _____ Antonio Banderas…
3. _____ Su profesor(a)…
4. _____ Jennifer López…
5. _____ El presidente…
6. _____ Óscar de la Hoya…

a. está trabajando en una película.
b. está hablando en las Naciones Unidas.
c. está cantando canciones románticas.
d. está corrigiendo (*correcting*) exámenes.
e. está practicando boxeo.
f. está haciendo un vídeo.

B. La familia de Rigoberto. Describa lo que están haciendo los miembros de la familia de Rigoberto, desde su perspectiva. Use la forma apropiada del gerundio. ¡OJO! Cuidado con los verbos que tienen un cambio en la raíz (*stem*).

1. Mi abuela está _____ (**dormir**) la siesta ahora.
2. Mi hermana María está _____ (**pedir**) $8.00 para ir al cine.
3. Mi padre está _____ (**servirse**) café.
4. Mis hermanos están _____ (**jugar**) al tenis.
5. Mi madre está _____ (**almorzar**) con una amiga.

   Está _____ (**divertirse**).

C. Mis padres (hijos) y yo. Sus padres (hijos) siempre hacen cosas muy diferentes de las que hace Ud. Cambie los infinitivos para mostrar lo que están haciendo ellos y lo que hace Ud. en este momento.

MODELO: leer el periódico / estudiar para un examen →
Mis padres (hijos) están leyendo el periódico, pero yo estoy estudiando para un examen.

1. jugar al golf / correr en un maratón _____
   _____

2. mirar la tele / aprender a esquiar _____
   _____

3. leer el periódico / escuchar música _____
   _____

4. acostarse / vestirme para salir _____
   _____

D. Descripción: ¿Qué están haciendo en este momento? Using the present progressive of the following verbs, tell what each person in the Hernández family is doing at the moment. For the exercise, don't attach the reflexive pronouns to the present participle. First, listen to the list of verbs.

afeitarse   bañarse   dormir   jugar   ponerse   vestirse

MODELO: (*you see*) **1.** (*you hear*) uno → (*you say*) El bebé está durmiendo.

2. ...   **3.** ...   **4.** ...   **5.** ...   **6.** ...

15. ¿*Ser* o *estar*? Summary of the Uses of *ser* and *estar*

¡RECUERDE!

¿Se usa **ser** o **estar**? Escriba el infinitivo apropiado en la columna de la izquierda. Luego complete las oraciones con la forma apropiada de **ser** o **estar** en la columna de la derecha.

1. *to talk about location of a person or thing:*

_____

Mis libros _____ al lado de mi silla.

2. *to talk about origin:* _____

Mi abuela _____ de España.

3. *to express possession with* **de:**

_____

¿De quién _____ este dinero?

4. *with adjectives, to express the norm or*

inherent qualities: _____

Los padres de Elena _____ altos.

La nieve _____ blanca.

5. *with adjectives, to express a change from*

the norm or to express conditions:

_____

Mi café _____ frío.

Tú _____ muy guapo esta noche.

¿_____ Uds. ocupados?

6. *to identify people or things:*

_____

Nosotros _____ estudiantes.

Miguel _____ el hijo de Julio.

7. *to express time:* _____

_____ las dos y media.

A. Minidiálogos. Complete los diálogos con la forma apropiada de **ser** o **estar.**

1. —¿De dónde _____ tú?

   —_____ de Buenos Aires.

2. —¿De quién _____ estas cosas?

   —Creo que _____ de Ana.

3. —Estos boletos (*tickets*) _____ para Uds. Vamos a entrar ahora, ¿eh? Las puertas

   del cine ya _____ abiertas.

   —Buena idea.

4. —Pablo, ya _____ la una y media. Tenemos que _____ en el aeropuerto

   a las dos y _____ difícil encontrar (*to find*) un taxi a estas horas.

   —De acuerdo. Vamos.

5. —Juan, tu cuarto _____ muy desordenado.

   —Sí, mamá. (Yo) _____ de acuerdo, ¡pero la puerta _____ cerrada!

6. —La novia de Tito _____ cariñosa y alegre. ¿Y él?

   —Él _____ muy formal y serio.

B. Sentimientos. Complete the sentences with the forms of **estar** and the most appropriate adjectives from the list below in order to describe how you might feel in the following situations. Use each adjective only once. ¡OJO! Be careful with adjective agreement.

aburrido/a   cansado/a   contento/a   furioso/a   nervioso/a   preocupado/a   triste

1. Cuando leo un libro que no me gusta, _____.

2. Cuando voy al cine con mis amigos, _____.

3. Antes de un examen difícil, _____.

4. Cuando mi novio/a no llama, _____.

5. Cuando mi hermano/a (compañero/a de cuarto,...) lleva mi chaqueta de seda favorita, _____

   _____.

6. Después de trabajar diez horas, _____.

7. Cuando no tengo dinero, _____.

C. Diálogo. Mari habla con Anita. Complete el diálogo con las formas apropiadas de **ser** o **estar.**

MARI: Hola, Anita. ¿Cómo _____[1]?

ANITA: Todavía _____[2] un poco enferma de gripe.[a]

MARI: Ay, lo siento.[b] ¿Quiénes _____[3] esos chicos que _____[4] con tu hermano?

ANITA: _____[5] nuestros primos. _____[6] de la Argentina.

MARI: ¿Y esta guitarra? ¿De quién _____[7]?

ANITA: De mi prima Rosario. Ella _____[8] una guitarrista fabulosa. Canta y toca como[c] profesional.

MARI: ¿Cuánto tiempo van a _____[9] aquí?

ANITA: Sólo dos semanas. ¿Por qué no vienes a casa el domingo? Vamos a dar[d] una fiesta.

MARI: Encantada, gracias.

[a]*flu* [b]*lo... I'm sorry* [c]*like a* [d]*give*

D. Minidiálogo: Una conversación por larga distancia. You will hear one side of a telephone conversation between a husband and his wife who is on a business trip. Then you will hear a series of questions from the dialogue. Circle the letter of the best response to each.

1. **a.** Estoy en Nueva York.   **b.** Estoy cansada, pero estoy bien.
2. **a.** Es el Sr. Miró.   **b.** Es muy moderno.
3. **a.** Estoy trabajando.   **b.** Hace buen tiempo.
4. **a.** Hace buen tiempo.   **b.** Son las once y media.

E. ¿Qué pregunta hiciste? (*What question did you ask?*) You will hear a series of statements that contain **ser** or **estar.** Each will be said twice. Circle the letter of the question that corresponds to each.

1. **a.** ¿Cómo estás?   **b.** ¿Cómo eres?
2. **a.** ¿Cómo están?   **b.** ¿Cómo son?
3. **a.** ¿Dónde estás?   **b.** ¿De dónde eres?
4. **a.** ¿Dónde está el consejero?   **b.** ¿De dónde es el consejero?
5. **a.** ¿De quién es la blusa?   **b.** ¿De qué es la blusa?

F. ¿Quiénes son? Imagine that the people in this photograph are your relatives. Tell who they are and describe them, using the oral cues and the appropriate forms of **ser** or **estar.** All the cues are about the couple on the right. Begin your first answer with **Son...**

1. ...   2. ...   3. ...   4. ...   5. ...   6. ...

Paso 3 Gramática

16. Describing • Comparisons

❖**A. Opiniones.** Complete las oraciones con **más/menos... que** o **tan... como.**

1. Soy _____ alto/a _____ mi padre/madre.

2. La salud (*Health*) es _____ importante _____ el dinero.

3. Mi cuarto está _____ limpio _____ el cuarto de mi mejor amigo/a.

4. Los hermanos de Michael Jackson son _____ ricos _____ él.

5. Mi padre es _____ serio _____ mi madre.

B. Hablando de Roberto, Ceci y Laura. Compare las cualidades indicadas de las personas nombradas.

MODELOS: Roberto **/** Ceci (delgado) → Roberto es tan delgado como Ceci.
Roberto **/** Ceci (estudioso) → Roberto es más estudioso que Ceci.

1. Ceci **/** Laura (delgado) _____

2. Ceci **/** Roberto (atlético) _____

3. Roberto **/** Laura (introvertido) _____

4. Ceci **/** Laura (alto) _____

5. Roberto **/** Laura (estudioso) _____

6. Roberto **/** Ceci (moreno) _____

❖Ahora haga tres comparaciones entre Ud. y Roberto, Laura y/o Ceci.

7. _____

8. _____

9. _____

C. **En el centro.** Conteste según el dibujo.

1. ¿Es el cine tan alto como la tienda Casa Montaño? _____

    _____

2. ¿Cuál es el edificio más pequeño de todos? _____

    _____

3. ¿Cuál es el edificio más alto? _____

    _____

4. ¿Es el cine tan alto como el café? _____

    _____

5. ¿Es el hotel tan grande como el cine? _____

    _____

 D. **Comparando dos ciudades**

Paso 1. La comparación. Listen as Uncle Ricardo compares Mexico City (**el Distrito Federal** [**D.F.**]) and Sevilla.

Paso 2. ¿Qué recuerda Ud.? Pause and complete the following sentences based on Ricardo's comparison. (Check your answers in the Appendix.)

Según (*According to*) Ricardo...

1. Sevilla es _____ bonita _____ la Ciudad de México.

2. Sevilla tiene _____ edificios altos _____ el D.F.

3. En el D.F. no hace _____ calor _____ en Sevilla.

4. Sevilla no tiene _____ habitantes _____ el D.F.

Now resume listening.

E. **Un desacuerdo.** Imagine that you and your friend Lourdes don't agree on anything! React to her statements negatively, following the model and using the cues.

MODELO: (*you hear and see*) Los amigos son más importantes que la familia.
(*you hear*) tan → (*you say*) No, los amigos son tan importantes como la familia.

1. El invierno es más bonito que el verano.
2. Hace tanto calor en Florida como en Alaska.
3. La clase de cálculo es menos difícil que la clase de física.
4. Los niños juegan más videojuegos (*video games*) que los adultos.

F. La rutina de Alicia. The following chart shows Alicia's routine for weekdays and weekends. You will hear a series of statements about the chart. Each will be said twice. Circle **C** if the statement is true or **F** if it is false, according to the chart. First pause and read the chart.

ACCIÓN	DE LUNES A VIERNES	SÁBADO Y DOMINGO
levantarse	6:30	9:30
bañarse	7:15	10:00
trabajar	8 horas	1 hora
almorzar	20 minutos	30 minutos
divertirse	1 hora	8 horas
acostarse	11:00	11:00

1. C   F   **2.** C   F   **3.** C   F   **4.** C   F   **5.** C   F

Un poco de todo

A. ¡Problemas y más problemas! Form complete sentences, using the words provided in the order given. Make any necessary changes, and add other words when necessary. Replace each **¿ ?** with the appropriate form of **ser** or **estar**. Write the progressive form of the underlined verbs. Write out all numbers. *Note:* **/ /** indicates a new sentence.

1. Carmen **/ ¿ ? /** ocupado **/** y **/** no **/** poder **/** ir **/** cine **/** este **/** noche

_____

2. ese **/** camisa **/ ¿ ? /** sucio **/ / /** (tú) deber **/** ponerse **/** otro

_____

3. ese **/** tiendas **/ ¿ ? /** cerrado **/** ahora **/ / /** no **/** (nosotros) poder **/** entrar

_____

4. (nosotros) deber **/** llevar **/** el paraguas (*umbrella*) **/ / ¿ ? /** <u>llover</u>

_____

_____

5. mi **/** primos **/ ¿ ? /** de Lima; **/** ahora **/** (ellos) <u>visitar</u> **/** su **/** tíos **/** en Texas, **/** pero **/** su **/** madre **/** ¿ ? **/** enfermo **/** y **/** (ellos) tener **/** regresar **/** su **/** país **/** semana **/** viene

_____

_____

B. Un hermano increíble. Fill in the blanks with the correct form of the infinitive or with the correct words in parentheses to complete the narration. Write out the numbers.

Yo tengo _____¹ (**21**) años. Mi hermano Miguel tiene sólo _____²

(**19**), pero _____³ (**ese / eso**) chico es increíble. Estudia menos _____⁴

(**que / como**) yo, pero recibe mejores notas^a _____⁵ (**de / que**) yo. También gana^b

más dinero _____⁶ (**de / que**) yo, aunque^c yo trabajo _____⁷

(**tanto / tan**) _____⁸ (**como / que**) él. En realidad,^d gana más _____⁹

(**de / que**) _____¹⁰ (**$200**) a la semana, pero nunca tiene dinero

_____¹¹ (**porque / por qué**) gasta^e todo su dinero en ropa. ¡Le gusta

_____¹² (**ser / estar**) muy de moda! Por ejemplo, cree que necesita más

_____¹³ (**de / que**) _____¹⁴ (**$150**) para comprar zapatos

de tenis. Yo creo que es una tontería^f _____¹⁵ (**paga / pagar**) tanto por zapatos.

^a*grades*   ^b*he earns*   ^c*although*   ^d*En... In fact*   ^e*he spends*   ^f*foolish thing*

C. En la plaza Santa Ana

Paso 1. ¿Qué pasa? You will hear a series of statements about the following drawing. Each will be said twice. Circle **C** if the statement is true or **F** if it is false. First, pause and look at the drawing.

1. C F   **2.** C F   **3.** C F   **4.** C F   **5.** C F

❖**Paso 2. Descripción.** Now pause and on a separate sheet of paper write five sentences that describe the drawing. You can talk about the weather, what the people are doing, how they seem to be feeling, their clothing, and so on. You can also make comparisons.

Paso 4 Un paso más

Videoteca*

Entrevista cultural: Guatemala

You will hear an interview with Deborah Davis. As you listen, complete the following paragraph with information from the interview. Check your answers in the Appendix. First, pause and read the incomplete paragraph.

Deborah es de _____¹ y es meteoróloga. Ella da pronósticos del

_____² para un canal de _____.³ El clima de Guatemala es

_____⁴: no hace ni mucho _____⁵ ni mucho

_____.⁶ A veces hay temporadas de _____⁷ tiempo con

_____⁸ y huracanes, pero el clima en general es superagradable, como en toda

Centroamérica. Los meses de lluvia son _____⁹ y _____.¹⁰

Now resume listening.

Entre amigos: A mí me encanta el verano.

The four friends answer questions about the climate and weather of their respective countries. Listen carefully and jot down notes about their responses. The names are listed in the order in which the first question is answered. Check your answers in the Appendix.

	PAÍS	CLIMA	ESTACIÓN FAVORITA
Karina			
Miguel René			
Rubén			
Tané			

Enfoque cultural: Guatemala

Complete las oraciones con la información apropiada.

1. Más del cincuenta por ciento de los guatemaltecos es descendiente de los _____.

2. Para documentar su historia y su cultura, los mayas tenían un sistema de

_____ jeroglífica y el _____ más exacto de su época.

3. En las ruinas de _____ se puede ver la grandeza de la civilización maya.

4. La violencia contra los indígenas de Guatemala ocurre entre los años _____.

5. Rigoberta Menchú pierde a cuatro miembros (*members*) de su _____, todos asesinados por el ejército (*army*).

6. En 1992, Menchú recibe el _____ por su trabajo a favor de los derechos humanos (*human rights*).

---

*The **Videoteca** videoclips is available on the CD to accompany *¿Qué tal?*, Seventh Edition.

❖■ ¡Repasemos!

A. Composición. On a separate sheet of paper, write two short paragraphs that answer the two sets of questions below. Remember that a paragraph is not a list of numbered answers but a connected composition. Use the following connectors to make your composition more interesting and meaningful: **por eso, y, aunque** (*although*), **también, luego,** and **porque.** However, do not use **porque** to begin a sentence; use **como** (*since*). For example, the two sentences **Hace calor** and **Voy a llevar un traje de baño** can be combined in the following ways:

> Como hace calor, voy a llevar un traje de baño.
>
> Voy a llevar un traje de baño porque hace calor.

- **1.** ¿En qué mes piensa ir de vacaciones este año? ¿Qué día va a salir? **2.** ¿Adónde va a ir? ¿Con quién(es) va? **3.** ¿Cuánto tiempo piensa estar allí? **4.** ¿Va a estar en un hotel o en la casa de unos amigos?

- **1.** ¿Qué tiempo hace allí? ¿Llueve con frecuencia? ¿Nieva mucho? ¿Hay contaminación? **2.** ¿Qué ropa piensa llevar? **3.** ¿Qué cosas quiere hacer durante el día? ¿y durante la noche? **4.** ¿En qué fecha piensa volver?

 B. *Listening Passage:* **Hablando del clima**

Antes de escuchar. Before you listen to the passage, pause and do the following prelistening exercises.

Paso 1. Read the following true/false statements. As you read them, try to infer the information the passage will give you, as well as the specific information for which you need to listen.

1. En las regiones tropicales, por lo general, hay una estación seca (*dry*) y una lluviosa (*rainy*).
2. En Latinoamérica, no hace frío en ninguna (*any*) región.
3. Hay climas muy variados en el mundo hispánico.
4. En Sudamérica, las estaciones del año son opuestas a las (*opposite to those*) de los países del Hemisferio Norte.

Paso 2. You probably do know quite a bit about the climate in most of Latin America. That information will be fairly easy for you to recognize in the listening passage. Read the next set of true/false statements, and try to infer what type of information you need to listen for regarding the person who will narrate the passage.

> La persona que habla…

1. es de Vermont.
2. prefiere el frío del invierno.
3. no sabe (*doesn't know how to*) esquiar.
4. quiere vivir en los Andes.

> A la persona que habla…

5. no le gustan las estaciones lluviosas en los países tropicales.

Now resume listening.

Listening Passage. Now, you will hear a passage about the climate in different regions of the Hispanic world. This passage is read by Nicanor, a friend of Susana's. The following words appear in the passage.

seca	*dry*
lluviosa	*rainy*
yo lo tengo claro	*it's clear to me*

Después de escuchar. Here is another version of the true/false statements you did in **Antes de escuchar.** Circle **C** if the statement is true or **F** if it is false. Then correct the statements that are false, according to the passage.

1. C   F   Nicanor es de Vermont.

    _____

2. C   F   A Nicanor no le gusta el frío.

    _____

3. C   F   En el mundo hispánico, hay climas muy variados.

    _____

4. C   F   En Sudamérica no hace frío en ninguna región.

    _____

5. C   F   A Nicanor le gustaría (*would like*) vivir en los Andes.

    _____

6. C   F   Cuando es verano en el Hemisferio Norte, también es verano en el Hemisferio Sur.

    _____

Now resume listening.

C.   Entrevista. You will hear a series of questions. Each will be said twice. Answer, based on your own experience. Write out all numbers. Pause and write the answers.

1.   _____
2.   _____
3.   _____
4.   _____
5.   _____
6.   _____

❖■ Mi diario

Escriba Ud. sobre tres cosas que hace, que piensa hacer o que le gusta hacer en cada estación del año.

MODELO: En la primavera me gusta ir de compras. En las vacaciones de primavera pienso visitar a mis amigos en Washington. Si todavía hay nieve, voy a esquiar (*to ski*) también. Me gusta mucho esquiar.

Vocabulario útil

celebrar mi cumpleaños   nadar (*to swim*)

esquiar   quedarme en casa

ir a la playa   visitar a mis abuelos (amigos)

Póngase a prueba

A ver si sabe...

A. Present Progressive: *estar* + *-ndo.* Complete la siguiente tabla con la forma correcta del gerundio.

cepillarse		hablar	hablando
divertirse		leer	
dormir	durmiendo	poner	
escribir		servir	
estudiar		tener	teniendo

B. ¿*Ser* o *estar*? Match the statements in the left-hand column with the appropriate use of **ser** or **estar** in the right-hand column.

1. _____ Estamos muy ocupados.

2. _____ Son las nueve.

3. _____ Ella está en Costa Rica.

4. _____ El reloj es de Carlos.

5. _____ Gracias, estoy bien.

6. _____ Ella es de Costa Rica.

7. _____ Marta es alta y morena.

8. _____ Están mirando la tele.

9. _____ Es importante salir ahora.

    a. to tell time
    b. with **de** to express origin
    c. to tell location of a person or thing
    d. to form generalizations
    e. with the present participle to form the progressive
    f. with adjectives to express a change from the norm or to express conditions
    g. with adjectives to express the norm or inherent qualities
    h. to speak of one's health
    i. with **de** to express possession

C. Comparisons. Subraye (*Underline*) las palabras apropiadas.

1. Paulina es (**más** / **tanta**) bonita (**que** / **como**) su hermana.

2. Tengo (**tan** / **tantos**) problemas (**que** / **como**) tú.

3. Este libro es bueno, pero el otro es (**menor** / **mejor**).

4. Tú cantas (**tan** / **tanto**) bien (**que** / **como**) Gloria.

5. Mis hermanos tienen (**tantos** / **menos**) clases (**que** / **como**) yo.

Prueba corta

A. Oraciones. Escriba oraciones con las siguientes palabras en el presente progresivo.

1. (yo) mirar **/** programa _____

2. Juan **/** leer **/** periódico _____

3. Marta **/** servir **/** café **/** ahora _____

4. niños **/** dormir _____

5. ¿almorzar (tú) **/** ahora? _____

B. ¿*Ser* o *estar*? Complete las oraciones con la forma apropiada de **ser** o **estar,** según el contexto.

1. —Buenas tardes. ¿Cómo _____ Ud., señorita?

   —_____ bien, gracias.

2. —¿De dónde _____ (tú), Pablo?

   —_____ de Bogotá, Colombia.

3. —¿En qué clase _____ Uds.?

   —_____ en la clase de Español 1.

4. —¿Qué te pasa (*What's the matter with you*)? ¿_____ enferma?

   —No, sólo _____ cansada.

5. Carlitos, debes ponerte otra camisa. Esa _____ sucia.

C. Arturo y Roberto. Study the following drawing. Then form complete sentences using the words provided, in the order given, to compare Arturo and Roberto.

1. Arturo **/** libros **/** Roberto _____

   _____

2. Arturo **/** gordo **/** Roberto _____

   _____

3. Roberto **/** alto **/** Arturo _____

   _____

4. Roberto **/** años **/** Arturo _____

   _____

5. Arturo **/** perros **/** Roberto _____

Arturo
22 años

Roberto
20 años

D. Comparaciones. You will hear a series of statements about the following chart. Each will be said twice. Circle **C** if the statement is true or **F** if it is false. First, pause and read the chart.

PAÍS	POBLACIÓN (HABITANTES)	ÁREA (MILLAS CUADRADAS) (SQUARE MILES)	TEMPERATURA COSTAL / TEMPERATURA INTERIOR EN GRADOS FAHRENHEIT	NÚMERO DE PERIÓDICOS DIARIOS (DAILY NEWSPAPERS)
Costa Rica	3.896.092	19.730	90° / 63°	4
Guatemala	13.909.384	42.042	82° / 68°	5
Nicaragua	5.128.517	50.838	77° / 79°	6
México	104.907.991	756.066	120° / 61°	285

Now resume listening.

1. C F   2. C F   3. C F   4. C F   5. C F   6. C F

E. La nueva profesora guatemalteca. Tell about the new professor, using the written cues. When you hear the corresponding number, form sentences using the words provided in the order given, making any necessary changes or additions. You will be given a choice of verbs. Choose the correct one.

MODELO: (you see) **1.** la profesora / (ser / estar) / Isabel Darío
(you hear) uno → (you say) La profesora es Isabel Darío.

2. la profesora / (ser / estar) / de Puerto Barrios, Guatemala
3. Puerto Barrios / (ser / estar) / lejos de la capital
4. la profesora / (ser / estar) / cansada por el viaje
5. ella / se (ser / estar) / quedando con unos amigos
6. la profesora / (ser / estar) / inteligente y simpática
7. los estudiantes / (ser / estar) / contentos con la nueva profesora

F. Hablando de viajes. Imagine that you will travel to a variety of places this year. Answer the questions you hear about each of your trips using the written cues. **¡ojo!** The questions may vary slightly from those in the model. Change your answers accordingly.

MODELO: (you see) 3/30 / fresco
(you hear) ¿Cuándo sales para Detroit? → (you say) Salgo el treinta de marzo.
(you hear) ¿Y qué tiempo hace allí? → (you say) Hace fresco.

1. 7/15 / calor
2. 12/1 / nevando
3. 1/10 / sol
4. 5/24 / viento

CAPÍTULO **6**

Paso 1 Vocabulario

 La comida

A. La comida. Complete las oraciones con las palabras apropiadas de la lista a continuación.

agua	helado	lechuga	té
arroz	huevos	pan	tomate
camarones	jugo	patatas fritas	verduras
carne	langosta	queso	zanahorias
galletas	leche	sed	

1. Un buen desayuno típico para mucha gente (*people*) en los Estados Unidos

   es _____ de naranja, dos _____ con jamón,

   _____ tostado y café, _____ o _____.

2. Dos mariscos favoritos son los _____ y la _____.

3. Las especialidades de McDonald's son las hamburguesas y las _____.

4. El _____ mineral es una bebida favorita de la gente que (*who*) no quiere

   engordar (*to gain weight*).

5. De (*For*) postre, ¿prefiere Ud. pastel, flan o _____ de vainilla o chocolate?

6. Un vegetariano no come _____; prefiere las _____ y las

   frutas.

7. El sándwich de jamón y _____ es popular para el almuerzo.

8. La ensalada se hace (*is made*) con _____ y _____.

9. Una combinación popular son las arvejas y las _____.

10. En la sopa de pollo hay _____ o fideos (*noodles*).

11. Cuando los niños vuelven de la escuela, tienen hambre y a veces quieren comer

    _____ con leche.

12. Cuando tengo _____, bebo agua fría.

❖B. **Preguntas personales.** Conteste estas preguntas sobre sus hábitos y preferencias con respecto a la comida.

1. ¿Dónde y a qué hora almuerza Ud., generalmente?

   _____

2. Cuando Ud. vuelve a casa después de sus clases o después de trabajar y tiene hambre, ¿qué le apetece (*do you feel like*) comer? ¿frutas? ¿galletas? ¿un sándwich? ¿ ?

   Me apetece comer _____.

3. Por lo general, ¿come Ud. más pescado, más pollo o más carne?

   _____

C. **Definiciones.** You will hear a series of definitions. Each will be said twice. Circle the letter of the word defined by each.

1.	**a.**	la zanahoria	**b.**	los huevos
2.	**a.**	la lechuga	**b.**	la langosta
3.	**a.**	la leche	**b.**	el vino blanco
4.	**a.**	un postre	**b.**	un sándwich
5.	**a.**	el almuerzo	**b.**	la cena
6.	**a.**	los espárragos	**b.**	el agua mineral

D. **Identificaciones.** Identify the following foods when you hear the corresponding number. Use the definite article in your answer.

1. 2. 3. 4.

5. 6. 7. 8.

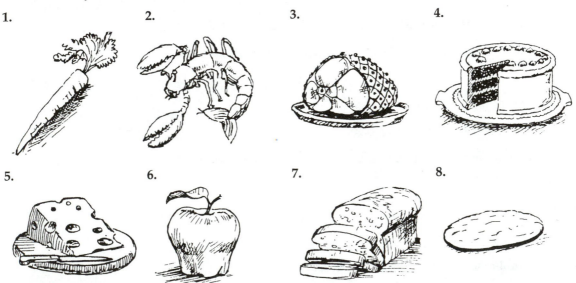

E. **Categorías.** You will hear a series of words. Repeat each word, telling in what category it belongs: **un tipo de carne, un marisco, una fruta, una verdura, un postre,** or **una bebida.**

MODELO: (*you hear*) el té → (*you say*) El té es una bebida.

1. … 2. … 3. … 4. … 5. …

¿Qué sabe Ud. y a quién conoce?

❖**A.** **¿Qué sabe Ud. y a quién conoce?** Indique si las siguientes declaraciones son ciertas o falsas para Ud.

1. C F Yo sé cocinar bien.

2. C F Conozco a la familia de mi mejor amigo/a.

3. C F Mi profesor(a) sabe tocar la guitarra.

4. C F Yo también sé tocar un instrumento musical.

5. C F Conozco a los dueños (*owners*) de un restaurante.

B. *¿Saber* o *conocer*? Complete las oraciones con la forma apropiada de **saber** o **conocer,** según el sentido (*meaning*).

1. Ellas no _____ a mi primo.

2. Yo no _____ a qué hora llegan del teatro.

3. ¿(*Tú*) _____ tocar el piano?

4. Necesitan _____ a qué hora vas a venir.

5. (*Nosotros*) _____ a los padres de Paquita, pero yo no _____ al resto de su familia.

6. Queremos _____ al presidente del club.

C. **La *a* personal.** Complete las oraciones con la **a** personal, cuando sea (*whenever it is*) necesario. ¡RECUERDE! **a + el = al.**

- No veo _____[1] el dueño y no conozco _____[2] los camareros (*waiters*). Todos son nuevos.

- —¿_____[3] quién buscan Uds.? —Buscamos _____[4] la Srta. Estrada. Creo que no está aquí todavía.

- Mis padres conocen _____[5] este restaurante. Creen que es muy bueno.

- ¿Por qué no llamas _____[6] el camarero ahora? Quiero ver _____[7] el menú mientras esperamos _____[8] María Elena.

D. **¿Qué sabe y a quién conoce?**

Paso 1. Mis amigos. You will hear a brief paragraph about some of the things your friends know and whom they know. Listen and write either **sí** or **no** under the corresponding item. Two items have been done for you.

NOMBRE	BAILAR	A JUAN	JUGAR AL TENIS	A MIS PADRES	ESTA CIUDAD
Enrique	sí	no			
Roberto					
Susana					

Paso 2. ¿Qué recuerda Ud.? Now pause and complete the following statements with information from the completed chart. Check the answers to **Paso 1** in the Appendix before you begin **Paso 2.**

1. Roberto y Susana _____ jugar al tenis.

2. Susana _____ bailar.

3. Nadie (*No one*) _____ a Juan.

4. Roberto y Enrique _____ bien la ciudad.

Now resume listening.

Pronunciación y ortografía: d

A. Repeticiones. Spanish **d** has two pronunciations. At the beginning of a phrase or sentence and after **n** or **l,** it is pronounced similarly to English *d* as in *dog:* [d], that is, as a stop. Listen to these words and repeat them after the speaker.

> [d]   diez   ¿dónde?   venden   condición   falda   el doctor

In all other cases, **d** is pronounced like the English sound *th* in *another* but softer: [đ], that is, as a fricative. Listen and repeat the following words.

> [đ]   adiós   seda   ciudad   usted   cuadros   la doctora

B. Entonación. Repeat the following sentences, imitating the speaker. Pay close attention to the intonation.

¿Dónde está el dinero?   ¿Qué estudia Ud.?

Dos y diez son doce.   Venden de todo, ¿verdad?

C. A escoger. You will hear a series of words containing the letter **d.** Each will be said twice. Circle the letter of the **d** sound you hear.

1. a. [d]   b. [đ]   3. a. [d]   b. [đ]   5. a. [d]   b. [đ]
2. a. [d]   b. [đ]   4. a. [d]   b. [đ]

Los hispanos hablan: ¿Qué no te gusta nada comer?

You will hear answers to this question from Clara, Xiomara, and Teresa. As they describe the foods that they do not like, check the appropriate boxes. Go back and listen again, if necessary. (Check your answers in the Appendix.) First, listen to the list of foods.

		CLARA	XIOMARA	TERESA
1.	huevos	☐	☐	☐
2.	verduras	☐	☐	☐
3.	oreja de cerdo (*pig's ear*)	☐	☐	☐
4.	mondongo (*tripe soup*)	☐	☐	☐
5.	hamburguesas con pepinillos (*pickles*)	☐	☐	☐
6.	caracoles (*snails*)	☐	☐	☐
7.	comida rápida	☐	☐	☐
8.	mantequilla	☐	☐	☐
9.	platos sofisticados	☐	☐	☐

Paso 2 Gramática

■ 17. Expressing *what* or *whom* • Direct Object Pronouns

A. El cumpleaños de Felipe. César Eco discusses plans for Felipe's birthday, answering everyone's questions but with a great deal of repetition. Rewrite César's answers, using direct object pronouns.

> MODELOS: —¿Quién llama a Felipe?
> —Yo llamo a Felipe. → Yo lo llamo.
>
> —¿Quién va a llevar las sillas?
> —Pepe va a llevar las sillas. (*two ways*) → Pepe va a llevarlas. (Pepe las va a llevar.)

1. —¿Quién prepara el pastel?

   —Yo preparo el pastel. _____

2. —¿Quién va a comprar los refrescos?

   —Yo voy a comprar los refrescos. (*two ways*) _____

   _____

3. —¿Quién va a hacer las galletas?

   —Dolores va a hacer las galletas. (*two ways*) _____

   _____

4. —¿Quién trae los discos?

   —Juan trae los discos. _____

5. —¿Quién invita a los primos de Felipe?

   —Yo invito a los primos de Felipe. _____

B. En casa, con la familia Buendía. Conteste las preguntas según los dibujos. Use los pronombres del complemento directo.

1. ¿A qué hora despierta el despertador (*alarm clock*) a los padres? _____

   _____

2. ¿Quién levanta al bebé? _____

3. ¿Quién lo baña? _____

4. ¿Quién divierte al bebé con una pelota (*ball*)? _____

5. ¿Qué hace la mamá con el bebé antes de darle de comer (*feeding him*)? _____

_____

6. ¿Quién acuesta al bebé? _____

C. **En la cocina.** Imagine that you are preparing a meal, and your friend Pablo is in the kitchen helping you. Answer his questions, using object pronouns and the written cues. You will hear each question twice.

> MODELO: (*you hear*) ¿Necesitas la olla (*pot*) ahora?
> (*you see*) sí → (*you say*) ¿La olla? Sí, la necesito.
> (*you see*) no → (*you say*) ¿La olla? No, no la necesito todavía.

1. no   2. sí   3. sí   4. no

D. **Entre amigos...** Imagine that your friend Manuel, who hasn't seen you for a while, wants to know when you can get together again. Answer his questions, using the written cues. You will hear each question twice.

1. esta noche   2. para mañana   3. 4:00   4. café La Rioja

Nota comunicativa: Talking About What You Have Just Done

A. **¿Qué acaban de hacer estas personas?**

> MODELO: Pete Sampras → Acaba de jugar al tenis.

1. Christina Aguilera _____

2. (en un restaurante) nosotros _____

3. (al final de la comida) el camarero _____

4. el profesor que sale de clase _____

❖5. yo, ¿ ? _____

B. **Hablando de los estudios.** You will hear a series of questions a parent or friend might ask about things you have already done. Each will be said twice. Answer, using **acabo de** and a direct object pronoun. Attach the direct object pronoun to the infinitive when you answer.

> MODELO: (*you hear*) ¿Por qué no escribes la composición? → (*you say*) Acabo de escribirla.

1. ...   2. ...   3. ...   4. ...

---

18. Expressing Negation • Indefinite and Negative Words

❖**A. Algo sobre comidas.** Indique si las siguientes declaraciones son ciertas o falsas para Ud.

1. C F No quiero comer nada esta noche. No tengo hambre.

2. C F Nadie tiene ganas de cocinar esta noche.

3. C F No hay ninguna comida sabrosa (*tasty*) en el refrigerador.

4. C F Y no hay nada para tomar tampoco.

5. C F No hay ningún restaurante chino cerca de mi casa.

6. C F Me gustan algunos platos vegetarianos.

7. C F Ninguno de mis amigos sabe cocinar. ¡Ni yo tampoco!

B. Federico, el pesimista. Su amigo Federico es muy pesimista y siempre contesta en forma negativa. Conteste las preguntas como si fuera (*as if you were*) él. Use la forma negativa de las palabras indicadas.

        Palabras útiles: contigo (*with you*), conmigo (*with me*)

        MODELO: ¿Sirven *algo* bueno en ese restaurante? → No, no sirven nada bueno.

1. ¿Vas a hacer *algo* interesante este fin de semana?

   No, _____.

2. ¿*Siempre* sales con *alguien* los sábados?

   No, _____.

3. ¿Tienes *algunos* nuevos amigos en la universidad? (¡OJO! Recuerde usar el singular.)

   No, _____.

4. ¿*Algunas* de esas chicas son tus amigas? (¡OJO!)

   No, _____.

5. ¿*Alguien* cena contigo *a veces*?

   No, _____.

C. Evita, la optimista. Federico es una persona negativa, pero su novia Evita es muy positiva. Escriba las reacciones positivas de Evita a los comentarios de Federico.

1. —No quiero comer nada. La comida aquí es mala.

   —Pues, yo sí _____.

2. —Nadie viene a atendernos (*wait on us*).

   —Pero aquí viene _____.

3. —Nunca cenamos en un restaurante bueno.

   —Yo creo que _____.

4. —No hay ningún plato sabroso (*tasty*).

   —Aquí hay _____.

D. ¿Y tú? Answer the questions, using **Yo tampoco** or **Yo también,** as appropriate.

1. Yo no tengo hambre. ¿Y tú?   (No) _____

2. Yo no tengo dinero. ¿Y tú?   (No) _____

3. Yo ceno a las seis. ¿Y tú?   (Sí) _____

4. Voy a tomar café. ¿Y tú?   (Sí) _____

❖**E. ¡Diga la verdad!** Escriba cuatro oraciones sobre cosas que Ud. nunca hace los sábados. Use **nunca** o **jamás.** Use expresiones de la lista o cualquier otra (*any other*).

afeitarse	ir al cine	quedarse en casa
despertarse temprano	lavar (*to wash*) la ropa	salir a bailar
estudiar	mirar la televisión todo el día	ver vídeos en casa

_____

_____

_____

_____

F. Descripción. You will hear a series of questions. Answer, according to the drawings.

MODELO: (*you hear*) ¿Hay algo en la pizarra? →
(*you say*) Sí, hay algo en la pizarra. Hay unas palabras.

1.

2.

3.

4.

5.

G. ¡Por eso no come nadie allí! You will hear a series of questions about a very unpopular restaurant. Each will be said twice. Answer, using the double negative.

MODELO: (*you hear*) ¿Sirven algunos postres especiales? →
(*you say*) No, no sirven ningún postre especial.

1. ...   2. ...   3. ...   4. ...

Paso 3 Gramática

19. Influencing Others • Formal Commands

A. Durante las vacaciones. The following flyer, distributed by the Spanish government, gives advice about how to prepare your house before going away on vacation. Scan it; then do the activities that follow.

Paso 1. Copy the command forms for the following infinitives from the flyer.

Título: acostumbrar _____

1. comprobar _____

2. encargar _____

3. no hacerlo _____

   dejarlas _____

4. no comentar _____

   dejar _____

5. no dejarlos _____

Paso 2. Express the basic idea of the following recommendations from the flyer by completing these sentences in English.

1. Make sure that _____

   _____.

2. Ask a neighbor to pick up

   _____.

3. Leave an extra set of keys with

   _____.

4. Don't leave notes indicating

   _____.

5. Don't leave objects of value or

   money _____

   _____.

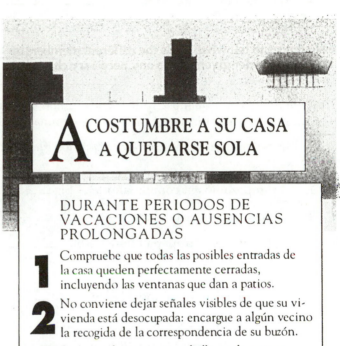

ACOSTUMBRE A SU CASA A QUEDARSE SOLA

DURANTE PERIODOS DE VACACIONES O AUSENCIAS PROLONGADAS

1 Compruebe que todas las posibles entradas de la casa queden perfectamente cerradas, incluyendo las ventanas que dan a patios.

2 No conviene dejar señales visibles de que su vivienda está desocupada: encargue a algún vecino la recogida de la correspondencia de su buzón.

3 Si quiere dejar un juego de llaves de reserva, no lo haga en escondites improvisados: déjelas a alguien de su confianza.

4 No comente su ausencia con personas desconocidas ni deje notas indicando cuándo piensa volver.

5 Existen diferentes entidades de crédito que durante sus vacaciones pueden hacerse cargo de sus objetos de valor: no los deje nunca en casa, ni tampoco deje dinero.

6 Conviene dejar a un vecino de confianza su dirección y teléfono de contacto mientras está usted fuera.

7 Existe la posibilidad de instalar un reloj programable que encienda y apague la luz o la radio en su vivienda, en diferentes horarios, disimulando su ausencia del domicilio.

B. Consejos. Sus amigos tienen los siguientes problemas. Déles (*Give them*) consejos apropiados con un mandato formal.

    MODELO: Estamos cansados. → Entonces, descansen.

    1. Tenemos hambre. _____

    2. Tenemos sed. _____

    3. Mañana hay un examen. _____

    4. Las ventanas están abiertas y tenemos frío. _____

    5. Siempre llegamos tarde. _____

    6. Somos impacientes. _____

C. ¡Qué amigos tan buenos! Your friends Emilio and Mercedes are helping you at dinner time. Answer their questions with affirmative or negative commands, as indicated. Change object nouns to pronouns.

    MODELO: ¿Lavamos (*Shall we wash*) los platos ahora? → Sí, lávenlos ahora.
                                           No, no los laven todavía.

    1. —¿Empezamos la comida ahora? —Sí, _____.

    2. —¿Servimos la cena ahora? —No, _____.

    3. —¿Llamamos a tu papá ahora? —Sí, _____.

    4. —¿Hacemos el café ahora? —No, _____.

    5. —¿Traemos las sillas ahora? —Sí, _____.

    6. —¿Ponemos la tele ahora? —No, _____.

D. ¿Qué acaban de decir? You will hear a series of commands. Write the number of the command you hear next to the corresponding drawing. You will hear each statement twice. **¡OJO!** There is an extra drawing.

    a. _____   **b.** _____   **c.** _____

    d. _____   **e.** _____

E. Profesora por un día... Imagine that you are the Spanish professor for the day. Practice telling your students what they should do, using the oral cues. Use **Uds.** commands.

    1. ...   **2.** ...   **3.** ...   **4.** ...   **5.** ...

F. La dieta del Sr. Casiano. Mr. Casiano is on a diet and you are his doctor. He will ask you whether or not he can eat certain things. Answer his questions, using affirmative or negative commands and direct object pronouns.

> MODELO: (*you hear*) ¿Puedo comer chocolate?   (*you see*) No,… →
> (*you say*) No, no lo coma.

1. No,…   **2.** No,…   **3.** No,…   **4.** Sí,…   **5.** Sí,…

Nota comunicativa: El subjuntivo

Un nuevo restaurante

Paso 1. You will hear an ad for a new restaurant that is opening soon. Listen carefully and circle the relevant actions (things you would do there) based on the information you hear in the ad. First, listen to the list of actions.

hacer reservaciones	pedir una hamburguesa	pagar con tarjeta de crédito
vestirse formalmente	llegar temprano	pagar al contado (*in cash*)
pedir el pescado		

Paso 2. Now pause and read the following recommendations. Check the recommendations that you would give a friend who wants to visit this restaurant. Remember to check your answers to **Paso 1** in the Appendix before beginning **Paso 2.**

1. ☐ No recomiendo que hagas reservaciones antes de ir a El Caribe.

2. ☐ Recomiendo que llegues temprano.

3. ☐ Recomiendo que vayas a El Caribe si te gusta mucho la carne.

4. ☐ Recomiendo que te vistas con ropa informal.

5. ☐ No recomiendo que lleves a toda tu familia.

6. ☐ Recomiendo que pagues con tarjeta de crédito o al contado.

Now resume listening.

Un poco de todo

A. Por teléfono. Fill in the blanks with the correct word(s) in parentheses to complete the dialogue between Ana and Pablo.

ANA: Oye, Pablo, ¿no _____[1] (**conoces / sabes**) tú _____[2] (**a / al / el**) profesor Vargas?

PABLO: No, no _____[3] (**él / lo**) _____[4] (**sé / conozco**). ¿Por qué?

ANA: Es profesor de historia. El viernes va a dar una conferencia[a] sobre la mujer en la Revolución mexicana. ¿No quieres ir? Yo _____[5] (**sé / conozco**) que va a ser muy interesante.

PABLO: ¡Qué lástima![b] Casi _____[6] (**siempre / nunca**) tengo tiempo libre[c] los viernes, pero este viernes tengo varios compromisos.[d]

ANA: Pues, yo no tengo mucho tiempo libre _____[7] (**también / tampoco**), pero voy a asistir. _____[8] (**Al / El**) Sr. Vargas siempre usa diapositivas[e] fascinantes y tengo ganas de verlas.

[a]dar... *give a lecture*   [b]¡Qué... *What a shame!*   [c]*free*   [d]*engagements*   [e]*slides*

B. Preparativos para una barbacoa. Imagine que Ud. vive en un nuevo apartamento, donde va a preparar una barbacoa. Conteste las siguientes preguntas sobre la barbacoa con pronombres de complemento directo.

MODELO: ¿A qué hora *me* llamas? → Te llamo a las ocho.

1. ¿Cuándo vas a preparar *la barbacoa*?

_____

2. ¿Piensas invitar *a Juan y a su novia*?

_____

3. ¿Puedo llamar *a dos amigas más*?

_____

4. ¿*Te* puedo ayudar el sábado?

_____

5. ¿Necesitas *las sillas de mi apartamento*?

_____

C. Preparativos para la fiesta. Marta calls to give you last-minute reminders of what to do for a party you and some friends are planning. First, write her command in the **Uds.** form. Then respond by telling her that you and José are already doing it. Use object pronouns in your response to avoid unnecessary repetition.

MODELO: limpiar la casa → LUISA: ¡Limpien la casa!
UD.: Ya estamos limpiándola. (Ya la estamos limpiando.)

1. lavar (*to wash*) los platos   LUISA: _____

UD.: _____

2. hacer la ensalada   LUISA: _____

UD.: _____

3. preparar las verduras   LUISA: _____

UD.: _____

4. empezar la paella   LUISA: _____

UD.: _____

D. ¿Qué va a pedir Juan? Juan and his friend Marta are in a restaurant. Listen to their conversation and circle the items that Juan is going to order. In this exercise, you will practice listening for specific information. First, pause and look at the drawing.

Paso 4 Un paso más

🎧 ▮ Videoteca*

Entrevista cultural: Panamá

You will hear an interview with Maír Citón. After listening, pause and choose the letter of the phrase that best completes each statement.

1. Maír es de...

   a. un restaurante. **b.** Panamá. **c.** Citón.

2. En el restaurante de Maír sirven comida...

   a. típica panameña. **b.** exclusiva. **c.** internacional.

3. Un plato típico panameño es...

   a. tacos. **b.** el arroz. **c.** la gallina.

4. El plato favorito de Maír son...

   a. los plátanos. **b.** los tamales. **c.** los tomates.

5. Maír trae...

   a. una mola. **b.** unas gallinas. **c.** la patria.

Now resume listening.

Entre amigos: ¿Quién cocina en tu casa?

Paso 1. ¿Cuál es tu comida favorita? The four friends will answer questions about food and its preparation. Listen carefully to the answers that each student gives to the first question and mark the foods that you hear. The names are listed in the order in which the friends answer. Check your answers in the Appendix.

1. Karina   ☐ las arepas   ☐ las zanahorias   ☐ los tamales   ☐ el arroz

2. Miguel René ☐ el arroz   ☐ las papas   ☐ la carne asada   ☐ los tacos

3. Tané   ☐ el pollo   ☐ los mariscos   ☐ los chiles   ☐ la carne

4. Rubén   ☐ los huevos rancheros ☐ los huevos fritos ☐ las papas fritas ☐ la sopa

Now resume listening

Paso 2. ¿Te gusta cocinar y quién cocina en tu familia? Listen carefully to the answers that each friend gives to this question and complete the following information. The names are listed in the order in which the friends answer. Check your answers in the Appendix.

		SÍ	NO	¿QUIÉN COCINA EN TU FAMILIA?
1.	Rubén	☐	☐	_____
2.	Karina	☐	☐	_____
3.	Miguel René	☐	☐	_____
4.	Tané	☐	☐	_____

---

*The **Videoteca** videoclips are available on the Video on CD to accompany *¿Qué tal?*, Seventh Edition.

Enfoque cultural: Panamá

Conteste las preguntas con la información apropiada.

1. ¿Qué significa la palabra Panamá? _____

2. ¿Qué carretera importante va de Alaska a Panamá? _____

   ¿Qué obstáculo natural la interrumpe en Panamá? _____

3. ¿Cómo se llama la primera presidenta de Panamá? _____. ¿En qué año ganó

   (*did she win*) las elecciones? _____

4. En 1534, ¿quién propone construir un canal a través del (*through the*) istmo de Panamá?

   _____

5. ¿En qué año se inaugura el Canal de Panamá?

   _____

6. Antes de la existencia del Canal de Panamá, ¿cómo pasaban (*used to pass*) los barcos del

   Océano Pacífico al Atlántico? _____

7. Desde el primero de enero del año 2000, ¿quién administra el Canal de Panamá?

   _____

¡Repasemos!

A. Una cena en El Toledano. En otro papel, conteste las preguntas (en la página 129) según los dibujos e invente los detalles necesarios. Luego, organice y combine sus respuestas en dos párrafos. ¡RECUERDE! Use palabras conectivas: **por eso, Como...** (*Since . . .*), **porque, aunque** (*although*), **luego,** etcétera.

1.

2.

3.

4.

5.

6.

- **1.** ¿Por qué llaman José y Miguel a Tomás? **2.** ¿Por qué cree Ud. que deciden llevarlo a El Toledano? **3.** ¿Conoce este lugar Tomás? ¿Le gusta la idea de salir con sus amigos? **4.** ¿A qué hora de la noche pasan por él[a]?

- **1.** Después de llegar al restaurante, ¿en qué sitio encuentran[b] una mesa desocupada[c]: cerca o lejos del escenario[d]? **2.** ¿Por qué hay tanta gente en el restaurante? **3.** ¿Qué platos pide cada joven? **4.** ¿Qué escuchan durante la cena? **5.** ¿Qué hacen después de comer? **6.** ¿Salen del restaurante contentos y satisfechos[e] o disgustados?

[a]pasan... *do they pick him up* [b]*do they find* [c]*empty* [d]*stage* [e]*satisfied*

B. *Listening Passage:* **La vida social en los bares de España**

Antes de escuchar. Before you listen to the passage, pause and do the following prelistening exercises.

Many aspects of social life and nightlife in Spain are different from those of the United States. Check the ones that you think apply *only* to Spain.

☐ Hay muchos bares. ¡A veces hay dos en cada calle (*street*)!

☐ La familia entera, padres e hijos pequeños, va al bar.

☐ Por lo general, no se sirve comida.

☐ Es costumbre pedir tapas: pequeños platos de comidas diversas.

Now resume listening.

Listening Passage. Now you will hear a passage about the many types of bars that are part of Spanish social life. The following words and phrases appear in the passage.

no tienen nada que ver con	*they have nothing to do with*
casero	*homemade, home-style*
sevillanos	personas de Sevilla
el ambiente	*atmosphere*

Después de escuchar. Go back and listen to the passage again. Then pause, and complete the following sentences with words chosen from the list.

amigos   bar   café   frío   Madrid   tapas   tarde   Sevilla

1. En España, los españoles van con frecuencia a un _____ o a un _____

   para pasar el tiempo con los _____ y los compañeros.

2. En los bares, sirven _____, que son pequeños platos de comidas diversas.

3. Julia dice que prefiere la ciudad de _____ para divertirse. Allí no hace

   _____ en el invierno y la gente puede salir muy _____ todo el año.

Now resume listening.

C. Entrevista. You will hear a series of questions. Each will be said twice. Answer, based on your own experience. Use direct object pronouns in your answers, if possible. Pause and write the answers.

1. _____
2. _____
3. _____
4. _____
5. _____
6. _____
7. _____

Mi diario

Ahora escriba en su diario lo que a Ud. le gusta mucho comer y la(s) comida(s) que no le gusta(n) nada. Si puede, mencione los ingredientes.

> **Palabras útiles:** el cocido (*stew*), los espaguetis, las remolachas (*beets*), el rosbif; caliente (*hot*), picante (*hot, spicy*); me encanta(n) (*I love*),* me gusta(n),* odiar (*to hate*); al horno (*baked, roasted*); bastante cocido (*medium*), bien cocido (*well done*), crudo (*raw*)

---

*If something you like is a plural noun, use the plural form of **gustar** or **encantar: Me gustan las zanahorias. Me encantan las arvejas.**

Póngase a prueba

A ver si sabe...

A. Direct Object Pronouns

1. Complete la tabla con la forma apropiada de los pronombres del complemento directo.

me	me	us	
you (*fam. sing.*)		you (*fam. pl.*)	**os**
you, him, it (*m.*)		you, them (*m.*)	**los**
you, her, it (*f.*)		you, them (*f.*)	

2. Rewrite using a direct object pronoun for the underlined direct object noun.

    a. Yo traigo <u>el postre</u>. _____

    b. ¡Traiga <u>el postre</u>! _____

    c. ¡No traiga <u>el postre</u>! _____

    d. Estamos esperando <u>al camarero</u>. (*two ways*) _____

    _____

    e. Voy a llamar <u>al camarero</u>. (*two ways*) _____

    _____

B. Negative Words. Write the negative form of the following words or phrases.

    1. alguien _____   **4.** algo _____

    2. también _____   **5.** algunos detalles (¡ojo!) _____

    3. siempre _____

C. Formal Commands. Complete la tabla con la forma apropiada de los mandatos formales.

pensar		Ud.	ser	sea	Ud.
volver		Ud.	buscar		Ud.
dar		Ud.	estar		Ud.
servir	sirva	Ud.	saber		Ud.
ir		Ud.	decir		Ud.

Prueba corta

A. ¿Saber o conocer? Escriba la forma apropiada de **saber** o **conocer**.

—Yo no _____[1] a la novia de Juan. ¿La _____[2] tú?

—No muy bien, pero (yo) _____[3] que ella se llama María Elena y que

_____[4] tocar bien la guitarra.

B. Oraciones afirmativas. Vuelva a escribir las oraciones en la forma afirmativa.

    1. No quiero comer nada. _____

    2. No busco a nadie. _____

    3. No hay nada para beber. _____

    4. —No conozco a ninguno de sus amigos. —Yo tampoco. _____

    _____

C. Preguntas. Conteste las preguntas usando pronombres de complemento directo.

1. ¿Vas a pedir la ensalada de fruta? _____

2. ¿Quieres zanahorias con la comida? _____

3. ¿Tomas café por la noche? _____

4. ¿Quién prepara la cena en tu casa? _____

D. Mandatos formales. Escriba la forma apropiada del mandato formal (**Uds.**) del verbo indicado.

1. _____ (*Uds.*: **Comprar**) tomates y lechuga.

2. No _____ (*Uds.*: **hacer**) ensalada hoy.

3. _____ (*Uds.*: **Traer**) dos sillas, por favor.

4. No _____ (*Uds.*: **tomar**) café por la noche.

5. Juan no está aquí todavía. _____ (*Uds.*: **Llamarlo**) ahora.

6. ¿El vino? No _____ (*Uds.*: **servirlo**) ahora.

E. *Los hispanos hablan:* **¿Qué te gusta mucho comer?** In this passage, Clara tells about two dishes typical of Spain: **el cocido** and **el gazpacho**. Then you will hear a series of statements. Circle **C** if the statement is true or **F** if it is false. The following words appear in the passage.

el hueso de codillo	*leg bone (as in ham)*
la morcilla	*blood sausage*
el pepino	*cucumber*
el pimiento	*pepper*
el ajo	*garlic*
el aceite de oliva	*olive oil*
el vinagre	*vinegar*
echarle por encima	*to sprinkle on top of it*
trocitos	*little bits (pieces)*

1. C F   **2.** C F   **3.** C F   **4.** C F

F. Cosas de todos los días. Practice talking about a new restaurant, using the written cues. When you hear the corresponding number, form sentences using the words provided in the order given, making any necessary changes or additions. When you are given a choice between verbs or words, choose the correct one.

MODELO: (*you see*) **1.** ¿(saber / conocer) / tú / un buen restaurante?
(*you hear*) uno → (*you say*) ¿Conoces un buen restaurante?

2. sí, yo / (saber / conocer) / un buen restaurante
3. ellos / (la / lo) / acabar de / abrir
4. yo / (saber / conocer) / al dueño (*owner*)
5. ellos / preparar / unos camarones deliciosos
6. ellos / (las / los) / cocinar / en vino blanco
7. no hay / (algo / nada) / malo en el menú
8. yo / (siempre / nunca) / cenar allí

G. ¡Qué maleducados! Mr. Alarcón's children have not been behaving lately, and he is constantly telling them what to do and what not to do. Play the role of Mr. Alarcón, using the oral cues.

MODELO: (*you hear*) no jugar en la sala → (*you say*) No jueguen en la sala.

1. ... **2.** ... **3.** ... **4.** ... **5.** ...

CAPÍTULO **7**

Paso 1 Vocabulario

De viaje

❖**A. Ud. y los viajes.** Lea las siguientes declaraciones y e indique si son ciertas o falsas para Ud.

1. C F Tengo mucho miedo de viajar en avión.

2. C F Siempre reservo los asientos con anticipación (*in advance*).

3. C F Cuando voy de viaje, hago las maletas a última hora (*at the last minute*).

4. C F Siempre llevo tantas maletas que tengo que pedirle ayuda a un maletero.

5. C F Pido un asiento en el pasillo (*aisle*) de un avión o tren porque me gusta levantarme con frecuencia.

6. C F Si hay una demora en la salida del avión (o del tren) no me importa. Me siento en la sala de espera y leo un libro o voy al bar.

B. Viajando en avión. Complete las oraciones con la forma apropiada de las palabras de la lista. Use cada expresión sólo una vez (*once*).

asistente	el control de	escala	salida
bajar	la seguridad	guardar	subir
boleto	demora	ida y vuelta	vuelo
cola	equipaje	pasajeros	

1. Cuando voy de viaje es más barato comprar mi _____ en el Internet.

2. Los boletos de _____ son más baratos que los de ida solamente.[a]

3. Quiero _____ del avión si hace _____ en Londres.[b]

4. Después de llegar al aeropuerto, un maletero me ayuda a facturar el _____.

5. Antes de llegar a la puerta,[c] hay que pasar por _____.

6. En la sala de espera hay muchos _____ que esperan su vuelo.

7. Un pasajero me _____ un asiento mientras[d] voy a comprar un libro.

8. Anuncian que el _____ #68 está atrasado; hay una _____ de media hora.

9. Cuando por fin anuncian la _____ de nuestro avión, los pasajeros hacemos

   _____ para _____.

10. Media hora después que el avión despega,[e] los _____ de vuelo sirven el desayuno. ¡Y qué hambre tengo!

[a]*only* [b]*London* [c]*gate* [d]*while* [e]*takes off*

C. Escenas. Describa los dibujos con los verbos indicados. Use el presente del progresivo cuando sea (*whenever it is*) posible.

1.

dormir, fumar, leer

2.

facturar, hacer cola, hacer una parada

3.

correr, estar atrasado, llover, subir

4.

mirar, servir algo de beber

1. _____
   _____

2. _____
   _____

3. _____
   _____

4. _____
   _____

D. Hablando de viajes... Using the oral and written cues, tell your friend Benito, who has never traveled by plane, the steps he should follow to make an airplane trip.

MODELO: (*you see*) Primero... (*you hear*) llamar a la agencia de viajes →
(*you say*) Primero llamas a la agencia de viajes.

1. pedir
2. El día del viaje,...
3. pasar por...
4. Después...
5. Cuando anuncian la salida del vuelo,...
6. Por fin...

E. Identificaciones. Identify the items after you hear the corresponding number. Begin each sentence with **Es un... , Es una... ,** or **Son...**

1. ... **2.** ... **3.** ... **4.** ... **5.** ...

De vacaciones

A. Las vacaciones

Paso 1. Identifique los lugares y objetos en el dibujo.

1. _____

2. _____

3. _____

4. _____

5. _____

Paso 2. Ahora explique qué hacen las siguientes personas.

1. El padre _____.

2. La madre _____.

3. Las hijas _____.

4. El hijo _____.

5. Toda la familia _____.

❖B. **Mis vacaciones.** Conteste las siguientes preguntas sobre las vacaciones que Ud. prefiere.

1. ¿Adónde prefiere Ud. ir de vacaciones? ¿a las montañas? ¿a la playa?

   _____

2. ¿Con quién le gusta ir de vacaciones?

   _____

3. ¿Cómo prefiere Ud. viajar?

   _____

4. ¿Le gusta a Ud. hacer *camping*? ¿Qué se necesita para hacer *camping*?

   _____

5. ¿Qué hace durante las vacaciones? ¿Le gusta sacar muchas fotos? ¿de qué? ¿Le gusta tomar el sol y nadar? ¿visitar museos o atracciones turísticas?

   _____

C. **Definiciones.** You will hear a series of definitions. Each will be said twice. Circle the letter of the word that is defined by each. ¡OJO! There may be more than one answer in some cases.

1. **a.** el avión   **b.** la playa   **c.** el océano
2. **a.** el billete   **b.** la estación de trenes   **c.** el aeropuerto
3. **a.** el hotel   **b.** el restaurante   **c.** la llegada
4. **a.** el puerto   **b.** el mar   **c.** las montañas

Nota comunicativa: Other Uses of *se*

¿Cuánto sabe Ud. de estas cosas? Seleccione la respuesta más apropiada.

1. Se habla portugués en...   **a.** el Paraguay.   **b.** Bolivia.   **c.** el Brasil.
2. Se factura el equipaje en...   **a.** el avión.   **b.** el mostrador (*counter*).   **c.** la sala de espera.
3. Se visitan las ruinas de Machu Picchu en...   **a.** Bolivia.   **b.** México.   **c.** el Perú.
4. Se ven ruinas mayas en Chichen Itzá,...   **a.** Colombia.   **b.** México.   **c.** el Perú.
5. Se venden bebidas alcohólicas en...   **a.** Francia.   **b.** Irán.   **c.** la Arabia Saudita.

Nombre _____ Fecha _____ Clase _____

Pronunciación y ortografía: *g, gu,* and *j*

A. Repeticiones. In Spanish, the letter **g** followed by **e** or **i** has the same sound as the letter **j** followed by any vowel. This sound [x] is similar to the English *h*. The pronunciation of this sound varies, depending on the region or country of origin of the speaker. Note the difference in the pronunciation of these words.

España:	Jorge	jueves	general	álgebra
el Caribe:	Jorge	jueves	general	álgebra

Repeat the following words, imitating the speaker.

1. [x] general   gigante   geranio   **2.** [x] jamón   Juan   pasaje

Now, say the following words when you hear the corresponding number. Repeat the correct pronunciation after the speaker.

3. gimnasio **4.** giralda **5.** rojo **6.** jipijapa

B. El sonido [g]. When the letter **g** is followed by the vowels **a, o,** or **u** or by the combination **ue** or **ui**, its pronunciation is very similar to the letter *g* in the English word *get:* [g]. It is also pronounced this way at the beginning of a word, after a pause, or after the letter **n.**

Repeat the following words, imitating the speaker.

[g] ángulo gusto gato Miguel guitarra

Now, say the following words when you hear the corresponding number. Repeat the correct pronunciation after the speaker.

1. gorila **2.** grande **3.** guerrilla **4.** Guevara

C. El sonido [g]. In all other positions, the Spanish **g** is a fricative [g]. It has a softer sound produced by allowing some air to escape when it is pronounced. There is no exact equivalent for this variant in English.

Repeat the following words, imitating the speaker.

1. [g] abrigo algodón el gato el gusto los gorilas
2. [g] / [g] un grupo el grupo gracias las gracias un gato el gato
3. [x] / [g] gigante jugos juguete

Now, read the following sentences when you hear the corresponding numbers. Repeat the correct pronunciation after the speaker.

4. ¡Qué ganga!
5. Domingo es guapo y delgado.
6. Tengo algunas amigas guatemaltecas.
7. La guitarra de Guillermo es de Gijón.

D. **¿G o j?** For the following Spanish words, indicate which are pronounced as [x] (similar to English *h*) or as [g] (similar to English *g* in *gate*). Some words have both sounds. Check your answers in the Appendix.

		[x]	[g]			[x]	[g]
1.	girafa	☐	☐	5.	guapo	☐	☐
2.	jugo	☐	☐	6.	gigante	☐	☐
3.	geranio	☐	☐	7.	gato	☐	☐
4.	general	☐	☐	8.	juguete	☐	☐

E. **Dictado.** You will hear four sentences. Each will be said twice. Listen carefully and write what you hear.

1. _____

2. _____

3. _____

4. _____

Los hispanos hablan: Unas vacaciones inolvidables (*unforgettable*)

You will hear Cecilia's description of an unforgettable vacation. Then you will hear a series of statements. Circle **C** if the statement is true or **F** if it is false. The following words appear in the description.

hace un año	*one year ago*	hacernos cargo de	*take care of*
veranear	*pasar el verano*	la aduana	*customs*
partimos	*we left*	las valijas	las maletas
el colectivo	*type of taxi shared by several passengers*	armamos la carpa	*we set up the tent*

1. C   F   Cecilia y su amiga pasaron (*spent*) el verano en las montañas.

2. C   F   Los padres de las muchachas pagaron (*paid for*) el viaje.

3. C   F   Cecilia y su amiga pasaron un mes en el Uruguay.

4. C   F   Había (*There were*) otra gente joven en la playa donde se quedaron Cecilia y su amiga.

Paso 2 Gramática

20. Expressing *to whom* or *for whom* • Indirect Object Pronouns; *Dar* and *decir*

A. Formas verbales. Complete las oraciones con la forma apropiada de los verbos entre paréntesis.

(**dar**) Hoy es el cumpleaños de Ana y todos lo celebramos con una fiesta. ¿Qué regalos le

_____¹ nosotros? Carmela le _____² una blusa, los padres de

Ana le _____³ un impermeable, tú le _____⁴ un suéter y yo le

_____⁵ un libro.

(**decir**) ¡No estamos de acuerdo! Yo _____⁶ que quiero salir, Jorge

_____⁷ que tiene que estudiar, Anita y Memo _____⁸ que no

tienen suficiente dinero, y tú _____⁹ que estás cansado. ¿Qué les (nosotros)

_____¹⁰ a los otros?

❖**B. Ud. y sus amigos.** Indique las cosas que Ud. hace y las cosas que hacen sus amigos. Después, Ud. va a decidir quién es más atento (*considerate*).

YO...

☐ siempre les regalo algo para su cumpleaños.

☐ les presto dinero.

☐ les ofrezco buenos consejos.

☐ les mando tarjetas postales cuando voy de vacaciones.

☐ les traigo flores en las ocasiones especiales.

☐ les hago favores.

☐ siempre les digo la verdad.

MIS AMIGOS...

☐ siempre me regalan algo para mi cumpleaños.

☐ me prestan dinero.

☐ me ofrecen buenos consejos.

☐ me mandan tarjetas postales cuando van de vacaciones.

☐ me traen flores en las ocasiones especiales.

☐ me hacen favores.

☐ siempre me dicen la verdad.

Y ahora, ¿qué opina Ud.?

☐ Yo soy más atento/a que mis amigos.

☐ Yo soy tan atento/a como ellos.

☐ Mis amigos son más atentos que yo.

C. ¿No recuerdas? Remind a friend of the things you do for him or her.

MODELO: (prestar dinero) → Te presto dinero.

1. (comprar regalos) _____

2. (mandar tarjetas postales) _____

3. (invitar a almorzar) _____

4. (explicar la tarea [*homework*]) _____

❖Now remind two other friends what you do for *them*. Use the following expressions or those from page 139.

> mandar flores   ofrecer consejos   prestar dinero

5. _____

6. _____

7. _____

D. Necesito consejos. Using the cues provided, ask a friend what you should do based on the following situations.

> MODELO: Mañana mi novio/a y yo vamos a un baile. (¿comprar **/** flores?) → ¿Le compro flores?

1. Mi hermano necesita $25 para ir a un concierto. (¿prestar **/** dinero?)

   _____

2. Mi novio/a quiere saber dónde estaba (*I was*) el sábado. (¿decir **/** verdad [*truth*]?)

   _____

3. Esta semana es el cumpleaños de Julia y Teresa. (¿dar **/** fiesta?)

   _____

4. Tengo problemas en esta clase. (¿pedir ayuda **/** profesor?)

   _____

5. Julio y Tomás quieren otra cerveza. (¿dar **/** más?)

E. Minidiálogo: Las vacaciones de primavera. You will hear a brief passage about what Javier told his parents. Then you will hear a series of incomplete statements. Circle the letter of the phrase that best completes each statement.

1. **a.** nunca les pide dinero.
   b. les pide mucho dinero para sus clases.
2. **a.** pedirles dinero para este semestre.
   b. pedirles dinero para el pasaje de avión.
3. **a.** Javier les pide mucho dinero.
   b. Javier es trabajador.
4. **a.** dinero para el boleto y comida.
   b. un cheque para sus clases.

F. En casa, durante la cena. Practice telling for whom the following things are being done, according to the model.

> MODELO: (*you see*) Mi padre sirve el guacamole.   (*you hear*) a nosotros →
>   (*you say*) Mi padre *nos* sirve el guacamole.

1. Mi madre sirve la sopa.
2. Ahora ella prepara la ensalada.
3. Mi hermano trae el café.
4. Rosalinda da postre.

G. Descripción. When you hear the corresponding number, tell what the following people are doing, using the written cues with indirect object pronouns.

En la fiesta de aniversario de los Sres. Moreno

1. Susana: regalar   2. Miguel: mandar   3. Tito: regalar

En casa, durante el desayuno

4. Pedro: dar
5. Marta: dar
6. Luis: servir / todos

21. Expressing Likes and Dislikes • *Gustar*

A. ¿Qué nos gusta de los aviones? Complete las oraciones con la forma correcta de **gustar** y la forma apropiada del complemento indirecto.

> MODELO: A mí **me gusta** llegar temprano al aeropuerto.

1. ¿A ti _____ _____ sentarte en el pasillo (*aisle*)?

2. A muchas personas no _____ _____ hacer paradas.

3. A mí también _____ _____ los vuelos directos.

4. A nosotros no _____ _____ la comida que sirven en la clase turística, pero a

    Jorge _____ _____ todo.

5. ¿Y qué línea aérea _____ _____ a Uds.?

B. Los gustos de la familia de Ernesto

Paso 1. Form complete sentences to tell what type of vacation activities or places the different members of Ernesto's family like, using the words provided in the order given. Make any necessary changes, and add other words when necessary. ¡RECUERDE! Use **a** in front of the indirect object noun or pronoun.

MODELO: su / padre / gustar / playa → A su padre le gusta la playa.

1. su / padre / gustar / vacaciones / montañas

   _____

2. su / madre / encantar / cruceros (*cruises*)

   _____

3. su / hermanos / gustar / deportes acuáticos

   _____

4. nadie / gustar / viajar en autobús

   _____

5. Ernesto / gustar / sacar fotos

   _____

❖**Paso 2.** Now write a statement to tell what kind of vacation the different members of *your* family like. After each statement, write your reaction to their preferences using one of the following:
a mí también; pero a mí, no.

MODELO: A mi padre le gusta la playa. A mí también. (Pero a mí, no.)

_____

_____

_____

_____

C. ¡Vamos de vacaciones! Pero... ¿adónde? You and your family can't decide where to go on vacation. You will hear what each person likes. Then decide where each person would like to go, using a location from the following list. There may be more than one answer in some cases. First, listen to the list. You will hear a possible answer.

Disneylandia	las playas de México
Florida	quedarse en casa
Nueva York	Roma

MODELO: (*you hear*) A mi padre le gusta mucho jugar al golf. →
(*you say*) Le gustaría ir a Florida.

1. ... 2. ... 3. ... 4. ... 5. ...

D. ¿Qué le gusta? ¿Qué no le gusta? Using the written cues, tell what you like or dislike about the following situations or locations. You will hear a possible answer.

MODELO: (*you see and hear*) ¿En la universidad? (*you see*) fiestas / exámenes →
(*you say*) Me gustan las fiestas. No me gustan los exámenes.

1. ¿En la playa? jugar al vólibol / sol
2. ¿En un restaurante? comida / música
3. ¿En un parque? flores / insectos
4. ¿En la cafetería? hablar con mis amigos / comida

Paso 3 Gramática

22. Talking About the Past (1) • Preterite of Regular Verbs and of *dar, hacer, ir,* and *ser*

A. El pretérito. Escriba la forma apropiada del pretérito de los verbos.

INFINITIVO	YO	TÚ	UD.	NOSOTROS	UDS.
hablar	hablé				
volver		volviste			
vivir			vivió		
dar				dimos	
hacer					hicieron
ser / ir	fui				
jugar		jugaste			
sacar			sacó		
empezar				empezamos	

❖**B. Un viaje que hice yo**

Paso 1. Piense en un viaje que hizo en el pasado. Ahora subraye (*underline*) las actividades que mejor describan sus experiencias en ese viaje.

1. Viajé en... avión / barco / tren / camioneta / motocicleta / ¿ ?
2. Fui a... la playa / las montañas / a hacer *camping* / otra ciudad / ¿ ?
3. Hice el viaje... con familia / con amigos / solo/a / ¿ ?
4. Fui para... visitar amigos / ver familia / pasar las vacaciones / ¿ ?
5. Llevé... una maleta / dos maletas / mi mochila / una tienda de campaña / ¿ ?
6. Saqué muchas fotos. / Hice vídeos. / No llevé ninguna cámara.
7. Comí... en restaurantes buenos / en casa de amigos o familia / comida rápida / ¿ ?
8. Conocí a varias personas. / No conocí a nadie. / ¿ ?

Paso 2. Ahora, en una hoja de papel aparte, combine lógicamente las oraciones que subrayó para describir su viaje. Use otros detalles para hacer más interesante su descripción.

Expresión útil hacer reservas (*reservations*)

MODELO: El verano pasado fui a Miami con dos amigos para pasar las vacaciones, nadar y descansar.

C. ¿Qué hicieron estas personas? Complete las oraciones con la forma apropiada de los infinitivos. ¡ojo! Recuerde los cambios ortográficos como almorcé, empecé, hizo, etcétera.

yo: Hoy _____[1] (**volver**) de la universidad a la una de la tarde.

_____[2] (**Hacerme**) un sándwich y lo _____[3] (**comer**) sentado[a]

delante del televisor. _____[4] (**Recoger**[b]) la ropa sucia y la

_____[5] (**meter**[c]) en la lavadora.[d] Antes de salir para el trabajo, le

_____[6] (**dar**) de comer[e] al perro.

tú: ¿Por qué no _____[1] (**asistir**) a tu clase de música esta mañana?

¿_____[2] (**Acostarte**) tarde? ¿Ya _____[3] (**empezar**) a estudiar

para el examen? ¿Adónde _____[4] (**ir**) anoche? ¿_____[5] (**Salir**)

con alguien interesante? ¿A qué hora _____[6] (**volver**) a casa?

Eva: El año pasado Eva _____[1] (**casarse**[f]) y _____[2] (**ir**) a vivir

a Escocia[g] con su esposo. Después de varios meses _____[3] (**matricularse**) en la

Universidad de Edimburgo y _____[4] (**empezar**) a estudiar para enfermera.[h]

Este verano _____[5] (**regresar**) para visitar a sus abuelos en Vermont por una

semana y luego _____[6] (**viajar**) a California, donde _____[7] (**ver**) a

muchos amigos y lo _____[8] (**pasar**) muy bien.[i]

Mi amiga y yo: El verano pasado, mi amiga Sara y yo _____[1] (**pasar**) dos

meses en Europa. _____[2] (**Vivir**) con una familia francesa en

Aix-en-Provence donde _____[3] (**asistir**) a clases en la universidad. También

_____[4] (**hacer**) viajes cortos. _____[5] (**Visitar**) la costa del sur de

Francia, _____[6] (**caminar**[j]) por las playas de Niza, _____[7]

(**comer**) muchos mariscos y _____[8] (**ver**) a muchas personas famosas allí.

Dos científicos[k]**:** Mi papá y otro profesor de astronomía _____[1] (**ir**) a Chile en

enero de 1986 para observar el cometa Halley. _____[2] (**Salir**) de Los Ángeles en

avión y _____[3] (**llegar**) a Santiago doce horas después. De allí

_____[4] (**viajar**) a un observatorio en los Andes donde _____[5]

(**ver**) el cometa todas las noches y _____[6] (**tomar**) muchas fotos. La comida y

el vino chilenos les _____[7] (**gustar**) mucho y _____[8]

(**volver**) de su viaje muy contentos.

[a]seated [b]To pick up [c]to put [d]washing machine [e]le... I fed [f]to get married [g]Scotland [h]para... to be a nurse [i]lo... she had a very good time [j]to walk [k]scientists

D. ¿Qué hizo Nadia anoche? You will hear a series of statements. Each will be said twice. Write the number of each statement next to the drawing that is described by that statement. First, pause and look at the drawings. Nadia's friend is Guadalupe.

a. _____

b. _____

c. _____

d. _____

e. _____

f. _____

g. _____

h. _____

i. _____

E. ¿Qué pasó ayer? Practice telling what the following people did yesterday, using the oral and written cues. Do not say the subject pronouns in parentheses.

Antes de la fiesta

1. (yo)

2. mi compañero

3. (nosotros)

Antes del examen de química

4. Nati y yo

5. (tú)

6. todos

Un poco de todo

A. Cosas que pasaron el semestre pasado. Use the expressions below to tell what you did for someone else, or what someone else did for you this past semester. Use the preterite and the appropriate indirect object pronouns. Use affirmative or negative sentences, following the model.

MODELO: escribir una carta → Les escribí una carta a mis abuelos.
(No le escribí a nadie.)
(Nadie me escribió a mí.)

1. mandar tarjetas postales _____

2. regalar flores _____

3. recomendar un restaurante _____

4. ofrecer ayuda _____

5. prestar una maleta _____

6. hacer un pastel _____

B. Situaciones. Cambie los verbos al pretérito.

1. *Salgo* temprano para las clases y *me quedo* allí _____ _____

   toda la mañana. *Almuerzo* al mediodía[a] y a las dos *voy* _____ _____

   al trabajo. *Vuelvo* a casa a las ocho. *Ceno* y luego _____ _____

   miro una película. A las once *subo* a mi alcoba, _____ _____

   me quejo de[b] la tarea, pero la *hago*. Por fin _____ _____

   duermo unas cinco o seis horas. _____

2. Luisa y Jorge *son* novios. Se *hacen* muchas _____ _____

   promesas[c] y él le *da* un anillo.[d] Un día _____

   Jorge *va* a Nueva York donde *se hace*[e] actor. _____ _____

   Se *escriben* muchas cartas, pero nunca *vuelven* _____ _____

   a verse[f] más.

3. La vida simple de Simón: *Busco* trabajo el lunes, _____

   me lo *dan* el martes, lo *pierdo* el miércoles, me _____ _____

   pagan el jueves, *gasto*[g] el dinero el viernes, el _____ _____

   sábado no *hago* nada y el domingo *descanso*. _____ _____

4. *Pasamos* los días muy contentos. *Comemos* bien, _____ _____

   vemos a nuestros amigos y *jugamos* al tenis. _____ _____

[a]noon [b]quejarse de = *to complain about* [c]*promises* [d]*ring* [e]se... *he becomes* [f]*see each other* [g]gastar = *to spend*

Paso 4 Un paso más

🎧 ▉ Videoteca*

Entrevista cultural: Honduras y El Salvador

Paso 1. Honduras. You will hear an interview with Heidi Luna. After listening, pause and choose the letter of the phrase that best completes each statement.

1. Heidi Luna es de...

   a. Tegucigalpa.   b. La Habana.   c. Panamá.

2. Heidi Luna es...

   a. cliente.   b. estudiante.   c. agente de viajes.

3. Muchos de sus clientes quieren viajar a...

   a. la Florida.   b. San Antonio.   c. Tegucigalpa.

4. Ella trae...

   a. un cuadro hecho en caoba.   b. un pueblo hondureño.   c. un objeto de Toronto.

Now resume listening.

Paso 2. El Salvador. You will hear an interview with Rubén Alexis Guillén. After listening, pause and circle **C** if the statement is true or **F** if the statement is false. First, pause and read the statements. This will help you get an idea of what to listen for.

1. C F Rubén es guía turístico.

2. C F Él trabaja en un hotel.

3. C F A Rubén no le gusta su trabajo.

4. C F Rubén necesita ser muy amable en su trabajo.

Now resume listening.

Entre amigos: El verano pasado me fui al Canadá.

Paso 1: Apuntes. The four friends will answer questions about their vacations. Listen carefully and jot down notes about their answers. Check your answers in the Appendix.

_____

_____

_____

_____

Now resume listening.

Paso 2. Now you will hear a series of statements about the answers that the students gave. Circle **C** if the statement is true *or* **F** if it is false.

   1. C F   2. C F   3. C F   4. C F

_____

*The **Videoteca** videoclips are available on the Video on CD to accompany *¿Qué tal?*, Seventh Edition.

Enfoque cultural: Honduras y El Salvador

Complete las oraciones con la información apropiada.

1. El centro ceremonial maya de Copán está en _____ y es hoy un parque nacional que tiene muchas _____.

2. La capital de Honduras es _____ y es un nombre indígena que significa «_____».

3. El volcán de Izalco en _____ se conoce como «el faro del Pacífico» porque estuvo encendido durante casi _____ años.

4. El Arzobispo Óscar Arnulfo Romero fue asesinado en el año _____.

5. Durante su vida, Romero criticó la violencia e injusticia de los _____ de su país y trabajó mucho para mejorar _____.

¡Repasemos!

A. Un viaje ideal. Imagine que Ud. acaba de recibir un regalo de $5.000 de su abuela (tía) rica. Le mandó el dinero para un viaje extraordinario. En otro papel, escríbale una carta de unas 100 palabras con la descripción de sus planes. Incluya la siguiente información.

1. ¿Adónde piensa ir y en qué mes va a salir?

2. ¿Cómo va a viajar?

3. ¿Qué ropa va a llevar?

4. ¿Qué piensa hacer en ese lugar?

5. ¿Cuánto tiempo piensa estar de viaje?

6. ¿Va a viajar solo/a o con otra persona (otras personas)?

7. ¿Dónde piensa quedarse?

MODELO:

Querida _____,

   ¡Mil gracias por el regalo tan fenomenal! Te escribo para darte detalles de mis planes para el viaje...

                    Un abrazo y muchos recuerdos cariñosos de tu (nieto/a, sobrino/a)...

B. *Listening Passage:* **Un anuncio turístico**

Antes de escuchar. Pause and do the following prelistening exercises.

Paso 1. Find out how much you know about Mexico's tourist attractions by answering the following questions. As you read the questions, try to infer the information the passage will give you, as well as the specific information for which you need to listen.

1. ¿Conoce Ud. México? ¿Sabe que la Ciudad de México es una de las ciudades más grandes del mundo, más grande aun (*even*) que Nueva York? ¡Tiene más de 25.000.000 de habitantes!

2. ¿Sabe Ud. el nombre de algunos de los pueblos indígenas (*native*) de México? Los olmecas y los toltecas son menos famosos que otros. ¿Cuáles son los más famosos?

Paso 2. Empareje (*Match*) el nombre de la ciudad mexicana con la atracción turística por la cual (*by which*) se conoce.

1. _____ la Ciudad de México

2. _____ Teotihuacán

3. _____ Acapulco

4. _____ Taxco

5. _____ Cancún

a. ruinas mayas y playas bonitas
b. objetos de plata (*silver*) y artesanías (*crafts*)
c. las Pirámides del Sol y de la Luna (*Moon*)
d. playas
e. el mejor museo antropológico del mundo

Now resume listening.

Listening Passage. Now, you will hear a travel ad about an excursion to Mexico. The following words appear in the passage.

mezclar	*to mix*	el submarinismo	*snorkeling*
la plata	*silver*	saborear	*to taste*
relajarse	*to relax*	tentadora	*templing*
broncearse	*to get a tan*	las plazas	*spaces (on the tour)*

Después de escuchar. Indicate the things that the tourists can do on this trip.

1. ☐ Pueden broncearse.

2. ☐ Hacen submarinismo.

3. ☐ Escalan (*They climb*) unas montañas muy altas.

4. ☐ Compran objetos de plata.

5. ☐ Pueden nadar en dos playas, por lo menos (*at least*).

6. ☐ Ven las ruinas de Machu Picchu.

7. ☐ Visitan un museo antropológico.

Now resume listening.

C. Entrevista. You will hear a series of questions. Each will be said twice. Answer, based on your own experience. Pause and write the answers.

1. _____

2. _____

3. _____

4. _____

5. _____

6. _____

Mi diario

Escriba sobre unas vacaciones que Ud. tomó *o* las de un amigo / una amiga. Incluya (*Include*) la siguiente información.

- adónde y con quién fue
- cuándo y cómo viajó
- el tiempo que hizo durante las vacaciones (llovió mucho, nevó, hizo mucho calor...)
- cuánto tiempo pasó allí
- qué cosas interesantes hizo
- lo que le gustó más (o menos)
- si le gustaría volver a ese lugar

Expresiones útiles   esquiar

hace un año (semana, mes) = *a year (week, month) ago*

tomar el sol

Póngase a prueba

 ## A ver si sabe...

A. Indirect Object Pronouns, *dar* and *decir*.

1. Place the indirect object pronoun **le** in the correct position in the following sentences.

   a. Siempre _____ digo _____ la verdad a mi amiga.

   b. _____ estoy diciendo _____ la verdad a mi amiga,

   o _____ estoy diciendo _____ la verdad a mi amiga.

   c. _____ voy a decir _____ la verdad a mi amiga,

   o _____ voy a decir _____ la verdad a mi amiga.

   d. (*aff. com, Ud.:* **decir**) ¡_____ la verdad a su amiga!

   e. (*neg. com, Ud.:* **decir**) ¡_____ la verdad a su amiga!

2. Complete la siguiente tabla.

INFINITIVO	YO	TÚ	ÉL	NOSOTROS	VOSOTROS	ELLOS
dar		das				
decir				decimos		

B. Gustar. Escriba oraciones con las siguientes palabras.

1. ¿(ellos) gustar / viajar? _____

2. a mí / no / gustar / tomates _____

3. Juan / gustar / aeropuertos _____

C. Preterite of Regular Verbs and of *dar*, *hacer*, *ir*, and *ser*.

INFINITIVO	YO	TÚ	ÉL	NOSOTROS	VOSOTROS	ELLOS
dar		diste				
hablar			habló			
hacer				hicimos		
ir / ser					fuisteis	
salir						salieron

▋ Prueba corta

A. Pronombres. Complete las oraciones con el pronombre apropiado del complemento indirecto.

1. Yo _____ compré un regalo. (a mi madre)

2. Ellos _____ escribieron una carta la semana pasada. (a nosotros)

3. Nosotros _____ compramos boletos para un concierto. (a nuestros amigos)

4. Roberto siempre _____ pide favores. (a mí)

5. ¿Qué _____ dieron tus padres para tu cumpleaños? (a ti)

B. Gustar. Use la forma apropiada de **gustar** y el complemento indirecto.

1. A mis padres no _____ _____ los asientos cerca de la puerta.

2. A mi mejor amigo _____ _____ viajar solo.

3. A mí no _____ _____ la comida que sirven en el avión.

4. A todos nosotros _____ _____ los vuelos sin escalas.

5. Y a ti, ¿adónde _____ _____ ir de vacaciones?

C. El pretérito. Complete las oraciones con la forma apropiada del pretérito del verbo entre paréntesis.

1. ¿A quién le _____ (*tú*: **mandar**) las flores?

2. Ayer _____ (*yo*: **empezar**) a hacer las maletas a las once.

3. Mi hermano _____ (**hacer**) un viaje al Mar Caribe.

4. ¿_____ (**Ir**) Uds. en clase turística?

5. ¿_____ (*Tú*: **Oír**) el anuncio (*announcement*) para subir al avión?

6. Ellos _____ (**volver**) de su viaje el domingo pasado.

7. Juan no me _____ (**dar**) el dinero para el boleto.

D. Cosas de todos los días: De vacaciones. Practice talking about you and your family's recent trip, using the written cues. When you hear the corresponding number, form sentences using the words provided in the order given, making any necessary changes or additions.

MODELO: (*you see*) **1.** mi familia y yo **/** ir de vacaciones   (*you hear*) uno →
(*you say*) Mi familia y yo *fuimos* de vacaciones.

2. el agente **/** recomendarnos **/** viaje a Cancún
3. (nosotros) viajar **/** Cancún **/** en avión
4. avión **/** no **/** hacer escalas
5. (nosotros) llegar **/** a **/** hotel **/** sin problemas
6. el recepcionista **/** darnos **/** cuarto con balcón (*balcony*)
7. mi **/** hermanos **/** nadar **/** la piscina (*swimming pool*)
8. (yo) tomar **/** el sol
9. nuestra madre **/** sacar **/** fotografías
10. nuestro padre **/** mandarles **/** tarjetas postales **/** a los amigos
11. gustarnos **/** mucho **/** viaje

E. Apuntes. You will hear a conversation between a tourist who is interested in traveling to Cancún and a travel agent. Listen carefully and write down the requested information. First, listen to the list of information that is being requested. (Check the answers in the Appendix.)

el tipo de boleto que el turista quiere: _____

la fecha de salida: _____

la fecha de regreso (*return*): _____

la sección y la clase en que va a viajar: _____

la ciudad de la cual (*from which*) va a salir el avión: _____

el tipo de hotel que quiere: _____

el nombre del hotel en el que se va a quedar: _____

CAPÍTULO **8**

Paso 1 Vocabulario

 La fiesta de Javier

❖**A. Ud. y las fiestas.** Indique si las siguientes declaraciones son ciertas o falsas para Ud.

1. C   F   Con frecuencia, en el Día de Acción de Gracias como demasiado y luego no me siento bien.

2. C   F   En la Noche Vieja bebemos, comemos, bailamos y nos divertimos mucho.

3. C   F   En mi universidad siempre hay una gran celebración el Cinco de Mayo.

4. C   F   Doy regalos el Día de los Reyes Magos.

5. C   F   Tengo guardadas (*I have saved*) algunas tarjetas del Día de San Valentín que me mandaron mis «viejos amores».

6. C   F   A veces tomo cerveza verde el Día de San Patricio.

7. C   F   Mi familia celebra el día de mi santo.

8. C   F   En la Pascua Florida, voy a la iglesia.

9. C   F   Mi familia gastó mucho dinero cuando celebró la quinceañera de mi hermana (prima, sobrina).

B. ¿Cuánto sabe Ud. de los días festivos? Complete las oraciones con el día festivo apropiado.

el Cinco de Mayo   la Navidad   la Pascua
el Día de Año Nuevo   la Nochebuena

1. El primero de enero es _____.

2. El 25 de diciembre los cristianos celebran _____.

3. _____ conmemora la huida (*escape*) de los judíos (*Jews*) de Egipto.

4. Muchos católicos asisten a la Misa del gallo (*midnight Mass*) durante

   _____.

5. La victoria de los mexicanos sobre los franceses en la batalla de Puebla (1862) se celebra

   _____.

C. El Día de los Inocentes. Lea la siguiente lectura sobre una fiesta popular y conteste las preguntas.

El 28 de diciembre en el mundo hispánico se celebra la fiesta tradicional que se llama el Día de los Inocentes. En esta fecha se conmemora el día en que murieron[a] muchos niños en Judea por orden de Herodes, quien esperaba hacer morir[b] al niño Jesús entre ellos.

Ese día, a la gente le gusta hacerles bromas[c] a sus amigos. Una broma común es decirle a un amigo:

—Un Sr. León te llamó hace veinte minutos[d] y quiere que lo llames porque es urgente. Aquí tienes su número de teléfono.

Todos esperan mientras el amigo inocente marca[e] el número.

—Buenos días —dice con un tono de mucha importancia—. Habla Enrique González. ¿Puedo hablar con el Sr. León, por favor? Me llamó hace unos minutos.

La joven que contesta el teléfono se ríe[f] y le dice:

—Lo siento. El Sr. León acaba de salir. ¿Quiere Ud. dejar[g] un mensaje? Yo soy su secretaria, la Srta. Elefante.

El amigo se da cuenta,[h] avergonzado,[i] de que ha llamado[j] al Jardín Zoológico[k] mientras todos le gritan[l]: —¡Por inocente, por inocente!

[a]*died* [b]*esperaba... hoped to kill* [c]*hacerles... to play tricks* [d]*hace... twenty minutes ago* [e]*dials*
[f]*se... laughs* [g]*to leave* [h]*se... realizes* [i]*embarrassed* [j]*ha... he has called* [k]*Jardín... Zoo* [l]*shout*

Comprensión

1. ¿Cuál es la fecha de un día festivo en los Estados Unidos que es similar al Día de los Inocentes?

   _____

2. En el mundo hispánico, ¿qué les hace la gente a sus amigos?

   _____

3. ¿Qué significa en inglés **león**? _____

D. ¿Una fiesta familiar típica? You will hear a description of Sara's last family gathering. Then you will hear a series of statements. Circle **C** if the statement is true or **F** if it is false. If the information is not given, circle **ND** (**No lo dice**).

1. C F ND Según lo que dice Sara, las fiestas familiares normalmente son muy divertidas.

2. C F ND A la tía Eustacia le gusta discutir (*argue*) con el padre de Sara.

3. C F ND Normalmente, los primos de Sara se portan mal en las fiestas familiares.

4. C F ND Sara no lo pasa bien nunca en las fiestas familiares.

5. C F ND Los hermanos de Sara discuten mucho con sus padres.

E. Asociaciones. With which of the following celebrations do you associate the descriptions that you hear? Each will be said twice. ¡OJO! There might be more than one possible answer in some cases.

1. a. La Navidad
   b. el Día de la Raza
   c. el cumpleaños
2. a. el día de los enamorados
   b. la Pascua
   c. el Cuatro de Julio

3. a. el Día de los Reyes Magos
   b. el Día de Acción de Gracias
   c. el Día de los Muertos
4. a. la quinceañera
   b. el Día de los Reyes Magos
   c. el día del santo

Emociones y condiciones

A. Profesores y estudiantes. ¿Cómo reaccionan? Use la forma apropiada de los verbos de la lista.

discutir	ponerse avergonzado (irritado,	quejarse
enfermarse	nervioso, triste)	reírse
enojarse	portarse	

1. Cuando Julián no contesta bien en clase, se ríe porque se pone nervioso. Cuando yo no

   recuerdo la respuesta correcta, yo _____.

2. Cuando nos olvidamos de entregar (*turn in*) la tarea a tiempo, los profesores

   _____.

3. Cuando llega la época de los exámenes, algunos estudiantes _____

   porque no duermen lo suficiente (*enough*). Y todos _____ porque
   dicen que tienen muchísimo trabajo.

4. Generalmente, los estudiantes universitarios son responsables y _____
   bien en clase.

5. A los profesores no les gusta _____ con los estudiantes sobre las
   notas (*grades*) que les dan.

B. ¿Cómo reacciona Ud.? Practice telling how you react to these situations, using the oral and written cues. Use the word **cuando** in each sentence.

MODELO: (*you see*) Me olvido del cumpleaños de mi madre.   (*you hear*) ponerme avergonzado →
(*you say*) Me pongo avergonzado cuando me olvido del cumpleaños de mi madre.

1. Mis padres me quitan (*take away*) el coche.
2. Veo una película triste.
3. Saco buenas notas (*grades*).
4. Tengo que hacer cola.

Nota comunicativa: Being Emphatic

¿Qué piensa Ud.? ¡Sea enfático/a, por favor! Use formas con **-ísimo/a.**

1. ¿Le parece larga la novela *Guerra y paz,* del autor ruso Tolstoi?

   _____

2. ¿Son ricos los Gate? _____

3. ¿Se siente Ud. cansado/a después de correr diez kilómetros?

   _____

4. ¿Es cara la vida en Tokio? _____

5. ¿Fueron difíciles las preguntas del último examen?

   _____

Pronunciación y ortografía: *c* and *qu*

A. El sonido [k]. The [k] sound in Spanish can be written two ways: before the vowels **a, o,** and **u** it is written as **c;** before **i** and **e,** it is written as **qu.** The letter **k** itself appears only in words that are borrowed from other languages. Unlike the English [k] sound, the Spanish sound is not aspirated; that is, no air is allowed to escape when it is pronounced. Compare the following pairs of English words in which the first [k] sound is aspirated and the second is not.

can / scan   cold / scold   kit / skit

B. Repeticiones. Repeat the following words, imitating the speaker. Remember to pronounce the [k] sound without aspiration.

1. casa	cosa	rico	loca	roca
2. ¿quién?	Quito	aquí	¿qué?	pequeño
3. kilo	kilogramo	kerosén	kilómetro	karate

Now, when you hear the corresponding number, read the following words. Repeat the correct pronunciation after the speaker.

4. paquete	**6.** química	**8.** camarones
5. quinceañera	**7.** comida	**9.** ¿por qué?

C. Dictado. You will hear a series of words. Each will be said twice. Listen carefully and write what you hear. **¡OJO!** Some of the words may be unfamiliar to you. Concentrate on the sounds.

1. _____   4. _____

2. _____   5. _____

3. _____   6. _____

Los hispanos hablan: Una fiesta inolvidable (*unforgettable*)

You will hear Karen and Xiomara talk about two unforgettable parties. The following words appear in the descriptions.

las damas	*ladies (maids of honor)*	orgulloso	*proud*
el vals	*waltz*	el brindis	*toast*
duró	*lasted*	he pasado	*I have spent*
estuvo presente	*were there*		

Now, pause and indicate the statements that can be inferred from the information in the two descriptions.

1. ☐ La quinceañera (fiesta de los quince años) es una fiesta importante para Karen y Xiomara.

2. ☐ Hay muchos invitados en estas fiestas.

3. ☐ La quinceañera es una fiesta que dura (*lasts*) hasta muy tarde.

4. ☐ Karen y Xiomara celebraron su quinceañera en los Estados Unidos.

5. ☐ En estas fiestas hay música.

Now resume listening.

Paso 2 Gramática

23. Talking About the Past (2) • Irregular Preterites

A. ¿Cuánto sabe Ud.?

Paso 1. ¿Son ciertos o falsos los siguientes hechos históricos?

1. C F Neil Armstrong fue el primer hombre que estuvo en la luna (*moon*).

2. C F Los Estados Unidos pusieron un satélite en el espacio antes que la Unión Soviética.

3. C F Magallanes quiso circunnavegar el mundo, pero murió en las Filipinas a manos de los indígenas (*natives*) en 1521.

4. C F En 1592 Cristóbal Colón pudo llegar a América.

5. C F Hitler no quiso dominar Europa.

6. C F Cortés no supo de la grandeza (*grandeur*) del imperio azteca hasta que llegó a Tenochtitlán en 1519.

7. C F Los españoles trajeron el maíz (*corn*) y el tomate a América.

8. C F En Berlín George Bush (padre) dijo: «Yo soy un berlinés».

9. C F Pocos inmigrantes irlandeses vinieron a los Estados Unidos en el siglo (*century*) XIX.

Paso 2. Ahora tache (*cross out*) la información incorrecta en cada respuesta falsa y corríjala (*correct it*).

B. Formas verbales. Escriba la forma indicada de los verbos.

INFINITIVO	YO	UD.	NOSOTROS	UDS.
estar				
	tuve			
		pudo		
			pusimos	
				quisieron
saber				
	vine			
		dijo		
			trajimos	

C. Situaciones. Complete las oraciones con el pretérito de los verbos entre paréntesis.

Durante la Navidad. La familia Román _____[1] (**tener**) una reunión familiar muy bonita para la Navidad. Todos sus hijos _____[2] (**estar**) presentes. _____[3] (**Venir**) de Denver y Dallas y _____[4] (**traer**) regalos para todos. Su mamá pensaba[a] hacer una gran cena para la Nochebuena, pero todos le _____[5] (**decir**) que no. Por la noche todos _____[6] (**ir**) a un restaurante muy elegante donde _____[7] (**comer**) bien y _____[8] (**poder**) escuchar música.

[a]*was planning*

Otro terremoto[a] en California. Esta mañana _____[1] (*nosotros:* **saber**) que _____[2] (**haber**) un terremoto en California. Lo _____[3] (*yo:* **oír**) primero en el radio y luego lo _____[4] (*yo:* **leer**) en el periódico. Algunas casas _____[5] (**romperse**[b]), pero en general, este terremoto no _____[6] (**hacer**) mucho daño.[c] Un experto _____[7] (**decir**): «No _____[8] (**ser**) el primero ni va a ser el último».

[a]*earthquake* [b]*to be destroyed* [c]*damage*

D. Después del examen. Jorge y Manuel hablan en la cafetería. Complete las oraciones con la forma apropiada de los verbos entre paréntesis.

JORGE: ¿Cómo _____[1] (**estar**) el examen?

MANUEL: ¡Terrible! No _____[2] (**poder**) contestar las últimas tres preguntas porque no _____[3] (**tener**) tiempo. ¿Por qué no _____[4] (**venir**) tú?

JORGE: _____[5] (**Querer**) venir, pero _____[6] (**estar**) enfermo todo el día. ¿Qué preguntas _____[7] (**hacer**) el profesor?

MANUEL: Muchas, pero ahora no recuerdo ninguna. ¿_____[8] (*tú:* **Saber**) que Claudia _____[9] (**tener**) un accidente y tampoco _____[10] (**venir**) al examen?

JORGE: Sí, me lo _____[11] (**decir**) María Inés esta mañana... Bueno, tengo que irme... ¡Caramba! ¿Dónde _____[12] (**poner**) mi cartera?

MANUEL: ¿No la _____[13] (**traer**) otra vez? Yo sólo _____[14] (**traer**) dos dólares. Vamos a buscar a Ernesto. Él siempre tiene dinero.

❖E. **Encuesta: Hablando de lo que pasó ayer.** You will hear a series of statements about what happened to you yesterday. For each statement, check the appropriate answer. No answers will be given. The answers you choose should be correct for you!

1. ☐ Sí ☐ No   5. ☐ Sí ☐ No

2. ☐ Sí ☐ No   6. ☐ Sí ☐ No

3. ☐ Sí ☐ No   7. ☐ Sí ☐ No

4. ☐ Sí ☐ No   8. ☐ Sí ☐ No

F. **Una fiesta de cumpleaños.** Tell what happened at the party, using the written and oral cues.

> MODELO: (*you see*) estar en casa de Mario (*you hear*) todos →
> (*you say*) Todos estuvimos en casa de Mario.

1. tener que preparar la comida   3. hacer mucho ruido
2. venir con regalos   4. ¡estar estupenda!

G. **Preguntas: ¿Qué hizo Ud. la Navidad pasada?** You will hear a series of questions. Each will be said twice. Answer, using the written cues. Use object pronouns when possible.

1. en mi casa   4. debajo del árbol (*tree*)
2. sí: venir todos mis tíos y primos   5. los niños
3. a su novia

24. Talking About the Past (3) • Preterite of Stem-Changing Verbs

A. **Formas verbales.** Escriba la forma indicada de los verbos.

INFINITIVO	YO	TÚ	UD.	NOSOTROS	UDS.
divertirse					
sentir					
dormir					
conseguir					
reír					
vestir					

B. Situaciones. Complete las oraciones con la forma apropiada del pretérito de uno de los verbos de la lista, según el significado de la oración.

dormirse   sentarse

1. Yo _____ delante del televisor y _____ poco después.

2. —¿A qué hora _____ Uds. a comer?

   —A las nueve y media. Y después de trabajar tanto, ¡nosotros casi _____ en la mesa!

3. Mi esposo se despertó a las dos y no _____ otra vez hasta las cinco de la mañana.

reírse   sentir[a]   sentirse

4. Esa película fue tan divertida que (nosotros) _____ toda la noche. Sólo Jorge

   no _____ mucho porque no la comprendió.

5. Rita y Marcial _____ mucho haber faltado[b] a tu fiesta, pero Rita se enfermó y

   _____ tan mal que se quedó en cama todo el fin de semana.

[a]*to regret*   [b]*haber... having missed*

C. La fiesta de sorpresa

Paso 1. You will hear a brief paragraph, narrated by Ernesto, about a surprise party. Listen carefully and check the appropriate actions for each person. First, pause and look at the chart.

PERSONA	VESTIRSE ELEGANTEMENTE	SENTIRSE MAL	DORMIR TODA LA TARDE	PREFERIR QUEDARSE EN CASA
Julia				
Verónica				
Tomás				
Ernesto (el narrador)				

Paso 2. You will hear a series of statements about the preceding paragraph. Each will be said twice. Circle **C** if the statement is true or **F** if it is false. If the information is not given, circle **ND** (**No lo dice**).

1. C   F   ND   2. C   F   ND   3. C   F   ND   4. C   F   ND   5. C   F   ND

D. ¿Qué le pasó a Antonio? Tell what happened to Antonio when you hear the corresponding number. First, listen to the beginning of Antonio's story.

Raquel Morales invitó a Antonio a una fiesta en su casa. Antonio le dijo a Raquel que él asistiría (*would attend*), pero todo le salió mal. En primer lugar…

1. no recordar llevar refrescos
2. perder la dirección de la Srta. Morales
3. llegar muy tarde a la fiesta
4. no divertirse
5. sentirse enfermo después de la fiesta
6. acostarse muy tarde
7. dormir mal esa noche
8. despertarse a las cinco de la mañana
9. tener que ir a clases de todas formas (*anyway*)

Paso 3 Gramática

25. Expressing Direct and Indirect Objects Together • Double Object Pronouns

> ¡RECUERDE!
>
> **Direct and Indirect Object Pronouns.** Cambie los complementos directos indicados o las frases indicadas (*a Ud., a nosotros, a ellos,* etcétera) a complementos pronominales. Luego identifique los pronombres (O.D. = objeto directo; O.I. = objeto indirecto).
>
> MODELOS: No dice la verdad. (*a Uds.*) → No les dice la verdad. (O.I.)
> No dice *la verdad.* → No la dice. (O.D.)
>
> 1. Yo traigo el café. (*a Ud.*) _____
>
> 2. Yo traigo *el café* ahora. _____
>
> 3. Ellos compran los boletos. (*a nosotros*) _____
>
> 4. Ellos compran *los boletos* hoy. _____
>
> 5. No hablo mucho. (*a ellas*) _____
>
> 6. No conozco bien *a tus primas.* _____

❖**A.** **¿Con qué frecuencia... ?** Indique la frecuencia con que Ud. y otras personas hacen estas cosas.

	SIEMPRE	A VECES	NUNCA
1. El coche: Mi padre me lo presta.	☐	☐	☐
2. El dinero: Mis amigos me lo piden.	☐	☐	☐
3. La cena: Me la prepara mi madre.	☐	☐	☐
4. La cena: Yo se la preparo a mi familia.	☐	☐	☐
5. La tarea: Nos la dan los profesores.	☐	☐	☐
6. La tarea: Se la explico a mis amigos.	☐	☐	☐

B. **¡Promesas, promesas!** (*Promises, promises!*) Estas personas prometen hacer las siguientes cosas. Vuelva a escribir lo que prometen, pero omita la repetición innecesaria del complemento directo.

MODELO: ¿Los discos? José nos trae *los discos* mañana. → José nos los trae mañana.

1. ¿El dinero? Te devuelvo (*I'll return*) *el dinero* mañana.

_____

2. ¿Las fotos? Te traigo *las fotos* el jueves.

_____

3. ¿La sorpresa? Nos van a revelar *la sorpresa* después.

_____

4. ¿Los pasteles? Me prometieron *los pasteles* para esta tarde.

_____

5. ¿Las fotos? Les mando *las fotos* a Uds. con la carta.

_____

¡RECUERDE!				

le **les**	lo la los las	→ **se**	lo la los las

6. ¿La bicicleta? Le devuelvo *la bicicleta* a Pablo mañana.

_____

7. ¿El dinero? Le doy *el dinero* a Ud. el viernes.

_____

8. ¿Los regalos? Le muestro *los regalos* a Isabel esta noche.

_____

C. La herencia (*inheritance*). Imagine que un pariente muy rico murió y les dejó (*he left*) varias cosas a Ud. y a diferentes personas e instituciones. ¿Qué le dejó a quién?

Ernesto y Ana

Memo

Cristina

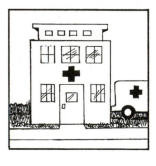

La Cruz Roja

La biblioteca

Yo

MODELO: ¿A quién le dejó su ropa? → Se la dejó a la Cruz Roja.

1. ¿A quién le dejó su Porsche? _____

2. ¿A quién le dejó su nueva cámara? _____

3. ¿A quién le dejó sus libros? _____

4. ¿A quién le dejó sus muebles? _____

5. ¿A quién le dejó su camioneta? _____

6. ¿A quién le dejó $20.000 dólares? _____

❖**D. Los regalos.** Haga una lista de cinco cosas que Ud. les regaló a su familia y amigos la Navidad pasada (*last*). Luego escriba a quiénes se las regaló.

MODELO: Un suéter: Se lo regalé a mi hermana.

1. _____
2. _____
3. _____
4. _____
5. _____

E. Dictado: Una fiesta de sorpresa para Lupita. You will hear a passage narrated by Olivia about a surprise party she gave recently. As you listen, write the missing words.

El viernes pasado, mis amigos y yo dimos una fiesta de sorpresa para una de nuestras amigas,

Lupita. Yo escribí las invitaciones y _____ _____¹ mandé a todos. Carmen hizo un pastel y

_____ _____² dio antes de la fiesta. Anita preparó una comida elegante y _____

_____³ sirvió en el comedor. Arturo y Patricio sacaron muchas fotos y _____ _____⁴

regalaron a Lupita. Todos llevamos regalos y _____ _____⁵ presentamos a Lupita al final

de la fiesta. ¡Lupita nos dijo que fue una fiesta maravillosa!

F. En casa, durante la cena. During dinner, your brother asks about the different foods that might be left. He will say each question twice. Listen carefully and circle the items to which he is referring.

MODELO: (*you hear*) ¿Hay más? ¿Me la pasas, por favor?
(*you see*) la sopa   el pan   el pescado →
(*you circle*) la sopa

1. las galletas   la fruta   el helado
2. la carne   el postre   los camarones
3. la leche   el vino   las arvejas
4. las papas fritas la cerveza   el pastel

G. ¿Dónde está? Carolina would like to borrow some things from you. Tell her to whom you gave each item, basing your answer on the written cues and selecting the correct pronouns. You will hear each of Carolina's questions twice.

MODELO: (*you hear*) Oye, ¿dónde está tu diccionario?
(*you see*) Se (**lo** / **la**) presté a Nicolás. Él (lo / la) necesita para un examen. →
(*you say*) Se lo presté a Nicolás. Él lo necesita para un examen.

1. Se (**lo** / **la**) presté a Nicolás. Él (**lo** / **la**) necesita para un viaje.
2. Se (**los** / **las**) presté a Teresa. Ella (**los** / **las**) necesita para su fiesta.
3. Se (**la** / **las**) presté a Juan. Él (**la** / **las**) necesita para escribir un trabajo.
4. Se (**lo** / **la**) presté a Nina. Ella (**lo** / **la**) necesita para ir al parque.

Un poco de todo

A. Preguntas personales. Conteste las preguntas con oraciones completas. Use los pronombres del complemento directo e indirecto.

> MODELO: ¿A quién le prestó Ud. su bicicleta? → Se la presté a mi hermano.
> (No se la presté a nadie.)

1. ¿A quién le mandó Ud. una tarjeta de San Valentín? _____

2. ¿A quién le dio Ud. regalos de Navidad? _____

3. ¿Quién le trajo flores a Ud. este año? _____

4. ¿Quién le pidió dinero a Ud. este mes? _____

5. ¿Quién le hizo una fiesta para su cumpleaños? _____

B. Una carta a un amigo

Paso 1. Complete la carta que Gerardo le escribe a un amigo que vive en Acapulco. Use el pretérito de los verbos entre paréntesis.

Querido Pepe:

La semana pasada _____[1] (*yo:* **hacer**) un corto viaje a Acapulco porque

_____[2] (**tener**) una reunión con mi agente de viajes. Aunque[a] _____[3]

(**estar**) ocupadísimo, _____[4] (**querer**) visitarte, pero _____[5] (**saber**)

por nuestro amigo Luis Dávila que estabas[b] fuera de la ciudad. Yo le _____[6] (**dar**)

a Luis unas fotos de la última vez que nosotros _____[7] (**estar**) juntos,[c] y le

_____[8] (*yo:* **pedir**) que te las diera[d] a tu vuelta a Acapulco.

Espero verte durante mi próximo viaje. Recibe un abrazo[e] de tu amigo,

Gerardo

[a]*Although* [b]*you were* [c]*together* [d]*he give* [e]*hug*

Paso 2. Conteste las preguntas con oraciones completas.

1. ¿Por qué fue Gerardo a Acapulco? _____

2. ¿Tuvo mucho tiempo libre o estuvo ocupado? _____

3. ¿Cómo supo Gerardo que Pepe estaba fuera de Acapulco? _____

4. ¿A quién le dio las fotos? _____

C. Un día típico. You will hear a description of a day in Ángela's life, narrated in the past. Then you will hear a series of statements. Circle **C** if the statement is true or **F** if it is false. If the information is not given, circle **ND** (**No lo dice**).

1. C F ND   Ángela se acostó tarde ayer.

2. C F ND   Ángela se levantó a las seis y media.

3. C F ND   Ángela se puso furiosa cuando llegó a la oficina.

4. C F ND   El jefe (*boss*) le dio mucho trabajo.

5. C F ND   Los padres de Ángela viven lejos de ella.

6. C F ND   Cuando Ángela se acostó, se durmió inmediatamente.

Paso 4 Un paso más

🎧 ◼ Videoteca*

Entrevista cultural: Cuba

You will hear an interview with Rocío García. As you listen, complete the following paragraph with information from the interview. Check your answers in the Appendix. First, pause and read the incomplete paragraph.

Rocío es de _____,[1]Cuba, pero ahora ella vive en _____.[2] Ella trabaja en

una tienda que vende artículos típicos de _____.[3] En Cuba, los _____[4]

se celebran con una gran fiesta, con globos y payasos (*clowns*). Su fiesta favorita es la

_____[5] porque se hace una gran fiesta con _____[6] típica cubana.

Rocío trae una _____[7] porque los cubanos _____[8] mucho café.

Now resume listening.

Entre amigos: Comemos las uvas de la suerte.

The four friends answer a question about the holidays that they celebrate. Listen carefully and jot down notes about their responses. The names are listed in the order in which they answer the question. Check your answers in the Appendix.

1. Karina _____
2. Rubén _____
3. Miguel René _____
4. Tané _____

◼ Enfoque cultural: Cuba

Conteste las preguntas con una palabra o frase corta.

1. ¿Cuándo obtuvo (*obtained*) Cuba su independencia de España? _____
2. ¿Adónde se fueron muchos cubanos después de la revolución de 1959?

   _____

3. Después de más de cuarenta años, ¿por qué no regresa la mayor parte de cubanos a Cuba?

   _____

4. ¿Cuál es la situación económica actual (*current*) en Cuba? _____
5. ¿Qué influencia refleja la poesía del poeta cubano Nicolás Guillén? _____

   _____

6. ¿Cuáles son dos de los temas importantes de su poesía? _____
7. ¿Qué mitos y leyendas aparecen en las obras de Guillén? _____

   _____

---

*The **Videoteca** videoclips are available on the Video on CD to accompany *¿Qué tal?*, Seventh Edition.

¡Repasemos!

A. ¡Saludos de España!

Paso 1. Lea la siguiente tarjeta postal.

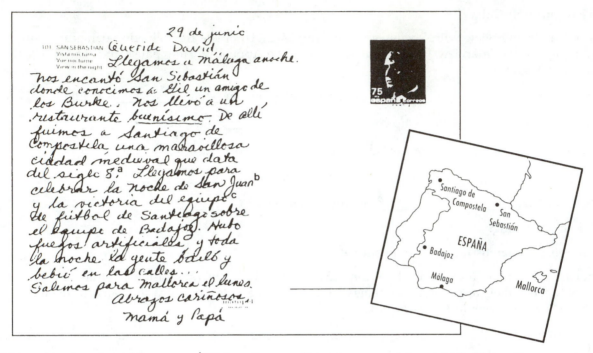

> 29 de junio
>
> 101 SAN SEBASTIAN
> Vista nocturna
> Vue nocturne
> View in the night
>
> Querido David,
> Llegamos a Málaga anoche.
> Nos encantó San Sebastián
> donde conocimos a Gil un amigo de
> los Burke. Nos llevó a un
> restaurante buenísimo. De allí
> fuimos a Santiago de
> Compostela una maravillosa
> ciudad medieval que data
> del siglo 8.ª Llegamos para
> celebrar la noche de San Juanᵇ
> y la victoria del equipoᶜ
> de fútbol de Santiago sobre
> el equipo de Badajoz. Hubo
> fuegos artificiales y toda
> la noche la gente bailó y
> bebió en las calles...
> Salimos para Mallorca el lunes.
> Abrazos cariñosos,
> Mamá y Papá

ᵃdata... *dates from the eighth century* ᵇNoche... fiesta tradicional que se celebra el 24 de junio ᶜ*team*

Paso 2. Ahora, escriba Ud. una tarjeta postal a un amigo o pariente, contándole de sus vacaciones. Mencione por lo menos un lugar que visitó y lo que vio o lo que pasó allí. Mencione también adónde piensa ir luego. Siga el modelo de la tarjeta. Puede inventar el viaje, si quiere.

_____

_____

_____

_____

_____

 B. *Listening Passage:* **El carnaval**

Antes de escuchar. You will hear a passage about carnival celebrations. The following words appear in the passage.

pagana	*pagan, not religious*
la Cuaresma	*Lent*
las máscaras	*masks*
los disfraces	*costumes*
caricaturescos	*cartoonish, satirical*
se mezclan	*are blended*
inolvidable	*unforgettable*

Listening Passage. Here is the passage. First, listen to it to get a general idea of the content. Then go back and listen again for specific information.

Después de escuchar. Indicate the statements that contain information that you *cannot* infer from the listening passage.

1. ☐ El carnaval es una tradición exclusivamente europea.

2. ☐ A pesar de (*In spite of*) las diferencias, las celebraciones de carnaval tienen muchas semejanzas (*similarities*).

3. ☐ El carnaval celebra la llegada del buen tiempo.

4. ☐ Los mejores carnavales se celebran en Europa.

5. ☐ La gran diferencia entre el carnaval de Río y los otros carnavales es que el de Río se celebra en un mes distinto (diferente).

6. ☐ La persona que habla tuvo gran dificultad con el idioma en Río de Janeiro.

7. ☐ La persona que habla quiere ir al *Mardi Gras* de Nueva Orleáns el próximo año.

Now resume listening.

C. Entrevista. You will hear a series of questions. Each will be said twice. Answer, based on your own experience. Pause and write the answers.

1. _____

2. _____

3. _____

4. _____

5. _____

6. _____

7. _____

❖ Mi diario

¿Cuál es el día festivo más importante para su familia (sus amigos)? ¿Cuándo se celebra? ¿Hay una cena especial o una fiesta? ¿Dónde es? ¿Quiénes asisten? ¿Cuáles son las costumbres (*customs*) y tradiciones más importantes para Uds.? ¿Qué comidas y bebidas se sirven? La preparación de la comida, ¿es una actividad cooperativa? ¿Lo prepara todo una sola persona?

Palabras útiles	dar las doce (*to strike 12*)
	decorar el árbol (*tree*)
	los fuegos artificiales (*fireworks*)
	el globo (*balloon*)
	normalmente (*normally*)

Póngase a prueba

■ **A ver si sabe...**

A. Irregular Preterites. Escriba las formas apropiadas de los verbos en el pretérito.

1. (**estar**) yo _____

2. (**poder**) tú _____

3. (**poner**) Ud. _____

4. (**querer**) nosotros _____

5. (**saber**) ellos _____

6. (**tener**) yo _____

7. (**venir**) tú _____

8. (**traer**) Ud. _____

9. (**decir**) ellos _____ /

10. (**ir**) nosotros _____

B. Preterite of Stem-Changing Verbs. Complete la siguiente tabla.

INFINITIVO	DORMIR	PEDIR	PREFERIR	RECORDAR	SENTIRSE
yo					
tú					
él/ella/Ud.					
nosotros/as					
ellos/Uds.					

C. Double Object Pronouns. Sustituya (*Substitute*) los complementos directos e (*and*) indirectos por sus respectivos pronombres.

MODELO: Alberto le sirvió *café* a *Jimena*. → Alberto __se__ __lo__ sirvió.

1. Ricardo le pidió *dinero* a *su padre*.   Ricardo _____ _____ pidió.

2. Clara le sugirió *una idea* a *Enrique*.   Clara _____ _____ sugirió.

3. Carmen les puso *el suéter* a *sus hijos*.   Carmen _____ _____ puso.

Prueba corta

A. Oraciones. Complete las oraciones con la forma correcta del pretérito de un verbo de la lista.

conseguir	dormir	reírse
despedirse	hacer	traer
divertirse	ponerse	vestirse

1. Cuando vimos esa película cómica, todos (*nosotros*) _____ mucho.

2. Después de comer ese pescado, Marcial _____ enfermo y se acostó, pero no

   _____ en toda la noche.

3. Yo _____ un boleto extra para el concierto de mañana. ¿Quieres ir?

4. Marcos _____ de sus amigos y volvió a su casa.

5. Para celebrar el Año Nuevo, Mirasol _____ con ropa elegante: pantalones

   negros y blusa de seda. Ella _____ muchísimo bailando con sus amigos.

6. Para celebrar el Año Nuevo, nosotros _____ una fiesta y unos amigos nos

   _____ champán.

B. Preguntas. Conteste las preguntas con la respuesta más apropiada.

1. ¿Cuándo nos traes el café?
   a. Se lo traigo en seguida (*right away*).
   b. Te los traigo en seguida.
   c. Te lo traigo en seguida.

2. ¿Cuándo me van a lavar (*wash*) el coche?
   a. Se lo vamos a lavar esta tarde.
   b. Me lo voy a lavar esta tarde.
   c. Te lo voy a lavar esta tarde.

3. ¿Quién te sacó estas fotos?
   a. Julio me los sacó.
   b. Julio te las sacó.
   c. Julio me las sacó.

4. ¿Quién les mandó estas flores a Uds.?
   a. Ceci nos los mandó.
   b. Ceci nos las mandó.
   c. Ceci se las mandó.

5. ¿A quién le vas a regalar esa camisa?
   a. Te la voy a regalar a ti.
   b. Se lo voy a regalar a Uds.
   c. Me las vas a regalar a mí.

6. ¿A quién le sirves ese vino?
   a. Se los sirvo a Uds.
   b. Se lo sirvo a Uds.
   c. Mario nos lo sirve.

C. Preparativos para la fiesta de Gilberto. The speaker will ask you several questions about Gilberto's birthday party. You will hear each question twice. Circle the letter of the best answer for each. Pay close attention to the object nouns and pronouns you hear in the question.

1. **a.** Sí, voy a mandártela. **b.** Sí, voy a mandártelos.
2. **a.** Sí, se lo tengo que hacer. **b.** Sí, te lo tengo que hacer.
3. **a.** Sí, nos los van a traer. **b.** Sí, se los voy a traer.
4. **a.** No, no van a traértelas. **b.** No, no van a traérmelas.
5. **a.** Sí, te las sirvo. **b.** Sí, se los sirvo.

D. Cosas de todos los días: el cumpleaños de Gilberto. Practice talking about the surprise birthday party that you gave a friend, using the written cues. When you hear the corresponding number, form sentences using the words provided in the order given, making any necessary changes or additions.

> MODELO: (*you see*) **1.** (yo) hacerle / una fiesta de sorpresa a Gilberto (*you hear*) uno →
> (*you say*) Le hice una fiesta de sorpresa a Gilberto.

2. venir / muchos de sus amigos
3. Tere / querer venir, / pero / no poder
4. todos / traer / o / mandar / regalos
5. Felicia y yo / tener que preparar todo
6. Fernando y Raúl / servir los refrescos
7. Fernando / contar chistes / como siempre
8. todos / divertirse / y / reírse
9. nadie / quejarse
10. Gilberto / tener que bailar / con todas las muchachas
11. ¡(él) / ponerse / muy nervioso!

Paso 1 Vocabulario

Pasatiempos, diversiones y aficiones

❖**A.** **¿Qué hace Ud.?** ¿Con qué frecuencia hace Ud. estas actividades durante un fin de semana típico?

	CASI NUNCA	A VECES	CON FRECUENCIA
1. Doy paseos (por un centro comercial, por la playa).	☐	☐	☐
2. Hago una fiesta con algunos amigos.	☐	☐	☐
3. Voy al cine.	☐	☐	☐
4. Visito un museo.	☐	☐	☐
5. Juego a las cartas.	☐	☐	☐
6. Paseo en bicicleta.	☐	☐	☐
7. Hago *camping* con amigos.	☐	☐	☐
8. Asisto a un concierto.	☐	☐	☐

B. **Diversiones.** Complete las oraciones según los dibujos.

1. **a.** A las personas en esta escena (*scene*) les gusta _____.

   b. Los dos hombres _____.

   c. Los tres amigos _____.

   d. La chica _____.

2. **a.** Los hombres en el parque _____.

   b. Tres personas hacen cola delante del _____ Colón.

   c. Dos personas van a visitar el _____ de Arte Moderno.

3. **Palabras útiles**   el cine   pasarlo bien

   divertido   la película

   ELSA: Estoy cansada de estudiar. Quiero

   hacer algo _____.[a]

   LISA: ¿Qué te parece si vamos al _____[b] Bretón? Ponen

   _____[c] *El señor de los anillos*.

   ELSA: Buena idea. Necesito salir de esta casa. ¡Quiero _____[d]!

❖C. ¿ A quién le gusta... ? ¿A cuál de sus amigos le gustan estos pasatiempos?

MODELO: (hacer *picnics*) → A Maritere le gusta hacer *picnics*.
(A ninguno de mis amigos le gusta hacer *picnics*.)

1. (montar a caballo) _____

2. (patinar) _____

3. (hacer *camping*) _____

4. (esquiar) _____

5. (nadar) _____

6. (pasear en bicicleta) _____

D. Gustos y preferencias. You will hear a series of descriptions of what people like to do. Each will be said twice. Listen carefully, and circle the letter of the activity or activities that are best suited to each person.

1.	**a.**	nadar	**b.**	jugar al ajedrez	**c.**	tomar el sol
2.	**a.**	dar fiestas	**b.**	ir al teatro	**c.**	ir a un bar
3.	**a.**	ir a un museo	**b.**	hacer *camping*	**c.**	hacer un *picnic*
4.	**a.**	pasear en bicicleta	**b.**	esquiar	**c.**	correr
5.	**a.**	jugar al fútbol	**b.**	ir a un museo	**c.**	ir al cine

E. Las actividades y el tiempo. You will hear a series of descriptions of weather and activities. Write the number of the description next to the corresponding picture. ¡OJO! Listen carefully. There is an extra description.

a. _____

b. _____

c. _____

d. _____

◼ Los quehaceres domésticos

A. Los quehaceres domésticos. Describa lo que hacen las personas en cada dibujo. Use el presente del progresivo cuando sea (*whenever it is*) posible.

1.  2.  3.

1. _____

2. _____

3. _____

B. Los aparatos domésticos. Dé el nombre del aparato apropiado.

1. Cocino en _____. 4. Tosto el pan en _____.

2. Lavos los platos en _____. 5. Preparo el café en _____.

3. Limpios la alfombra con _____. 6. Lavo la ropa en _____.

❖**B. Preguntas personales.** Haga un inventario de los aparatos eléctricos que tiene y de los que le gustaría tener en su cocina.

Tengo _____.

Me gustaría tener _____.

🎧 **C. Mandatos para el nuevo robot.** Imagine that your family has been chosen to test a model robot in your home. Tell the robot what to do in each of the following situations, using the oral cues. ¡OJO! You will be using **Ud.** command forms.

MODELO: (*you hear*) uno (*you see*) →
(*you say*) Lave los platos.

1.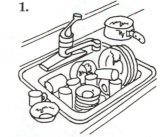

2.  3.  4.  5.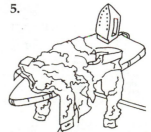

Pronunciación y ortografía: *p* and *t*

A. Repeticiones. Like the [k] sound, Spanish **p** and **t** are not aspirated as they are in English. Compare the following pairs of aspirated and nonaspirated English sounds.

pin / spin   pan / span   tan / Stan   top / stop

Repeat the following words, imitating the speaker.

1. pasar   patinar   programa   puerta   esperar
2. tienda   todos   traje   estar   usted

Now, read the following phrases and sentences after you hear the corresponding number. Repeat the correct pronunciation after the speaker.

3. una tía trabajadora
4. unos pantalones pardos

5. Tomás, toma tu té.
6. Pablo paga el periódico.

B. Repaso: [p], [t], [k]. You will hear a series of words. Each will be said twice. Circle the letter of the word you hear.

1. **a.** pata   **b.** bata
2. **a.** van   **b.** pan
3. **a.** coma   **b.** goma

4. **a.** dos   **b.** tos
5. **a.** de   **b.** té
6. **a.** callo   **b.** gallo

C. Dictado. You will hear four sentences. Each will be said twice. Listen carefully and write what you hear.

1. _____

2. _____

3. _____

4. _____

Los hispanos hablan: ¿Cuál es tu pasatiempo favorito?

Paso 1. You will hear two answers to this question. Listen carefully and, on a separate sheet of paper, jot down notes about what each person says. The following words appear in the answers.

los aparadores   *display windows*
las sodas   *soda fountains*
los bancos   *benches*

Paso 2. Now, pause and answer these questions. (Check your answers in the Appendix.)

1. ¿Qué actividades tienen en común las dos jóvenes?

_____

_____

2. ¿Qué pasatiempos no tienen en común Gabriela y Xiomara?

_____

_____

Paso 2 Gramática

26. Descriptions and Habitual Actions in the Past • Imperfect of Regular and Irregular Verbs

A. El cumpleaños de Clara. Lea la siguiente descripción de cómo pasaba los cumpleaños Clara López Rubio cuando era niña. Escriba abajo las formas del imperfecto que encuentra en su descripción.

Los cumpleaños que más recuerdo son los que celebraba de pequeña. La casa siempre se llenaba de[a] gente: parientes, amiguitos míos[b] con sus padres... Mis amigos y yo debíamos hacer muchísimo ruido. Corríamos por la casa, comíamos patatas fritas y luego, al final, cortábamos la torta.[c] Yo siempre era la última en recibir un pedazo[d] y eso me molestaba mucho, sobre todo[e] porque en los cumpleaños de mi amigo Pablo, él siempre era el primero porque era «el anfitrión».[f]

[a]se... *would fill up with* [b]*of mine* [c]*pastel* [d]*piece* [e]sobre... *especialmente* [f]*host*

1. _____   6. _____

2. _____   7. _____

3. _____   8. _____

4. _____   9. _____

5. _____   10. _____

B. Recuerdos juveniles. (*Youthful Memories.*) Complete la narración con la forma apropiada del imperfecto de los verbos entre paréntesis.

Cuando _____[1] (*yo:* **tener**) catorce años, _____[2] (*nosotros:* **vivir**)

en el campo.[a] _____[3] (*yo:* **Ir**) al colegio[b] en una ciudad cerca de casa y a veces

_____[4] (*yo:* **volver**) tarde porque _____[5] (**preferir**) quedarme a

jugar con mis amigos. Ellos a veces _____[6] (**venir**) a visitarnos, especialmente

cuando _____[7] (**ser**) el cumpleaños de mi madre. Siempre lo

_____[8] (*nosotros:* **celebrar**) con una gran fiesta y ese día mi padre

_____[9] (**hacer**) todos los preparativos y _____[10] (**cocinar**) él

mismo.[c] Nos _____[11] (**visitar**) parientes de todas partes y siempre

_____[12] (**quedarse**) algunos con nosotros por dos o tres días.

Durante esos días _____[13] (*nosotros:* **dormir**) poco porque mis primos y yo

_____[14] (**acostarse**) en la sala de recreo y allí siempre _____[15]

(**haber**) gente hasta muy tarde. Todos nosotros lo _____[16] (**pasar**) muy bien. Pero

esos _____[17] (**ser**) otros tiempos, claro.

[a]*country(side)* [b]*high school* [c]él... *himself*

C. La mujer de ayer y hoy. Compare la vida de la mujer de la década de los años 50 con la vida que lleva hoy día. Use los infinitivos indicados. Siga el modelo. Luego escriba dos contrastes que Ud. ha observado (*have observed*) en la vida de su propia familia o de sus amigos.

MODELO: tener muchos hijos **/ /** tener familias pequeñas →
Antes tenía muchos hijos. Ahora tiene familias pequeñas.

1. depender de su esposo **/ /** tener más independencia económica

_____

2. quedarse en casa **/ /** preferir salir a trabajar

_____

3. sólo pensar en casarse (*getting married*) **/ /** pensar en seguir su propia carrera (*own career*)

_____

4. su esposo sentarse a leer el periódico **/ /** ayudarla con los quehaceres domésticos

_____

❖5. _____

❖6. _____

❖**D. Su pasado.** Conteste las preguntas sobre su vida cuando tenía 15 años.

1. ¿Dónde y con quién vivía Ud.? _____

2. ¿Cómo era su casa? _____

3. ¿A qué escuela asistía? ¿Cómo se llamaba su maestro preferido / maestra preferida en la
escuela secundaria? ¿Cómo era él/ella? _____

_____

4. ¿Qué materia le gustaba más? _____

5. ¿Qué tipo de estudiante era? ¿Siempre recibía buenas notas (*grades*)? _____

_____

6. Generalmente, ¿qué hacía después de volver a casa? Y los fines de semana, ¿qué hacía? _____

_____

E. Minidiálogo: Diego habla de los aztecas.

Paso 1. Dictado. You will hear the following paragraph in which Diego, a student from California who studied for one year in Mexico City, describes some aspects of Aztec culture. Listen carefully and write the missing words.

Los aztecas construyeron grandes pirámides para sus dioses.

En lo alto de cada pirámide _____[1] un

templo donde _____[2] lugar las ceremonias y

se _____[3] los sacrificios. Las pirámides _____[4]

muchísimos escalones, y _____[5] necesario subirlos todos para llegar a los templos.

Cerca de muchas pirámides _____⁶ un terreno como el de una cancha de

basquetbol. Allí se _____⁷ partidos que _____⁸ parte de una

ceremonia. Los participantes _____⁹ con una pelota de goma dura, que sólo

_____¹⁰ mover con las caderas y las rodillas…

Paso 2. ¿Qué recuerda Ud.? Now pause and complete the following sentences with words chosen from the list. (Check the answers in the Appendix.)

ceremonia   dioses   pirámides   religiosa   sacrificios

1. Los aztecas ofrecían _____ a sus _____.

2. El juego de pelota que se jugaba era parte de una _____.

3. Las _____ eran estructuras altas que tenían una función _____.

Now resume listening.

❖F. Encuesta: ¿Qué hacía Ud. y cómo era cuando era joven? You will hear a series of statements about what you used to do or what you were like when you were younger. For each statement, check the appropriate answer. No answers will be given. The answers you choose should be correct for you!

1. ☐ Sí ☐ No   4. ☐ Sí ☐ No   6. ☐ Sí ☐ No

2. ☐ Sí ☐ No   5. ☐ Sí ☐ No   7. ☐ Sí ☐ No

3. ☐ Sí ☐ No

G. Describiendo el pasado: En la primaria. Practice telling what you and others used to do in grade school, using the oral and written cues.

MODELO: (*you see*) (yo)   (*you hear*) jugar mucho → (*you say*) Jugaba mucho.

1. Rodolfo   2. (tú)   3. todos   4. (nosotros)

27. Expressing Extremes • Superlatives

A. Opiniones sobre los deportes. Expand the information in these sentences according to the model. Then if you don't agree with the statement, give your opinion on the line below.

MODELO: El golf es más aburrido que el fútbol. (todos) →
El golf es el deporte más aburrido de todos.
No estoy de acuerdo. El fútbol es el más aburrido.

1. El béisbol es más emocionante que el basquetbol. (todos)

_____

_____

2. Shaquille O'Neal es mejor jugador que Allen Iverson. (mundo)

_____

_____

3. El equipo de los Dallas Cowboys es peor que el de (*that of*) los 49ers. (todos)

_____

_____

4. El estadio (*stadium*) de Río de Janeiro, Brasil, es más grande que el de Pasadena. (mundo)

_____

_____

B. Las opiniones de Margarita

Paso 1. Apuntes. You will hear a brief paragraph in which Margarita gives her opinions about a variety of topics. Listen carefully and write down her opinions. First, listen to the list of topics.

1. la fiesta más divertida del año: _____

2. el peor mes del año: _____

3. la mejor película del mundo: _____

4. el quehacer doméstico más aburrido: _____

❖**Paso 2.** Now pause and express your own opinion about the same topics. No answers will be given. The answers you choose should be correct for you!

En mi opinión…

1. La fiesta más divertida del año es _____

2. El peor mes del año es _____

3. La mejor película del mundo es _____

4. El quehacer doméstico más aburrido es _____

Now resume listening.

C. Sólo lo mejor… Imagine that your friend's **quinceañera** has the best of everything. Answer some questions about it, using the written cues.

MODELO: (*you see and hear*) Los vestidos son elegantes, ¿no? (*you see*) fiesta →
(*you say*) Sí, son los vestidos más elegantes de la fiesta.

1. Antonio es un chico guapo,
¿verdad? / fiesta
2. La música es buena, ¿no? / mundo
3. Y la comida, qué rica, ¿no? / mundo
4. La fiesta es divertida, ¿verdad? / año

Paso 3 Gramática

28. Getting Information • Summary of Interrogative Words

A. Situaciones. Imagine that you have just met Rafael Pérez, an up-and-coming baseball player. Rafael's answers are given below. Write your questions, using the appropriate interrogative from each group. Use the **Ud.** form of verbs.

¿Qué?   ¿Dónde?   ¿Adónde?   ¿De dónde?   ¿Cómo?   ¿Cuál(es)?

1. —¿_____? —Me llamo Rafael Pérez.

2. —¿_____? —(Soy) de Bayamón, Puerto Rico.

3. —¿_____? —(Vivo) En el sur de California.

4. —¿_____? —Ahora voy al estadio.

5. —¿_____? —Voy a entrenarme con el equipo.

6. —¿_____? —(Mis pasatiempos favoritos) Son jugar al tenis y nadar.

¿Cuándo?   ¿Quién(es)?   ¿Por qué?   ¿Cuánto/a?   ¿Cuántos/as?

Palabras útiles   ganar (*to earn*)   lo suficiente (*enough*)

7. —¿_____? —Empecé a jugar en 1998.

8. —¿_____? —(Mis jugadores preferidos) Son Barry Bonds y Alex Rodríguez.

9. —¿_____? —Porque son los mejores jugadores del béisbol de todos los tiempos.

10. —¿_____? —Gano lo suficiente para vivir bien.

B. Una amiga entrometida (*nosy*). Una amiga llama a Cristina por teléfono. Complete el diálogo con las palabras interrogativas apropiadas.

AMIGA: Hola, Cristina, ¿_____[1] estás?

CRISTINA: Muy bien, gracias, ¿y tú?

AMIGA: ¡Bien, gracias! ¿_____[2] estás haciendo?

CRISTINA: Estaba estudiando con Gilberto Montero pero ya se fue.

AMIGA: ¿_____[3] es Gilberto Montero?

CRISTINA: Es un amigo de la universidad.

AMIGA: ¿Ah, sí? ¿_____[4] es?

CRISTINA: De Bogotá.

AMIGA: ¡Ah! ¡Colombiano! Y, ¿_____[5] años tiene?

CRISTINA: Veintitrés.

AMIGA: ¿_____[6] es él?

CRISTINA: Es moreno, bajo, guapo y muy simpático.

AMIGA: ¡Ajá! ¿_____[7] regresa tu amigo a su país?

CRISTINA: En julio, pero antes vamos juntos[a] a San Francisco.

AMIGA: ¡A San Francisco! ¿_____[8] van a San Francisco?

CRISTINA: Porque él quiere visitar la ciudad y yo tengo parientes allí...

AMIGA: ¿Y _____[9] van a ir? ¿En avión?

CRISTINA: No, vamos en coche.

AMIGA: ¿_____[10] coche van a usar?

CRISTINA: El coche de Gilberto. ¿Qué te parece?[b]

AMIGA: ¡Fantástico! Adiós, Cristina. Ahora tengo que llamar a Luisa.

[a]*together*   [b]¿Qué... *What do you think?*

C. Preguntas y respuestas. You will hear a series of questions. Each will be said twice. Circle the letter of the best answer to each.

1. a. Es de Juan.   b. Es negro.
2. a. Están en México.   b. Son de México.
3. a. Soy alto y delgado.   b. Bien, gracias. ¿Y Ud.?
4. a. Mañana.   b. Tengo cinco.
5. a. Es gris.   b. Tengo frío.
6. a. Con Elvira.   b. Elvira va a la tienda.
7. a. A las nueve.   b. Son las nueve.

D. ¿Qué dijiste? Your friend Eva has just made several statements, but you haven't understood everything she said. You will hear each statement only once. Choose either **¿Qué?** or **¿Cuál?** and form a question to elicit the information you need.

MODELO: (*you hear*) La capital del Perú es Lima.
(*you see*) **a.** ¿qué? **b.** ¿cuál? →
(*you say*) **b.** ¿Cuál es la capital del Perú?

1. a. ¿qué?   b. ¿cuál?
2. a. ¿qué?   b. ¿cuál?
3. a. ¿qué?   b. ¿cuál?
4. a. ¿qué?   b. ¿cuál?
5. a. ¿qué?   b. ¿cuál?

E. Entrevista con la Srta. Moreno. Interview Ms. Moreno, an exchange student, for your campus newspaper, using the written cues. Add any necessary words. You will hear the correct question, as well as her answer. Use her name only in the first question.

MODELO: (*you see*) **1.** ¿dónde? / ser   (*you hear*) uno →
(*you say*) Srta. Moreno, ¿de dónde es Ud.? (*you hear*) Soy de Chile.

2. ¿dónde? / vivir
3. ¿dónde? / trabajar
4. ¿qué? / idiomas / hablar
5. ¿cuál? / ser / deporte favorito

Un poco de todo

A. ¿Un día desastroso (*disastrous*) **o un día de suerte** (*lucky*)? Complete la siguiente narración haciendo estos cambios.

1. Complete la narración en el pretérito (P) o el imperfecto (I), según las indicaciones.
2. Cambie los verbos marcados con * por la forma del gerundio solamente: esquiar* → esquiando.

Hace cinco o seis semanas,[a] Fernando Sack-Soria, un joven anglohispano del sur de España,

_____ [1] (*I,* **pasar**) unas vacaciones _____ [2] (**esquiar***) en Aspen,

Colorado. Allí _____ [3] (*P,* **conocer**) por casualidad[b] a María Soledad Villardel,

también española, pero de Barcelona. Ella _____ [4] (*I,* **visitar**) a unos amigos que

_____ [5] (*I,* **vivir**) en Aspen.

El primer encuentro[c] entre Fernando y Marisol (así llaman a María Soledad) fue casi

desastroso. Fernando _____ [6] (*I,* **esquiar**) montaña abajo[d] a la vez[e] que Marisol

_____ [7] (*I,* **estar**) cruzando distraída la pista de esquí.[f] Cuando Fernando la

_____ [8] (*P,* **ver**), trató de evitar un choque.[g] _____ [9] (*P,* **Doblar**[h]) brusca-

mente[i] a la izquierda y perdió el equilibrio. El joven se cayó[j] y _____ [10] (*P,* **perder**)

uno de sus esquís. Marisol paró,[k] _____ [11] (*P,* **ponerse**) muy avergonzada y, casi sin

pensarlo, le habló... en español.

—¡Hombre, cuánto lo siento[l]! ¡No sé dónde llevaba la cabeza[m]! ¿_____ [12]

(*P, Tú:* **Hacerse**) daño[n]?

—¡No, de ninguna manera! La culpa fue mía.[o] Venía muy rápido —le dijo Fernando.

—¡Por Dios! ¡Hablas español! —contestó ella muy sorprendida.

—¡Claro! Soy español, de Jerez de la Frontera.

—Y yo, de Barcelona. ¿Qué haces por aquí?

—Ya ves, _____ [13] (**esperar***) a una chica guapa con quien chocar[p] en Colorado

—dijo Fernando, _____ [14] (**sacudirse***[q]) la nieve y _____ [15] (**sonreír***)—.

¿Y tú?

—¿Yo? Estaba en las nubes,[r] como siempre, y casi te causé un accidente serio.

Para hacer corta la historia, desde ese día _____ [16] (*P,* **hacerse**[s]) muy amigos y

ahora se escriben y se visitan cuando pueden.

[a]Hace... *Five or six weeks ago*   [b]por... *by chance*   [c]*meeting*   [d]montaña... *down the mountain*   [e]a... *at the same time*   [f]cruzando... *crossing the ski slope absentmindedly*   [g]trató... *he tried to avoid a collision*   [h]*To turn*   [i]*sharply*   [j]se... *fell down*   [k]*stopped*   [l]cuánto... *I'm so sorry*   [m]*head*   [n]Hacerse... *To hurt oneself*   [o]La... *It was my fault.*   [p]*to bump into*   [q]*to shake off*   [r]*clouds*   [s]*to become*

B. ¡Nunca cambian! Mire los dibujos y describa las acciones de las personas. Use el presente del progresivo (ahora), el pretérito (ayer) y el imperfecto (de niño/a).

Vocabulario útil

bailar

hacer ejercicio

jugar

nadar

pasear en bicicleta

Amada   Joaquín   Rosalía   Rogelio   David

1. Amada: Ahora, _____ .

                Ayer, _____ .

                De niña, _____ .

2. Joaquín: Ahora, _____ .

                Ayer, _____ .

                De niño, _____ .

3. Rosalía: Ahora, _____ .

                Ayer, _____ .

                De niña, _____ .

4. Rogelio: Ahora, _____ .

                Ayer, _____ .

                De niño, _____ .

5. David: Ahora, _____ .

                Ayer, _____ .

                De niño, _____ .

C. Descripción. En casa de los Delibes. You will hear a series of statements about the following drawing. Each will be said twice. Circle **C** if the statement is true or **F** if it is false. First, pause and look at the drawing.

1. C   F
2. C   F
3. C   F
4. C   F
5. C   F
6. C   F

Paso 4 Un paso más

🎧 Videoteca*

Entrevista cultural: Colombia

You will hear an interview with Mauricio. After listening, pause and choose the letter of the phrase that best completes each statement.

1. Mauricio es de...
   - **a.** Caracas.
   - **b.** Bogotá.
   - **c.** Costa Rica.

2. Mauricio juega...
   - **a.** tenis.
   - **b.** basquetbol.
   - **c.** fútbol.

3. Él también practica...
   - **a.** natación.
   - **b.** béisbol.
   - **c.** polo.

4. Además (*Besides*) de ser futbolista, Mauricio es...
   - **a.** estudiante.
   - **b.** maestro.
   - **c.** profesor.

5. El objeto que trae Mauricio es...
   - **a.** una cultura.
   - **b.** un colombiano.
   - **c.** una balsa dorada.

Now resume listening.

Entre amigos: ¿Sabes bailar salsa?

Paso 1. The four friends answer a question about what they like to do in their free time. Listen carefully and jot down notes about their responses. The names are listed in the order in which they answer.

1. Rubén _____
2. Karina _____
3. Miguel René _____
4. Tané _____

Now resume listening.

Paso 2. Now listen as they answer a question about the sports that are played in their countries. Write down the sport they mention and whether or not they play it now or played it before. Check your answers for both **Pasos** in the Appendix.

1. Tané _____
2. Rubén _____
3. Karina _____
4. Miguel René _____

---

*The **Videoteca** videoclips are available on the Video on CD to accompany *¿Qué tal?*; Seventh Edition.

Enfoque cultural: Colombia

A. Colombia. Complete las oraciones con la información apropiada.

1. La República de Colombia obtuvo su independencia de _____ en

   _____ (año). Su primer presidente fue _____.

2. Colombia produce mucho _____, platino y esmeraldas, y exporta mucho

   petróleo y _____.

3. Un 14 por ciento de la población colombiana es de origen _____.

4. Se cree que las misteriosas estatuas de _____ son del siglo

   _____ antes de Cristo.

B. Juanes. Complete el siguiente párrafo.

Juanes nació en _____.[1] Fundó el grupo Ekhymosis cuando tenía

_____.[2] En 2002 ganó _____.[3] En 2003 dedicó su concierto en

Bogotá a _____.[4]

¡Repasemos!

A. Un día típico. Use the following verbs or phrases in the order given to write a composition (on page 185) in the imperfect tense, describing a typical day when you were a high school student. Use phrases such as **casi siempre, nunca, muchas veces, generalmente.**

1. despertarse
2. bañarse/ducharse
3. cepillarse los dientes
4. vestirse
5. desayunar
6. despedirse
7. ir a la escuela
8. asistir a clases
9. almorzar
10. conversar y reírse con los amigos
11. volver a casa
12. estudiar
13. sentarse a cenar a las seis
14. si no tener que estudiar
15. mirar la televisión
16. leer
17. decirle «buenas noches» a _____
18. quitarse la ropa
19. acostarse

_____

_____

_____

_____

_____

_____

_____

_____

_____

_____

_____

_____

_____

_____

_____

_____

B. *Listening Passage: ¿Cómo se pasan los fines de semana y los días de fiesta?*

Antes de escuchar. Pause and do the following prelistening exercise.

Before you listen to the passage, read the following statements about how some people spend weekends or holidays. Check those statements that are true for you and your family.

☐ Los fines de semana son ocasiones familiares.

☐ Pasamos los fines de semana o los días de fiesta en nuestra casa en el campo.

☐ Mi madre siempre prepara una comida especial los domingos.

☐ Paso el fin de semana con mis amigos y no con mi familia.

☐ Después de comer, toda la familia sale a dar un paseo por el parque.

☐ Paso el fin de semana con mis abuelos.

Now resume listening.

Listening Passage. Now you will hear a passage about how some Hispanics spend their weekends and holidays. The following words appear in the passage.

adinerados	personas que tienen mucho dinero
a mediodía	*at noon*
se casan	*get married*
el hogar	*home*
el descanso	*rest*
se suele	*it is the custom (to)*
elegir	*to choose, pick*
los columpios	*swings*
los críos	*young children*
charlando	hablando, conversando
relajados	*relaxed*

Después de escuchar. Read the following statements. Circle **C** if the statement is true or **F** if it is false. If the statement is false, according to the passage, correct it.

1. C F Muchos hispanos tienen otra casa fuera de la ciudad.

   _____

2. C F Normalmente los abuelos no pasan tiempo con sus hijos y nietos.

   _____

3. C F Los domingos se almuerza rápidamente para poder ir al cine o al teatro.

   _____

4. C F Por lo general, los padres no pasan tiempo con sus hijos durante el fin de semana.

   _____

Now resume listening.

 C. Entrevista. You will hear a series of questions. Each will be said twice. Answer, based on your own experience. Pause and write the answers.

1. _____

2. _____

3. _____

4. _____

5. _____

6. _____

❖■ Mi diario

¿Qué quehaceres domésticos le tocaba hacer a Ud. cuando estaba en la escuela secundaria? ¿Con qué frecuencia debía hacerlos? Escriba algo en su diario sobre estos quehaceres.

MODELO: Yo debía hacer mi cama todos los días, ¡y lo hacía! También me tocaba...

Póngase a prueba

 ## A ver si sabe...

A. Imperfect of Regular and Irregular Verbs

1. Complete la siguiente tabla.

INFINITIVO	CANTAR	IR	LEER	SER	VER
yo	cantaba				
nosotros					

2. Match the following uses of the imperfect with the examples.

1. _____ To express *time* in the past.

2. _____ To describe a repeated or habitual action in the past.

3. _____ To describe an action in progress.

4. _____ To express *age* in the past.

5. _____ To describe ongoing physical, mental, or emotional states in the past.

6. _____ To form the past progressive.

a. ¿Estabas estudiando?
b. Tenía ocho años.
c. Cenaba con mis padres cuando llamaste.
d. Eran las doce.
e. Siempre comíamos a las seis.
f. No me gustaba practicar.

B. Superlatives. Complete las oraciones.

1. (*happiest*) Soy _____ persona _____ feliz _____ mundo.

2. (*best*) Son los _____ jugadores _____ equipo.

3. (*worst*) Es el _____ estudiante _____ _____ clase.

C. Summary of Interrogative Words. ¿Qué o cuál(es)? Complete la pregunta con la palabra interrogativa apropiada.

1. ¿_____ significa (*means*) ciclismo?

2. ¿_____ es tu teléfono?

3. ¿_____ son tus libros?

4. ¿_____ restaurante me recomiendas?

5. ¿_____ es el mejor restaurante de la ciudad?

Prueba corta

A. Mafalda. Complete el párrafo con el imperfecto de los verbos entre paréntesis.

Cuando Mafalda _____¹ (**ser**) una niña más pequeña, ella no _____² (**asistir**) a la escuela. Siempre _____³ (**estar**) en casa con su madre, y a veces la _____⁴ (**ayudar**) con los quehaceres. Muchas veces, durante el día, otras niñas que _____⁵ (**vivir**) cerca _____⁶ (**ir**) a visitarla y todas _____⁷ (**jugar**) en el patio de su casa. Su mamá les _____⁸ (**servir**) galletas y leche y cuando todas sus amiguitas _____⁹ (**cansarse**^a) de jugar, ellas _____¹⁰ (**volver**) a casa.

^a*to become tired*

B. Preguntas. Complete las preguntas con la palabra interrogativa apropiada.

1. ¿_____ van Uds. ahora? ¿A casa o al centro?

2. ¿_____ es la chica de pelo rubio?

3. ¿_____ se llama la profesora de francés?

4. ¿_____ están los otros estudiantes? No los veo.

5. ¿_____ es tu clase favorita este semestre?

6. ¿_____ pagaste por tu nuevo coche?

C. Recuerdos. You will hear a passage about a person's childhood memories. Then you will hear a series of questions. Circle the letter of the best answer for each.

1. **a.** Trabajaba en Panamá.   **b.** Vivía en Panamá.
2. **a.** Hacía calor.   **b.** No hacía calor.
3. **a.** Jugaba béisbol.   **b.** Patinaba con sus amigos.
4. **a.** Iba al cine.   **b.** Iba al centro.
5. **a.** Patinaba con sus padres.   **b.** Patinaba con sus amigos.
6. **a.** Daba paseos en el parque.   **b.** Daba paseos en el cine.
7. **a.** Su quehacer favorito era lavar los platos.   **b.** No le gustaba lavar los platos.

D. Cosas de todos los días: una niñez feliz. Practice talking about your imaginary childhood, using the written cues. When you hear the corresponding number, form sentences using the words provided in the order given, making any necessary changes or additions.

MODELO: (*you see*) **1.** (yo) / ser / niño muy feliz   (*you hear*) uno →
(*you say*) *Era* un niño muy feliz.

2. cuando / (yo) / ser/ niño, / vivir / Colombia
3. mi familia / tener / una casa / bonito / Medellín
4. mi hermana y yo / asistir / escuelas públicas
5. todos los sábados, / mi mamá / ir de compras
6. me / gustar / jugar / con mis amigos
7. los domingos / (nosotros) / reunirse / con / nuestro / abuelos

ANSWER KEY

Appendix: Answers

CAPÍTULO PRELIMINAR

Primer paso

Saludos y expresiones de cortesía **A.** (*Possible answers*) 1. Hola. ¿Qué tal? 2. Buenas noches, señora Alarcón. 3. Buenas tardes, señor Ramírez. 4. Buenos días, señorita Cueva. ¡RECUERDE! 1. usted 2. tú 3. ¿Cómo te llamas? 4. ¿Cómo se llama usted? **B.** (*Possible answers*) 1. ¿Qué tal? (¿Cómo estás?) 2. ¿Y tú? 3. hasta 4. Hasta luego. (Hasta mañana.) **C.** 1. Buenas 2. está usted 3. gracias 4. se llama 5. Me llamo ____. 6. gusto 7. Mucho gusto. (Igualmente. / Encantado/a.) **El alfabeto español** **A.** 1. ñ 2. h **B.** 1. ge 2. ve (uve) 3. equis 4. zeta 5. ce 6. i 7. con hache **Nota comunicativa** **B.** **Paso 2.** 1. C 2. F 3. F 4. C 5. C 6. C **¿Cómo es usted?** **B.** (*Possible answers*) 1. inteligente, realista, responsable 2. optimista, idealista (*and so on*) **Nota cultural** **A.** Northeast d; Southwest a, c; Southeast a. b **Pronunciación y ortografía** **F.** **Paso 1.** 1. rodilla 2. Maribel 3. unilateral 4. salvavidas 5. olvidadizo **Paso 2.** 1. Muñoz 2. Robles 3. Casimira 4. Gamorro

Segundo paso

Los números 0–30; *hay* **A.** 1. una 2. cuatro 3. siete 4. trece 5. once 6. un 7. veinte 8. veintitrés (veinte y tres) 9. veintiséis (veinte y seis) 10. veintiún (veinte y un) 11. veintiuna (veinte y una) 12. treinta **B.** 1. 8 / ocho 2. 11 / once 3. 5 / cinco 4. 6 / seis 5. 7 / siete 6. 22 / veintidós (veinte y dos) 7. 30 / Treinta **Gustos y preferencias** **A.** (*Possible answers*) 1. ¿le gusta jugar a la lotería? Sí, (No, no) me gusta. 2. ¿le gusta la música jazz? Sí, (No, no) me gusta. 3. ¿te gusta esquiar? Sí, (No, no) me gusta. 4. ¿te gusta beber café? Sí, (No, no) me gusta. 5. ¿te gusta el programa «American Idol»? Sí, (No, no) me gusta. 6. ¿te gusta el chocolate? Sí, (No, no) me gusta. **¿Qué hora es?** **A.** 1. c 2. f 3. d 4. a 5. e 6. b **Nota comunicativa** 1. Son las doce y veinte de la mañana. 2. Es la una y cinco de la tarde. 3. Son las dos en punto de la mañana. 4. La recepción es a las siete y media de la noche. 5. La clase es a las once menos diez de la mañana. 6. Son las diez menos cuarto (quince) de la noche. 7. Es la una y media de la mañana. 8. Son las ocho y cuarto (quince) de la mañana. ¡OJO! a. 4:05 P.M. b. 8:15 P.M. c. 10:50 P.M. **A leer** 1. a 2. c 3. f 4. b 5. e 6. d

Un paso más

Videoteca **Entre amigos** 1. 23, México 2. 21, Cuba 3. 23, España 4. 20, Venezuela **Póngase a prueba** **A ver si sabe...** **A.** 1. soy 2. eres 3. es **B.** 1. Hola 2. Buenos / Buenas / Buenas 3. te llamas 4. De nada / No hay de qué **C.** 1. gusta 2. me gusta **D.** 1. Qué hora es 2. Es / Son **Prueba corta** **A.** 1. ¿Cómo se llama usted? 2. ¿Cómo te llamas? 3. ¿De dónde eres? 4. Gracias. 5. De nada. / No hay de qué. 6. (*Possible answer*) Eres inteligente, paciente y rebelde. 7. ¿Le gusta el jazz? 8. ¿Te gusta el chocolate? 9. seis / doce / quince / veintiuno / treinta 10. Son las once y quince (cuarto) de la noche.

CAPÍTULO 1

Paso 1: Vocabulario

En la clase **A.** 1. el edificio 2. la librería 3. la oficina 4. la secretaria 5. el escritorio 6. el bolígrafo 7. el lápiz 8. el papel 9. el estudiante 10. la calculadora 11. la ventana 12. el cuaderno 13. la mochila 14. la clase 15. la silla 16. la profesora 17. la pizarra 18. la puerta 19. el libro (de texto) 20. la biblioteca 21. la mesa 22. el bibliotecario 23. el diccionario **B.** 1. La calculadora, porque es una cosa. No es una persona.   2. La mochila, porque es una cosa. No es un lugar.   3. El hombre, porque es una persona. No es una cosa.   4. El edificio, porque es un lugar. No es una cosa.   5. La bibliotecaria, porque es una persona. No es un lugar.   **C.** *Here is the text of Luisa's list. Check your chart against it.*   A ver... para este semestre necesito algunas cosas para mis clases. Necesito cinco cuadernos, siete libros de texto, tres bolígrafos y un lápiz. También debo comprar una mochila y una calculadora.   **Las materias   A.**   1. Gramática alemana, La novela moderna, Francés 304   2. Cálculo 1, Contabilidad, Trigonometría, Computación   3. Antropología, Sociología urbana, Sicología del adolescente   4. Astronomía, Biología 2, Química orgánica, Física   **Nota comunicativa A.**   1. Cuánto   2. A qué hora (Cuándo)   3. Cómo   4. Cuál   5. Dónde   6. Quién   7. Cuándo   8. Qué **B.**   1. Cómo   2. Quién   3. Cómo   4. Cuánto   5. Dónde   6. A qué hora   7. Qué   **Pronunciación y ortografía   A.**   1. five   2. a, e, o   3. i, u   4. strong, weak, weak   **B.**   1. es-tu-dian-te   2. dic-cio-na-rio   3. puer-ta   4. cua-der-no   5. bi-lin-güe   6. gra-cias   7. es-cri-to-rio   8. sie-te   9. seis **F.**   1. *ciencias*   2. *Patricio*   3. *seis*   4. *buenos*   5. *auto*   6. *soy*   **Los hispanos hablan**   1. JOSÉ: *No:* matemáticas; *Sí:* química, física, biología, sicología (literatura)   2. RAÚL: *No:* idiomas; *Sí:* ciencias 3. JULIA: *No:* historia, química; *Sí:* matemáticas, sicología

Paso 2: Gramática

Gramática 1   A.   1. la   2. la   3. la   4. el   5. el   6. la   7. la   8. el   **B.**   1. un   2. una   3. un 4. una   5. un   6. una   7. una   8. un   **C.**   1. (No) Me gusta la clase de español.   2. (No) Me gusta la universidad.   3. (No) Me gusta la música de Bach.   4. (No) Me gusta el Mundo de Disney. 5. (No) Me gusta la limonada.   6. (No) Me gusta la comida mexicana.   7. (No) Me gusta la física. 8. (No) Me gusta el programa «CSI».   **E.   Paso 1.**   1. el   2. programa   3. el   4. libro   5. un   6. una 7. lista   8. novelas   9. el   10. problema   11. el   12. tiempo   **Gramática 2   A.**   1. las amigas   2. los bolígrafos   3. las clases   4. unos profesores   5. los lápices   6. unas extranjeras   7. las universidades 8. unos programas   **B.**   1. el edificio   2. la fiesta   3. una cliente   4. un lápiz   5. el papel   6. la universidad   7. un problema   8. una mujer   **C.**   1. Hay unos libros.   2. Hay un cuaderno.   3. Hay unos lápices.   4. Necesita una mochila.   5. Necesita unos bolígrafos.   6. Necesita un diccionario. 7. Necesita una calculadora.   **G.**   1. Hay *unos estudiantes* en *la oficina.*   2. *Los diccionarios* están en *la biblioteca.*   3. No hay *clientes* en *la clase.*   4. ¿Hay *una calculadora* en *la mochila*?

Paso 3: Gramática

Gramática 3   A.   1. ellas   2. él   3. yo   4. ellos   5. ellos   6. nosotros/as   **B.**   1. tú   2. vosotros / Uds.   3. Uds.   4. Ud.   5. tú / tú   **C.**   1. Él no trabaja en una oficina.   2. Ella no canta en japonés. 3. No tomamos cerveza en la clase.   4. Ella no regresa a la universidad por la noche.   5. Ellos no bailan en la biblioteca.   6. No enseño español.   **D.**   1. hablo / canta / bailan / toman / paga / trabaja   2. escuchamos / busca / necesita   3. enseña / estudian / practican / regresa   **Nota comunicativa   A.**   1. Raúl y Carmen están en la oficina.   2. Yo estoy en la biblioteca.   3. Tú estás en la clase de biología.   4. Uds. están en el laboratorio de lenguas.   **B.**   1. estamos   2. bailan   3. cantan   4. toco 5. toma / escucha   **Un poco de todo   A.**   (*Possible answers*)   1. Sí, estudiamos español.   2. El Sr. (La Sra./Srta.) _____ enseña la clase.   3. Es de _____.   4. Hay _____ estudiantes en la clase.   5. Sí, me gusta.   6. No, no habla inglés en la clase.   7. No, no necesitamos practicar en el laboratorio todos los días.   8. (La clase) Es a la (las) ____.   **B.**   1. (Martín) Compra libros en la librería.   2. Sí, hay libros en italiano.   3. Hay cuadernos, bolígrafos y lápices.   4. Compra dos libros.   5. No, hablan inglés. 6. No, paga veintidós dólares.

Paso 4: Un paso más

Videoteca   Entrevista cultural   1. b   2. a   3. a   4. c   **Entre amigos**   1. *Miguel René:* muy bien, muy contento *Tané:* bien, cansada *Karina:* muy bien *Rubén:* bien, cansado   2. *Karina:* ingeniería *Rubén:* ciencias sociales *Miguel René:* ¿? *Tané:* comunicación social   3. *Rubén:* tres: informática, inglés, literatura *Karina:* cuatro: informática, inglés, literatura, matemáticas *Tané:* cinco: computación, historia (universal), historia (del teatro), inglés, literatura *Miguel René:* informática, inglés, literatura   4. *Tané:* bailar, descansar *Miguel René:* bailar, estudiar, ir al cine, leer, trabajar *Rubén:* bailar, descansar, leer *Karina:* descansar, leer   **Enfoque cultural**   1. C   2. F   3. C   4. F   **Póngase a prueba   A ver si sabe...**

A. 1. el / los 2. la / las 3. un / unos 4. una / unas **B.** 1. busco 2. buscas 3. busca
4. buscamos 5. buscáis 6. buscan **C.** 1. Yo no deseo tomar café. 2. No hablamos alemán en la
clase. **D.** 1. ¿Dónde? 2. ¿Cómo? 3. ¿Cuándo? 4. ¿Quién? 5. ¿Qué? 6. ¿Por qué?
E. 1. nosotros estamos 2. estáis 3. están 4. ellos están **Prueba corta** **A.** 1. el 2. la 3. la 4. el
5. la 6. los 7. los 8. los **B.** 1. una 2. unos 3. unos 4. un 5. una 6. unas 7. una 8. unas
C. 1. estudian 2. practico 3. hablamos 4. Toca 5. enseña 6. Necesito 7. regresa

CAPÍTULO 2

Paso 1: Vocabulario

La familia y los parientes **A.** 1. Joaquín es el abuelo de Julián. 2. Julio es el primo de Julián.
3. Miguel y Mercedes son los tíos de Julián. 4. Estela y Julio son los primos de Julián. 5. Josefina es la
abuela de Julián. 6. Pedro y Carmen son los padres de Julián. 7. Chispa es el perro de Julián.
8. Tigre es el gato de Julián. **B.** 1. sobrino 2. tía 3. abuelos 4. abuela 5. nieta 6. parientes
7. mascota **C.** Gregorio el abuelo; Julia la abuela; Marta la tía; Juan el tío; Sara la madre; Manuel el
padre; Elena la prima; Juanito el primo; Manolito el hermano **Nota cultural** 1. c 2. d **Los
números 31–100** **A.** 1. cien 2. treinta y una 3. cincuenta y siete 4. noventa y un 5. setenta y
seis **B.** cuarenta y cinco mochilas; noventa y nueve lápices; cincuenta y dos cuadernos; setenta y
cuatro novelas; treinta y una calculadoras; cien libros de español **Adjetivos** **B.** 1. bajo, feo, listo,
trabajador 2. soltero, viejo, simpático, moreno **C.** **Paso 1.** (*Possible answers*) 1. Billy Crystal es
simpático, cómico, delgado y bajo. 2. Arnold Schwarzenegger es alto, grande, casado, serio y
valiente. 3. James Gandolfini es serio, alto, gordo y cruel. 4. El presidente es moreno, casado y rico.
D. 1. No, David es joven y moreno. 2. No, Luis tiene 48 años. 3. No, Carlos es soltero y delgado.
4. No, a Luis le gusta la música clásica. 5. No, es el siete, catorce, veintiuno, setenta y siete.
Pronunciación y ortografía ¡RECUERDE! 1. a 2. b **A.** 1. do<u>c</u>tor 2. mu<u>j</u>er 3. mo<u>ch</u>ila 4. a<u>c</u>tor
5. per<u>m</u>iso 6. po<u>s</u>ible 7. <u>g</u>eneral 8. profe<u>s</u>ores 9. univer<u>s</u>idad 10. <u>C</u>armen 11. I<u>s</u>abel 12. biblio<u>tec</u>a
13. us<u>t</u>ed 14. liber<u>t</u>ad 15. ori<u>g</u>en 16. ani<u>m</u>al **D.** 1. con - *trol* 2. e - le - *fan* - te 3. mo - nu -
men - *tal* 4. com - pa - *ñe* - ra 5. *bue* - nos 6. us - *ted*

Paso 2: Gramática

Gramática 4 **A.** 1. bonita, grande, interesante 2. delgados, jóvenes, simpáticos 3. delgada,
pequeña, trabajadora 4. altas, impacientes, inteligentes **B.** 1. alemana 2. italiano 3. norteamer-
icano 4. inglesa 5. mexicana 6. ingleses 7. francesas **C.** 1. Ana busca otro coche italiano.
2. Buscamos una motocicleta alemana. 3. Paco busca las otras novelas francesas. 4. Busco el gran
drama inglés *Romeo y Julieta*. 5. Jorge busca una esposa ideal. **D.** *For each person, you should have
checked:* SU TÍO: bajo, soltero; LOS ABUELOS: viejos, activos; SUS PRIMOS: jóvenes, activos; SU HERMANA:
casada; SU PADRE: bajo **Gramática 5** **A.** 1. soy de Barcelona 2. son de Valencia 3. eres de Granada
4. somos de Sevilla 5. son de Toledo 6. sois de Burgos **C.** 1. —¿De quién son los libros? —Son de
la profesora. 2. —¿De quién es la mochila? —Es de Cecilia. 3. —¿De quién son los bolígrafos? —Son
del Sr. Alonso. 4. —¿De quién es la casa? —Es de los Sres. Olivera. **D.** 1. El programa de «Weight
Watchers» es para mi hermana. Es gorda. 2. La casa grande es para los Sres. Walker. Tienen cuatro
niños. 3. El dinero es para mi hermano. Desea comprar un *iPod*. 4. El televisor nuevo es para mis
abuelos. Su televisor es viejo. **E.** **Paso 2.** 1. es, hija 2. es, español 3. son, España 4. es, delgada,
alto

Paso 3 Gramática

Gramática 6 ¡RECUERDE! 1. (Ella) Es la hermana de Isabel. 2. (Ellos) Son los parientes de Mario.
3. (Ellos) Son los abuelos de Marta. **A.** 1. Mi 2. Nuestra 3. mis 4. mis 5. Mis 6. mi **B.** 1. Sí,
es su suegra. 2. Sí, es nuestro hermano. 3. Sí, son sus padres. 4. Sí, somos sus primos. 5. Sí, es su
sobrina. 6. Sí, soy su nieto (nieta). **Gramática 7** **A.** 1. Luis come mucho. 2. Gloria estudia
francés. 3. José y Ramón beben Coca-Cola. 4. Inés escribe una carta. 5. Roberto mira un vídeo.
6. Carlos lee un periódico. **C.** 1. vivimos 2. asisto 3. hablamos 4. leemos 5. escribimos
6. aprendemos 7. abren 8. comemos 9. debemos 10. prepara

Paso 4 Un paso más

Videoteca Entre amigos Paso 1. 1. Moreno Gómez 2. Martínez Placencia 3. Ramírez Sánchez 4. Zamora Egert **Paso 2.** 1. Karina 2. Miguel René 3. Rubén 4. Tané **Enfoque cultural** 1. F 2. C 3. F 4. C 5. C 6. C **Póngase a prueba A ver si sabe... A.** 1. a. casada b. casados c. casadas 2. a. grandes b. sentimentales c. franceses **B.** 1. c 2. a 3. b 4. d **C.** 1. mi hermano 2. su tío 3. nuestros abuelos 4. su casa **D.** *leer:* leo / leemos / leéis // *escribir:* escribes / escribe / escriben **Prueba corta A.** 1. italiano 2. francesa 3. alemán 4. inglesas **B.** 1. es 2. soy 3. son 4. eres 5. somos **C.** 1. mi 2. mi 3. Mis 4. su 5. nuestra 6. sus 7. su (tu) **D.** 1. comprendemos / habla 2. Escuchas / estudias 3. lee 4. venden 5. recibe 6. bebo 7. asistimos

CAPÍTULO 3

Paso 1: Vocabulario

De compras: La ropa A. 1. a. un traje b. una camisa c. una corbata d. unos calcetines e. unos zapatos f. un impermeable 2. a. un abrigo b. un vestido c. unas medias d. una bolsa e. un sombrero **B.** 1. centro 2. almacén 3. venden de todo 4. fijos 5. tiendas 6. rebajas 7. mercado 8. regatear 9. gangas **C.** 1. algodón 2. corbatas / seda 3. suéteres / faldas / lana **¿De qué color es? A.** 1. verdes 2. verde / blanca / roja 3. roja / blanca / azul 4. anaranjada / amarillo 5. gris 6. morado 7. rosado 8. color café **Más allá del número 100 A.** 1. 111 2. 476 3. 15.714 4. 700.500 5. 1.965 6. 1,000.013 **B.** 1. veintiocho mil quinientos diez nuevos pesos 2. catorce mil seiscientos veinticinco nuevos pesos 3. siete mil trescientos cincuenta y cuatro nuevos pesos 4. tres mil setecientos ochenta y dos nuevos pesos 5. mil ochocientos cuarenta y un nuevos pesos 6. novecientos veinte nuevos pesos **C.** pares de medias de nilón: 1.136; camisas blancas: 567; suéteres rojos: 9.081; pares de zapatos de tenis: 3.329: blusas azules: 111; faldas negras: 843 **Pronunciación y ortografía ¡RECUERDE!** 1. a 2. b 3. b **A.** 3. matrícula 4. bolígrafo 7. Pérez 9. alemán **C.** *The following words require a written accent:* 1. métrica 4. Rosalía 6. sabiduría 7. jóvenes 8. mágico

Paso 2: Gramática

Gramática 8 ¡RECUERDE! 1. este 2. estos 3. esta 4. estas **A.** 1. Este 2. ese 3. aquel 4. este *(possible answer)* / es económico **B.** 1. Sí, esta chaqueta es de Miguel. 2. Sí, esos calcetines son de Daniel. 3. Sí, ese impermeable es de Margarita. 4. Sí, estos guantes son de Ceci. 5. Sí, este reloj es de Pablo. 6. Sí, esos papeles son de David. **Gramática 9 A. Paso 1.** 1. Quieres 2. puedo 3. tengo 4. Prefiero 5. vengo 6. quiero **Paso 2.** *(Verb forms)* Quieren / podemos / tenemos / Preferimos / venimos por Uds. / queremos **B.** 1. Tengo sueño. 2. Tengo que estudiar mucho. 3. Tengo miedo. 4. Tengo prisa. 5. Tengo razón. **C.** LUIS: ¿A qué hora vienes a la universidad mañana? MARIO: Vengo a las ocho y media. ¿Por qué? LUIS: ¿Puedo venir contigo? No tengo coche. MARIO: ¡Cómo no! Paso por ti a las siete y media. ¿Tienes ganas de practicar el vocabulario ahora? LUIS: No. Ahora prefiero comer algo. ¿Quieres venir? Podemos estudiar para el examen después. MARIO: Buena idea. Creo que Raúl y Alicia quieren estudiar con nosotros.

Paso 3: Gramática

Gramática 10 A. 1. va 2. van 3. vas 4. vamos 5. voy **B.** 1. Eduardo y Graciela van a buscar... 2. David y yo vamos a comprar... 3. Todos van a ir... 4. Ignacio y Pepe van a venir... 5. Por eso vamos a necesitar... 6. Desgraciadamente Julio no va a preparar... **C.** 1. Vamos a estudiar esta tarde. 2. Vamos a mirar en el Almacén Juárez. 3. Vamos a buscar algo más barato. 4. Vamos a descansar ahora. **Un poco de todo A.** 1. la 2. quiere 3. ir 4. pequeñas 5. venden 6. especiales 7. grandes 8. prefiere 9. españolas 10. esta 11. especializadas 12. populares 13. existen 14. elegantes 15. famosos **B.** 1. Tengo 2. ganas 3. miedo 4. razón 5. sueño **C.** 1. estás 2. estos 3. tus 4. esos 5. nuestro 6. vas 7. voy 8. vamos 9. nosotras 10. tu 11. esta 12. queremos 13. prisa 14. Adiós

Paso 4 Un paso más

Videoteca   Entrevista cultural   1. Nicaragua   2. 24   3. tienda   4. mujeres   5. pantalones   6. zapatos
7. mamá   **Enfoque cultural**   1. Cristóbal Colón   2. el Lago de Nicaragua / trescientas   3. agua /
tiburones   4. William Walker / derrotado   5. historia / conservadoras / liberales   **Póngase a prueba
A ver si sabe...   A.**   1. este   2. estos   3. esa   4. esos   5. aquella   6. aquellos   **B.**   1. Ellos van a
comprar...   2. ¿No vas a comer?   3. Van a tener...   4. Voy a ir...   **C.**   1. *poder:* puedo / puede /
podemos // *querer:* quiero / queréis / queremos // *venir:* vengo / viene / venís / venimos
2. a. tener miedo (de)   b. tener razón (no tener razón)   c. tener ganas (de)   d. tener que   **Prueba
corta   A.**   1. Quiero comprar ese impermeable negro.   2. ¿Buscas este traje gris?   3. Juan va a comprar esa chaqueta blanca.   4. Mis padres trabajan en aquella tienda nueva.   **B.**   1. venimos / tenemos
2. prefieres (quieres) / prefiero (quiero)   3. tiene   4. pueden   **C.**   1. Roberto va a llevar traje y corbata.
2. Voy a buscar sandalias baratas.   3. Vamos a tener una fiesta.   4. ¿Vas a venir a casa esta noche?
F.   1. mil ciento veinticinco dólares   2. doscientos sesenta y cinco   3. trescientos cuarenta y nueve
4. lana   5. seda   6. camisa   7. dos dólares

CAPÍTULO 4

Paso 1: Vocabulario

¿Qué día es hoy?   A.   (*Possible answers*)   1. El lunes también va a hablar (tiene que hablar) con el
consejero.   2. El martes va (tiene que ir) al dentista.   3. El miércoles va a estudiar (tiene que estudiar)
física.   4. El jueves va (tiene que ir) al laboratorio de física.   5. El viernes tiene un examen y va a
cenar con Diana.   6. El sábado va (a ir) de compras y (por la noche) va a un concierto.   7. El
domingo va (a ir) a la playa.   **B.**   1. fin / el sábado / el domingo   2. El lunes   3. miércoles   4. jueves   5. pasado mañana   6. el / los   7. próxima   **C.   Paso 1.**   *lunes:* mañana: 10:45, clase de conversación *martes:* mañana: 8:30, dentista; 10:15, librería; tarde: 3:00, clase de español *miércoles:* mañana:
9:00, profesora Díaz; tarde: 1:00, biblioteca *jueves:* tarde: 3:00, clase de español *viernes:* mañana: 10:45,
clase de conversación; tarde: 7:30, fiesta   **Los muebles, los cuartos y otras partes de la casa
A.**   1. la sala   2. el comedor   3. la cocina   4. la alcoba   5. el baño   6. el garaje   7. el patio
8. la piscina   9. el jardín   **¿Cuándo? Las preposiciones   A.**   (*Possible answers*)   1. Tengo sueño antes
de descansar.   2. Regreso a casa después de asistir a clase.   3. Tengo ganas de comer antes de estudiar.   4. Preparo la comida después de ir al supermercado.   5. Lavo los platos después de comer.
Pronunciación y ortografía   B.   1. Alberto viene en veinte minutos.   2. ¿Trabajas el viernes o el
sábado?   3. La abuela de Roberto es baja.   4. No hay un baile el jueves, ¿verdad?   5. ¿Vas a llevar
esa corbata?   **Los hispanos hablan**   Equipo de estéreo, reloj despertador, biblioteca, televisor, aba-
nico, lámpara para estudiar, escritorio, cama, tocador, dos *closets*, alfombras, cuadros, fotos, *posters*,
una gata de peluche

Paso 2: Gramática

Gramática 11   A.   1. veo   2. salimos   3. Pongo   4. traigo   5. oyen   6. hago   7. Salgo   **B.**   1. pongo
2. hago   3. trae   4. salimos   5. Vemos   6. salimos   **D.   Paso 1.**   1. salir   2. ponen   3. hacen
4. traer   **Gramática 12   ¡RECUERDE!**   *querer:* quiero / quieres / quiere / quieren *preferir:* prefiero /
prefiere / preferimos / prefieren *poder:* puedo / puedes / podemos / pueden   **B.**   1. piensan /
pensamos / piensas   2. volvemos / vuelve / vuelven   3. pide / piden / pedimos   **C.**   1. Sale de
casa a las siete y cuarto.   2. Su primera clase empieza a las ocho.   3. Si no entiende la lección, hace
muchas preguntas.   4. Con frecuencia almuerza en la cafetería.   5. A veces pide una hamburguesa y
un refresco.   6. Los lunes y miércoles juega al tenis con un amigo.   7. Su madre sirve la cena a las seis.
8. Hace la tarea por la noche y duerme siete horas.

Paso 3: Gramática

Gramática 13   B.   1. me / se   2. se   3. te   4. Se   5. nos / nos   6. te   **C.**   1. Nos despertamos...
2. Nos vestimos después de ducharnos.   3. Nunca nos sentamos...   4. ...asistimos... y nos divertimos.
5. ...hacemos la tarea.   6. ...tenemos sueño, nos cepillamos los dientes y nos acostamos.   7. Nos

dormimos... **Un poco de todo A.** 1. me levanto 2. tengo 3. despertarme 4. quiero 5. jugar
6. empezamos 7. pongo 8. salgo 9. puedo 10. almorzamos 11. pierde 12. tiene 13. pierdo
14. tengo 15. vuelvo

Paso 4: Un paso más

Videoteca Entre amigos Paso 1. *Miguel René:* apartamento, con otras personas, mediano, dos alcobas, un baño, con cocina; *Karina:* apartamento, sola, mediano, una alcoba, un baño; *Tané:* casa, con
otras personas, grande, cuatro, tres baños, con cocina; *Rubén:* apartamento, solo, pequeño, una alcoba,
un baño, con cocina **Enfoque cultural A.** 1. democracias 2. 1821 3. neutro 4. el Premio Nóbel
5. la paz y el progreso humano **B.** 1. C 2. F 3. F 4. F **Póngase a prueba A ver si sabe...**
A. *hacer:* hago / haces / hacen *traer:* traigo / traes / traemos *oír:* oigo / oímos / oyen *poner:* pongo /
pones / ponemos / ponen *ver:* veo / ves / vemos / ven *salir:* salgo / sales / salimos / salen
B. 1. piensas 2. empiezo a 3. volver a 4. pedir **C.** 1. a. me b. te c. se d. nos e. os f. se
2. a. Yo me acuesto tarde. b. ¿Cuándo te sientas a comer? c. Me visto en cinco minutos. **Prueba
corta A.** 1. se duermen 2. sentarme 3. me divierto 4. levantarte 5. se pone 6. haces 7. salimos **B.** (*Possible answers*) 1. me despierto, me levanto, me visto 2. me baño, me afeito, me cepillo
los dientes 3. el sofá, el sillón, la mesa 4. un escritorio, una lámpara, una cama 5. Almuerzo en la
cocina. / Duermo en la alcoba. / Estudio en la sala. **E.** El número de alcobas: *4*; El número de
baños: *2*; ¿Cuántos metros mide la sala?: *4 metros por 5 metros*; Esta casa está cerca de *las escuelas* y
enfrente de *un parque*; La dirección de la casa: *calle Miraflores, número 246*

CAPÍTULO 5

Paso 1: Vocabulario

¿Qué tiempo hace hoy? A. 1. Hace sol. 2. Hace calor. 3. Hace fresco. 4. Hace frío. 5. Hay
mucha contaminación. **B.** 1. Llueve. 2. Hace (mucho) frío. 3. Hace calor. 4. Hace fresco.
5. Hace buen tiempo. 6. Hay mucha contaminación. **Los meses y las estaciones del año A.** 1. el
primero de abril 2. junio / julio / agosto 3. invierno 4. llueve 5. otoño 6. cuatro de julio
7. nieva 8. enero / mayo **¿Dónde está? Las preposiciones B.** 1. entre 2. al norte 3. al sur
4. al este 5. al oeste 6. lejos 7. cerca 8. en 9. al oeste **Pronunciación y ortografía ¡RECUERDE!**
r / rr A. 1. Rosa 3. perro 4. Roberto 5. rebelde 6. un horrible error 7. una persona rara
8. Raquel es rubia **Los hispanos hablan** JOSÉ: Ciudad: *Río Segundo*, País: *Costa Rica*, El clima: *fresco y
agradable*, La gente: *amable*, ¿Hay una universidad en la ciudad?: *No*; CLARA: Ciudad: *Granada*, País:
España, El clima: *inviernos fríos y hay nieve*, La gente: *joven.* ¿Hay una universidad en la ciudad?: *Sí*;
DIANA: Ciudad: *Cali*, País: *Colombia*, El clima: *hace mucho calor*, La gente: *alegre y amable*, ¿Hay una
universidad en la ciudad?: *Sí*

Paso 2: Gramática

Gramática 14 A. 1. c 2. a 3. d 4. f 5. b 6. e **B.** 1. durmiendo 2. pidiendo 3. sirviéndose
4. jugando 5. almorzando / divirtiéndose **C.** 1. Mis padres están jugando al golf, pero yo estoy
corriendo en un maratón. 2. Mis padres están mirando la tele, pero yo estoy aprendiendo a esquiar.
3. Mis padres están leyendo el periódico, pero yo estoy escuchando música. 4. Mis padres están acos-
tándose (se están acostando), pero yo estoy vistiéndome (me estoy vistiendo) para salir. **Gramática 15**
¡RECUERDE! 1. estar / están 2. ser / es 3. ser / es 4. ser / son / es 5. estar / está / estás / Están
6. ser / somos / es 7. ser / Son **A.** 1. eres / Soy 2. son / son 3. son / están 4. es / estar / es
5. está / Estoy / está 6. es / es **B.** (*Possible answers*) 1. estoy aburrido/a 2. estoy contento/a
3. estoy nervioso/a 4. estoy preocupado/a 5. estoy furioso/a 6. estoy cansado/a 7. estoy triste
C. 1. estás 2. estoy 3. son 4. están 5. Son 6. Son 7. es 8. es 9. estar

Paso 3: Gramática

Gramática 16 B. 1. Ceci es más delgada que Laura. 2. Ceci es más atlética que Roberto.
3. Roberto es más introvertido que Laura. 4. Ceci es tan alta como Laura. 5. Roberto es tan

estudioso como Laura.   6. Roberto es tan moreno como Ceci.   **C.**   1. Sí, el cine es tan alto como la tienda.   2. El café es el más pequeño de todos.   3. El hotel es el más alto (de todos).   4. No, el cine es más alto que el café.   5. No, el hotel es más grande que el cine.   **D.   Paso 2.**   1. Sevilla es *tan* bonita *como* la Ciudad de México.   2. Sevilla tiene *menos* edificios altos *que* el D.F.   3. En el D.F. no hace *tanto* calor *como* en Sevilla.   4. Sevilla no tiene *tantos* habitantes *como* el D.F.   **Un poco de todo A.**   1. Carmen está ocupada y no puede ir al cine esta noche.   2. Esa camisa está sucia. Debes ponerte otra.   3. Esas tiendas están cerradas ahora. No podemos entrar.   4. Debemos llevar el paraguas. Está lloviendo.   5. Mis primos son de Lima; ahora están visitando a sus tíos en Texas, pero su madre está enferma y tienen que regresar a su país la semana que viene.   **B.**   1. veintiún   2. diecinueve   3. ese   4. que   5. que   6. que   7. tanto   8. como   9. de   10. doscientos dólares   11. porque   12. estar   13. de   14. ciento cincuenta dólares   15. pagar

Paso 4: Un paso más

Videoteca   Entrevista cultural   1. Guatemala   2. tiempo   3. televisión   4. templado (moderado)   5. frío   6. calor   7. mal   8. lluvias   9. febrero   10. marzo   **Entre amigos**   *Karina:* Venezuela; mucho calor, tropical; verano; *Miguel René:* México; norte: frío en invierno, calor en verano; sur; calor; verano; *Rubén:* España; variado, frío en invierno, mucho calor en verano; llueve en primavera y otoño; invierno; *Tané:* Cuba; calor todo el tiempo; primavera   **Enfoque cultural**   1. mayas   2. escritura / calendario   3. Tikal   4. 1978 y 1985   5. familia   6. Premio Nóbel de la Paz   **Póngase a prueba A ver si sabe...   A.**   cepillándose / divirtiéndose / escribiendo / estudiando / leyendo / poniendo / sirviendo   **B.**   1. f   2. a   3. c   4. i   5. h   6. b   7. g   8. e   9. d   **C.**   1. más / que   2. tantos / como   3. mejor   4. tan / como   5. menos / que   **Prueba corta   A.**   1. Estoy mirando un programa.   2. Juan está leyendo el periódico.   3. Marta está sirviendo el café ahora.   4. Los niños están durmiendo.   5. ¿Estás almorzando ahora?   **B.**   1. está / Estoy   2. eres / Soy   3. están / Estamos   4. Estás / estoy   5. está   **C.**   1. Arturo tiene tantos libros como Roberto.   2. Arturo es más gordo que Roberto.   3. Roberto es más alto que Arturo.   4. Roberto es menor (tiene dos años menos) que Roberto.   5. Arturo tiene menos perros que Roberto.

CAPÍTULO 6

Paso 1: Vocabulario

La comida   A.   1. jugo / huevos / pan / té / leche   2. camarones / langosta   3. patatas fritas   4. agua   5. helado   6. carne / verduras   7. queso   8. lechuga / tomate   9. zanahorias   10. arroz   11. galletas   12. sed   **¿Qué sabe Ud. y a quién conoce?   B.**   1. conocen   2. sé   3. Sabes   4. saber   5. Conocemos / conozco   6. conocer   **C.**   1. al   2. a   3. A   4. a   5. ø   6. al   7. ø   8. a   **D.   Paso 1.**   ENRIQUE: *Sí:* bailar, a mis padres; *No:* a Juan, jugar al tenis, esta ciudad. ROBERTO: *Sí:* bailar, jugar al tenis, a mis padres; *No:* a Juan, esta ciudad. SUSANA: *Sí:* jugar al tenis, a mis padres, esta ciudad; *No:* bailar, a Juan.   **Paso 2.**   1. saben   2. no sabe   3. conoce   4. no conocen   **Los hispanos hablan**   *You should have checked the following boxes for each person:* CLARA: oreja de cerdo, caracoles; XIOMARA: verduras, mondongo, platos sofisticados; TERESA: huevos, mondongo, hamburguesas con pepinillos, comida rápida, mantequilla

Paso 2: Gramática

Gramática 17   A.   1. Yo lo preparo.   2. Yo voy a comprarlos. / Yo los voy a comprar.   3. Dolores va a hacerlas. / Dolores las va a hacer.   4. Juan los trae.   5. Yo los invito.   **B.**   1. Los despierta a las seis y media.   2. El padre lo levanta.   3. La madre lo baña.   4. Su hermana lo divierte.   5. Lo sienta en la silla.   6. El padre lo acuesta.   **Nota comunicativa   A.**   (*Possible answers*)   1. Acaba de cantar y bailar.   2. Acabamos de comer.   3. Acaba de traer la cuenta.   4. Acaba de enseñar.   **Gramática 18   B.**   1. No, no voy a hacer nada interesante.   2. No, nunca (jamás) salgo con nadie los sábados.   3. No, no tengo ninguno (ningún nuevo amigo).   4. No, ninguna es mi amiga.   5. No, nadie cena conmigo nunca (jamás).   **C.**   1. Pues yo sí quiero (comer) algo. La comida aquí es buena.   2. Pero aquí viene alguien.   3. Yo creo que siempre cenamos en un restaurante bueno.   4. Aquí hay algunos platos sabrosos.   **D.**   1. Yo tampoco.   2. Yo tampoco.   3. Yo también.   4. Yo también.

Paso 3: Gramática

Gramática 19 **A.** **Paso 1.** Título: acostumbre 1. compruebe 2. encargue 3. no lo haga / déjelas 4. no comente / deje 5. no los deje **Paso 2.** 1. your house is well–locked 2. your mail 3. someone you know 4. when you will return 5. in your house **B.** (*Possible answers*) 1. Entonces, coman algo 2. Entonces, beban (tomen) algo. 3. Entonces, estudien. 4. Entonces, ciérrenlas. 5. Entonces, lleguen (salgan) (más) temprano. 6. No sean impacientes. **C.** 1. empiécenla ahora 2. no la sirvan todavía 3. llámenlo ahora 4. no lo hagan todavía 5. tráiganlas ahora 6. no la pongan todavía **Nota comunicativa** **Paso 1** *You should have circled* hacer reservaciones, pedir el pescado, llegar temprano, pagar con tarjeta de crédito, pagar al contado **Un poco de todo** **A.** 1. conoces 2. al 3. lo 4. conozco 5. sé 6. siempre 7. tampoco 8. El **B.** (*Possible answers*) 1. Voy a prepararla (La voy a preparar) este sábado. 2. Sí, pienso invitarlos (los pienso invitar). 3. Sí, puedes llamarlas (las puedes llamar) si quieres. 4. Sí, me puedes ayudar (puedes ayudarme). 5. Sí, las necesito. **C.** 1. ¡Laven los platos! / Ya los estamos lavando. (Ya estamos lavándolos.) 2. ¡Hagan la ensalada! / Ya la estamos haciendo. (Ya estamos haciéndola.) 3. ¡Preparen las verduras! / Ya las estamos preparando. (Ya estamos preparándolas.) 4. ¡Empiecen la paella! / Ya la estamos empezando. (Ya estamos empezándola.)

Paso 4: Un paso más

Videoteca **Entrevista cultural** 1. b 2. a 3. b 4. b 5. a **Entre amigos** **Paso 1.** 1. las arepas 2. el arroz, la carne asada 3. los mariscos 4. los huevos fritos **Paso 2.** 1. sí, él y su madre 2. sí, su madre 3. sí, él 4. sí, su abuela **Enfoque cultural** 1. Tierra de muchos peces 2. La Carretera Panamericana / la selva Darién 3. Mireya Moscoso / 1998 4. el emperador Carlos V (de España) 5. 1914 6. Tenían que darle vuelta a Sudamérica. 7. la República de Panamá **Póngase a prueba** **A ver si sabe...** **A.** 1. te / lo / la / nos / las 2. a. Yo lo traigo. b. ¡Tráigalo! c. ¡No lo traiga! d. Estamos esperándolo. / Lo estamos esperando. e. Voy a llamarlo. / Lo voy a llamar. **B.** 1. nadie 2. tampoco 3. nunca / jamás 4. nada 5. ningún detalle **C.** piense / vuelva / dé / vaya / busque / esté / sepa / diga **Prueba corta** **A.** 1. conozco 2. conoces 3. sé 4. sabe **B.** 1. Quiero comer algo. 2. Busco a alguien. 3. Hay algo para beber. 4. —Yo conozco a algunos de sus amigos. —Yo también. **C.** (*Possible answers*) 1. No, no voy a pedirla. (No, no la voy a pedir.) 2. Sí, las quiero. 3. No, no lo tomo por la noche. 4. Yo la preparo. **D.** 1. Compren 2. hagan 3. Traigan 4. tomen 5. Llámenlo 6. lo sirvan

CAPÍTULO 7

Paso 1: Vocabulario

De viaje **B.** 1. boleto 2. ida y vuelta 3. bajar / escala 4. equipaje 5. el control de la seguridad 6. pasajeros 7. guarda 8. vuelo / demora 9. salida / cola / subir 10. asistentes **C.** (*Possible answers*) 1. En la sala de espera (En la sección de no fumar) un hombre está durmiendo; en la sección de fumar dos pasajeros están fumando y una mujer está leyendo el periódico. 2. Los pasajeros están haciendo cola para facturar su equipaje. El vuelo 68 a Madrid hace una parada en Chicago. 3. Está lloviendo. Un hombre está corriendo porque está atrasado. Los otros pasajeros están subiendo al avión. 4. Los asistentes de vuelo están sirviendo algo de beber. Los pasajeros están mirando una película. **De vacaciones** **A.** **Paso 1.** 1. las montañas 2. la tienda de campaña 3. la playa 4. la camioneta 5. el mar / el océano **Paso 2.** 1. El padre saca fotos (de la madre). 2. La madre toma sol en la playa. 3. Las hijas juegan en la playa. 4. El hijo nada en el mar/océano. 5. Toda la familia hace *camping*. **Nota comunicativa** 1. c 2. b 3. c 4. b 5. a **Pronunciación y ortografía** **D.** 1. [x] 2. [x], [g] 3. [x] 4. [x] 5. [g] 6. [x], [g] 7. [g] 8. [x], [g] **E.** 1. Don Guillermo es viejo y generoso. 2. Por lo general, los jóvenes son inteligentes. 3. Juan estudia geografía y geología. 4. A mi amiga Gloria le gustan los gatos.

Paso 2: Gramática

Gramática 20 **A.** 1. damos 2. da 3. dan 4. das 5. doy 6. digo 7. dice 8. dicen 9. dices 10. decimos **C.** 1. Te compro regalos. 2. Te mando tarjetas postales. 3. Te invito a almorzar.

4. Te explico la tarea.   **D.**   1. ¿Le presto el dinero?   2. ¿Le digo la verdad?   3. ¿Les doy una fiesta?   4. ¿Le pido ayuda al profesor?   5. ¿Les doy más?   **Gramática 21   A.**   1. te gusta   2. les gusta   3. me gustan   4. nos gusta / le gusta   5. les gusta   **B.   Paso 1.**   1. A su padre le gustan las vacaciones en las montañas.   2. A su madre le encantan los cruceros.   3. A sus hermanos les gustan los deportes acuáticos.   4. A nadie le gusta viajar en autobús.   5. A Ernesto le gusta sacar fotos.

Paso 3: Gramática

Gramática 22   A.   *hablar:* hablaste / habló / hablamos / hablaron *volver:* volví / volvió / volvimos / volvieron *vivir:* viví / viviste / vivimos / vivieron *dar:* di / diste / dio / dieron *hacer:* hice / hiciste / hizo / hicimos *ser/ir:* fuiste / fue / fuimos / fueron *jugar:* jugué / jugó / jugamos / jugaron *sacar:* saqué / sacaste / sacamos / sacaron *empezar:* empecé / empezaste / empezó / empezaron   **C.** *yo:* 1. volví   2. Me hice   3. comí   4. Recogí   5. metí   6. di   *tú:* 1. asististe   2. Te acostaste   3. empezaste   4. fuiste   5. Saliste   6. volviste   *Eva:* 1. se casó   2. fue   3. se matriculó   4. empezó   5. regresó   6. viajó   7. vio   8. pasó   *Mi amiga y yo:* 1. pasamos   2. Vivimos   3. asistimos   4. hicimos   5. Visitamos   6. caminamos   7. comimos   8. vimos   *Dos científicos:* 1. fueron   2. Salieron   3. llegaron   4. viajaron   5. vieron   6. tomaron   7. gustaron   8. volvieron   **Un poco de todo   A.**   (*Possible answers*)   1. Les mandé tarjetas postales a mis abuelos. (No le mandé tarjetas postales a nadie. / Nadie me mandó tarjetas postales a mí.)   2. Le regalé flores a mi madre. (No le regalé flores a nadie. / Nadie me regaló flores a mí.)   3. Les recomendé un restaurante a mis amigos. (No le recomendé un restaurante a nadie. / Nadie me recomendó un restaurante a mí.)   4. Le ofrecí ayuda a una amiga. (No le ofrecí ayuda a nadie. / Nadie me ofreció ayuda a mí.)   5. Le presté una maleta a mi hermano. (No le presté una maleta a nadie. / Nadie me prestó una maleta a mí.)   6. Le hice un pastel a un amigo. (No le hice un pastel a nadie. / Nadie me hizo un pastel a mí.)   **B.**   1. Salí / me quedé / Almorcé / fui / Volví / Cené / miré / subí / me quejé / hice / dormí   2. fueron / hicieron / dio / fue / se hizo / escribieron / volvieron   3. Busqué / dieron / perdí / pagaron / gasté / hice / descansé   4. Pasamos / Comimos / vimos / jugamos

Paso 4 Un paso más

Videoteca   Enfoque cultural   1. Honduras, ruinas mayas   2. Tegucigalpa, cerros de plata   3. El Salvador, doscientos   4. 1980   5. líderes políticos, las condiciones económicas y sociales de El Salvador   **Póngase a prueba   A ver si sabe...   A.**   1. a. Siempre le digo...   b. Le estoy diciendo... / Estoy diciéndole...   c. Le voy a decir... / Voy a decirle...   d. Dígale...   e. No le diga...   2. *dar:* doy / da / damos / dais / dan *decir:* digo / dices / dice / decís / dicen   **B.**   1. ¿Les gusta viajar?   2. A mí no me gustan los tomates.   3. A Juan le gustan los aeropuertos.   **C.** *dar:* di / dio / dimos / disteis / dieron *hablar:* hablé / hablaste / hablamos / hablasteis / hablaron *hacer:* hice / hiciste / hizo / hicisteis / hicieron *ir/ser:* fui / fuiste / fue / fuimos / fueron *salir:* salí / saliste / salió / salimos / salisteis   **Prueba corta   A.**   1. le   2. nos   3. les   4. me   5. te   **B.**   1. les gustan   2. le gusta   3. me gusta   4. nos gustan   5. te gusta   **C.** 1. mandaste   2. empecé   3. hizo   4. Fueron   5. Oíste   6. volvieron   7. dio   **E.** el tipo de boleto que el turista quiere: *un boleto de ida y vuelta* / la fecha de salida: *el doce de noviembre* / la fecha de regreso: *el veintisiete de noviembre* / la sección y la clase en que va a viajar: *la sección de no fumar, primera clase* / la ciudad de la cual va a salir el avión: *Chicago* / el tipo de hotel que quiere: *uno que esté cerca de la playa y que tenga aire acondicionado* / el nombre del hotel en el que se va a quedar: *Hotel Presidente*

CAPÍTULO 8

Paso 1: Vocabulario

La fiesta de Javier   B.   1. el Día de Año Nuevo   2. la Navidad   3. La Pascua   4. la Nochebuena   5. el Cinco de Mayo   **C.**   1. Es el primero de abril.   2. Les hace bromas.   3. Significa *lion*.   **Emociones y condiciones   A.**   (*Possible answers*)   1. me pongo avergonzado/a   2. se enojan (se ponen irritados)   3. se enferman / se quejan   4. se portan   5. discutir   **Nota comunicativa**   1. Sí, me parece larguísima.   2. Sí, son riquísimos.   3. Sí, me siento cansadísimo/a.   4. Sí, es carísima.   5. Sí, fueron dificilísimas. **Pronunciación y ortografía** **C.** **Dictado** 1. quemar 2. quince 3. campaña 4. compras 5. coqueta 6. comedor

Paso 2: Gramática

Gramática 23 **A.** **Paso 1.** 1. C 2. F 3. C 4. F 5. F 6. C 7. F 8. F 9. F **Paso 2.** 2. La Unión Soviética puso un satélite antes que los Estados Unidos. 4. En 1492... 5. Hitler sí quiso dominar Europa. 7. Los españoles llevaron el maíz y el tomate a Europa. 8. John Kennedy dijo: «Yo soy un berlinés». 9. Muchos inmigrantes irlandeses vinieron en el siglo XIX. **B.** *estar:* estuve / estuvo / estuvimos / estuvieron *tener:* tuvo / tuvimos / tuvieron *poder:* pude / pudimos / pudieron *poner:* puse / puso / pusieron *querer:* quise / quiso / quisimos *saber:* supe / supo / supimos / supieron *venir:* vino / vinimos / vinieron *decir:* dije / dijimos / dijeron *traer:* traje / trajo / trajeron **C.** *Durante la Navidad:* 1. tuvo 2. estuvieron 3. Vinieron 4. trajeron 5. dijeron 6. fueron 7. comieron 8. pudieron *Otro terremoto...* 1. supimos 2. hubo 3. oí 4. leí 5. se rompieron 6. hizo 7. dijo 8. fue **D.** 1. estuvo 2. pude 3. tuve 4. viniste 5. Quise 6. estuve 7. hizo 8. Supiste 9. tuvo 10. vino 11. dijo 12. puse 13. trajiste 14. traje **Gramática 24** **A.** *divertirse:* me divertí / te divertiste / se divirtió / nos divertimos / se divirtieron *sentir:* sentí / sentiste / sintió / sentimos / sintieron *dormir:* dormí / dormiste / durmió / dormimos / durmieron *conseguir:* conseguí / conseguiste / consiguió / conseguimos / consiguieron *reír:* reí / reíste / rio / reímos / rieron *vestir:* / vestí / vestiste / vistió / vestimos / vistieron **B.** 1. me senté / me dormí 2. se sentaron / nos dormimos 3. se durmió 4. nos reímos / se rio 5. sintieron / se sintió **C.** **Paso 1.** *You should have checked the following actions for each person:* JULIA: vestirse elegantemente; VERÓNICA: vestire elegantemente; TOMÁS: sentirse mal, dormir toda la tarde, preferir quedarse en casa; ERNESTO (el narrador): vestirse elegantemente

Paso 3: Gramática

Gramática 25 ¡RECUERDE! 1. Yo le traigo el café. (O.I.) 2. Yo lo traigo ahora. (O.D.) 3. Ellos nos compran los boletos. (O.I.) 4. Ellos los compran hoy. (O.D.) 5. No les hablo mucho. (O.I.) 6. No las conozco bien. (O.D.) **B.** 1. ¿El dinero? Te lo devuelvo mañana. 2. ¿Las fotos? Te las traigo el jueves. 3. ¿La sorpresa? Nos la van a revelar después. 4. ¿Los pasteles? Me los prometieron para esta tarde. 5. ¿Las fotos? Se las mando a Uds. con la carta. 6. ¿La bicicleta? Se la devuelvo a Pablo mañana. 7. ¿El dinero? Se lo doy a Ud. el viernes. 8. ¿Los regalos? Se los muestro a Isabel esta noche. **C.** (*Possible answers*) 1. Se lo dejó a Cristina. 2. Se la dejó a Memo. 3. Se los dejó a la biblioteca. 4. Se los dejó a la Cruz Roja. 5. Se la dejó a Ernesto y Ana. 6. ¡Me los dejó a mí! **E.** 1. se las 2. me lo 3. nos la 4. se las 5. se los **Un poco de todo** **A.** (*Possible answers*) 1. Se la mandé a mi novio/a. 2. Se los di a mi familia y a mis amigos. 3. Nadie me las trajo. 4. Mi hermano me lo pidió. 5. Mis amigos me la hicieron. **B.** **Paso 1.** 1. hice 2. tuve 3. estuve 4. quise 5. supe 6. di 7. estuvimos 8. pedí **Paso 2.** 1. Fue porque tuvo una reunión con su agente de viajes. 2. No tuvo mucho tiempo libre. (Estuvo ocupadísimo.) 3. Lo supo porque se lo dijo su amigo Luis Dávila. 4. Se las dio a Luis.

Paso 4 Un paso más

Videoteca **Entrevista cultural** 1. La Habana 2. México 3. fiesta 4. cumpleaños 5. Navidad 6. comida 7. taza de café 8. toman **Entre amigos** 1. las bodas, los bautizos, los cumpleaños, la quinceañera, los carnavales 2. la Navidad, los cumpleaños 3. el cumpleaños, el Día de las Madres, el Día del Padre, el Día de Muertos, la Navidad, el Año Nuevo 4. los cumpleaños, la Navidad **Enfoque cultural** 1. 1898 2. (la) Florida 3. Porque Fidel Castro todavía gobierna a Cuba. 4. Es difícil. 5. Refleja la influencia africana. 6. la injusticia social y una crítica al colonialismo 7. los mitos y las leyendas afrocubanas **Póngase a prueba** **A ver si sabe...** **A.** 1. estuve 2. pudiste 3. puso 4. quisimos 5. supieron 6. tuve 7. viniste 8. trajo 9. dijeron 10. fuimos **B.** *yo:* dormí / pedí / preferí / recordé / me sentí *tú:* dormiste / pediste / preferiste / recordaste / te sentiste *él/ella/Ud.:* durmió / pidió / prefirió / recordó / se sintió *nosotros/as:* dormimos / pedimos / preferimos / recordamos / nos sentimos *ellos/Uds.:* durmieron / pidieron / prefirieron / recordaron / se sintieron **C.** 1. se lo 2. se la 3. se lo **Prueba corta** **A.** 1. nos reímos 2. se puso / durmió

3. conseguí   4. se despidió   5. se vistió / se divirtió   6. hicimos / trajeron   **B.**   1. a   2. a   3. c   4. b
5. a   6. b

CAPÍTULO 9

Paso 1: Vocabulario

Pasatiempos, diversiones y aficiones   **B.**   1. a. hacer *camping*   b. juegan a las cartas   c. dan un
paseo d. toma el sol   2. a. juegan al ajedrez   b. Teatro   c. Museo   3. a. divertido   b. cine   c. la película   d. pasarlo bien   **Los quehaceres domésticos**   **A.**   1. Está sacudiendo los muebles.   2. Está
barriendo el piso.   3. Está poniendo la mesa.   **B.**   1. la estufa   2. el lavaplatos   3. la aspiradora
4. el tostador   5. la cafetera   6. la lavadora   **Pronunciación y ortografía**   **C.**   1. Paco toca el piano
para sus parientes.   2. Los tíos de Tito son de Puerto Rico.   3. ¿Por qué pagas tanto por la ropa?
4. Tito trabaja para el padre de Pepe.   **Los hispanos hablan**   **Paso 1.**   *Here is the text of Xiomara and
Gabriela's answers. Compare it with the notes you took.* XIOMARA: Mi pasatiempo favorito es salir con mis
amigas a dar paseos por la ciudad o ir a la piscina a nadar un rato. También me gusta muchísimo
hacer aeróbicos en mi casa. Mi mejor amiga es Teresa y con ella es con quien salgo. Nos gusta ver los
aparadores de las tiendas, ir de compras, hablar con nuestros novios, ir a buscar amigos o amigas,
conversar en mi casa, tomar refrescos en las sodas, sentarnos en los bancos de los parques y ver
películas. GABRIELA: Bueno, no tengo sólo un pasatiempo favorito. En realidad son muchas las cosas
que me gusta hacer en mi tiempo libre. Me gusta leer y escuchar música, me gusta ir a mi club y
reunirme con mis amigos. Allí practicamos deportes —tenis, natación, *squash*. Algo que hacemos muy
a menudo, generalmente los fines de semana, es organizar *picnics*, y más tarde, en la noche, nos
reunimos en fiestas o vamos al cine o a algún café.   **Paso 2.**   (*Answers may vary.*)   1. Las actividades
que tienen en común las dos jóvenes son el salir o reunirse con sus amigos, nadar y ver películas.
2. Algunos de los pasatiempos que no tienen en común son el ir de compras, el leer, el escuchar música,
el hacer aeróbicos, el conversar en casa, el ir al club, el jugar al tenis/*squash* y el organizar *picnics*.

Paso 2: Gramática

Gramática 26   **A.**   1. celebraba   2. se llenaba   3. debíamos   4. Corríamos   5. comíamos   6. cortábamos   7. era   8. me molestaba   9. era   10. era   **B.**   1. tenía   2. vivíamos   3. Iba   4. volvía   5. pre-
fería   6. venían   7. era   8. celebrábamos   9. hacía   10. cocinaba   11. visitaban   12. se quedaban
13. dormíamos   14. nos acostábamos   15. había   16. pasábamos   17. eran   **C.**   1. Antes dependía de
su esposo. Ahora tiene más independencia económica.   2. Antes se quedaba en casa. Ahora prefiere
salir a trabajar.   3. Antes sólo pensaba en casarse. Ahora piensa en seguir su propia carrera.   4. Antes
su esposo se sentaba a leer el periódico. Ahora (su esposo) la ayuda con los quehaceres domésticos.
E.   **Paso 1.**   1. había   2. tenían   3. ofrecían   4. tenían   5. era   6. había   7. celebraban   8. eran
9. jugaban   10. podían   **Paso 2.**   1. sacrificios, dioses   2. ceremonia   3. pirámides, religiosa
Gramática 27   **A.**   (*Possible answers*)   1. El béisbol es el más emocionante de todos los deportes.
2. Shaquille O'Neal es el mejor jugador del mundo   3. El equipo de los Dallas Cowboys es el peor
equipo de todos.   4. El estadio de Río de Janeiro es el más grande del mundo.   **B.**   **Paso 1.**   1. el
carnaval   2. mayo   3. *Como agua para chocolate*   4. pasar la aspiradora

Paso 3: Gramática

Gramática 28   **A.**   1. ¿Cómo se llama Ud.?   2. ¿De dónde es Ud.?   3. ¿Dónde vive Ud.?
4. ¿Adónde va Ud. ahora?   5. ¿Qué va a hacer?   6. ¿Cuáles son sus pasatiempos favoritos?
7. ¿Cuándo empezó a jugar?   8. ¿Quiénes son sus jugadores preferidos?   9. ¿Por qué (son sus preferidos)?   10. ¿Cuánto gana Ud. al año?   **B.**   1. cómo   2. Qué   3. Quién   4. De dónde   5. cuántos
6. Cómo   7. Cuándo   8. Por qué   9. cómo   10. Qué   **Un poco de todo**   **A.**   1. pasaba   2. esquiando
3. conoció   4. visitaba   5. vivían   6. esquiaba   7. estaba   8. vio   9. Dobló   10. perdió   11. se puso
12. Te hiciste   13. esperando   14. sacudiéndose   15. sonriendo   16. se hicieron   **B.**   1. Ahora Amada
está jugando al basquetbol. Ayer jugó... De niña jugaba...   2. Ahora Joaquín está nadando. Ayer nadó...
De niño nadaba...   3. Ahora Rosalía está bailando. Ayer bailó. De niña bailaba.   4. Ahora Rogelio está

paseando en bicicleta. Ayer paseó... De niño paseaba...   5. Ahora David está haciendo ejercicio. Ayer hizo... De niño hacía...

Paso 4 Un paso más

Videoteca   Entre amigos   Paso 1.   1. leer, ir al cine, dormir   2. leer, bailar, ir de compras   3. salir con amigos, tomar café, leer, ir al cine o a un bar   4. descansar, dormir tarde, ver fotos   **Paso 2.**   1. el béisbol; ahora no, antes sí   2. el fútbol, sí   3. el béisbol, no   4. el fútbol, no   **Enfoque cultural**
A.   1. España / 1819 / Simón Bolívar   2. oro / café   3. africano   4. San Agustín / VI   **B.**   1. Medellín
2. 14 años   3. tres Grammys Latinos   5. las víctimas de la violencia y las personas que las protegen
Póngase a prueba   A ver si sabe...   A.   1. *yo:* iba / leía / era / veía *nosotros:* cantábamos / íbamos / leíamos / éramos / veíamos   2. 1. d   2. e   3. c (a)   4. b   5. f   6. a   **B.**   1. Soy la persona más feliz del mundo.   2. Son los mejores jugadores del equipo.   3. Es el peor estudiante de la clase.
C.   1. Qué   2. Cuál   3. Cuáles   4. Qué   5. Cuál   **Prueba corta   A.**   1. era   2. asistía
3. estaba   4. ayudaba   5. vivían   6. iban   7. jugaban   8. servía   9. se cansaban   10. volvían
B.   1. Adónde   2. Quién   3. Cómo   4. Dónde   5. Cuál   6. Cuánto